Orton-Gillingham Word List Dictionary: Syllables

Volume 4:

Multi-Syllable words

Syllable Types

Syllable Division

Syllable Patterns

Contractions

ION/TION & related endings

Orton-Gillingham Word List Dictionary Series

Volume 1	Volume 2	Volume 3	Volume 4 Syllables (this book)
Consonants Short Vowels FLOSS Blends End Blends Compound Words Closed Syllable Exceptions	Digraphs & Trigraphs VCE (silent E) Vowel Teams Sounds of Y Compound Words	R-Controlled W-Combinations Soft C & G -CLE (Stable Syllables) Silent Letter teams Complex Letter Teams -ED, -ES, -EST	Multi-syllable Words Syllable Types Syllable Division Syllable Patterns Contractions ION/TION & related endings

Other Books by Valerie Arredondo

Morphology Word List Dictionary Series
Due for publication 2023 Volume 1: Prefixes Volume 2: Latin and Greek Roots Volume 3: Suffixes

Phoneme-Based Word Family Dictionary
This book of word lists focuses on bringing word family instruction into alignment with the science of reading. It emphasizes phoneme/grapheme correspondences and explains how word families can be taught in conjunction with phoneme-level instruction. Included in this book are lists of word families that can be combined to make word sorts, word building activities, and word chains.

Table of Contents

Extended Table of Contents

2 of 4

Extended Table of Contents

3 of 4

Extended Table of Contents

What is a Syllable?

A syllable is a word part that has one vowel sound. Words may have only one syllable (ball), or they may have many syllables (in-ter-dis-ci-pli-nar-y).

Each time you say a vowel sound, your jaw lowers slightly.

ball (1 syllable)

ti-ger (2 syllables)

but-ter-fly (3 syllables)

A syllable can include consonants, or it can be a vowel all by itself.

The word **OPEN** is divided **O-PEN**.

The **O** is a syllable all by itself, with no additional consonants.

PEN is a syllable with the vowel **E** plus two attached consonants.

A syllable has only one vowel sound, but a syllable can have more than one vowel letter. Two or more letters can make one vowel sound.

The word **train** is only one syllable. The **A** and **I** are two vowel letters that make up the **AI** letter team (phonogram). The letter team **AI** only represents one vowel sound.

The word **bake** has two vowels that are separated (b**a**k**e**). The word **bake** is only one syllable because it has only one vowel sound (long **A**).

Most words have 1-4 syllables, but some words can have 5 or more syllables.

1 syllable: **dish** 2 syllables: **rob-in** 3 syllables: **po-ta-to** 4 syllables: **in-tel-li-gent**	5 syllables: **ir-re-ver-si-ble** 6 syllables: **au-to-bi-og-ra-phy** 7 syllables: **so-ci-o-ec-o-nom-ic**

Students with dyslexia and other language-based learning disabilities may have trouble hearing the syllable beats in a word. One way to help them to "feel" the syllables is for the students to hold their lips shut and say a word. They will feel their lips pulling apart for each vowel sound. Another method is for the students to hold their hands under their jaw while they say the word. their jaw will drop for each syllable. These methods work for *most* multi-syllable words. There are some words that are exceptions. Sometimes making a consonant sound will feel like an additional jaw drop, such as in the word *prism*.

Why Teach Syllables?

The main reason we teach syllables is to give students a valuable tool for reading and spelling longer words. When students can divide a long multi-syllable word into syllables, it makes that word much easier to read, and it also makes that word much easier to spell.

In addition, brain studies have shown that breaking a word down into smaller parts helps the brain to encode or "map" the word into memory. This process of encoding words in the brain is called **orthographic mapping.**

The brain encodes or "maps" on multiple levels.[1] One of the most important ways the brain encodes is by connecting sounds (phonemes) to letters (graphemes). Researchers have also found that the brain encodes words not just on a phonogram level, but on a syllable level and a morpheme level, as well.[2] Drawing the student's attention to the syllables in a word helps them to encode those longer words in their brain.

A longer word like **socioeconomic** can be intimidating to a struggling reader, but when it is divided into syllables, it becomes much easier to read: **so-ci-o-ec-o-nom-ic**.

As a good reader, you may already have the word **socioeconomic** in your reading "lexicon," so let's try two examples of words that could be new even to a seasoned reader.

The longest (non-medical, non-technical) word in the English language[3] is

antidisestablishmentarianism

The longest word in a standard dictionary is

pseudopseudohypoparathyroidism

If you divide those words into syllables, you will find that they are much easier to read.

an-ti-dis-es-tab-lish-men-tar-i-an-ism (11 syllables)

pseu-do-pseu-do-hy-po-pa-ra-thy-roid-ism (11 syllables)

Dividing by morphemes (units of meaning, prefixes, suffixes, and roots) is another good way to divide longer words. A good understanding of phonograms (letters, letter teams, and their associated sounds) is a necessary prerequisite to being able to read morphemes. Experience with syllables is also helpful in being able to read morphemes. Below are our two long words divided by morphemes:

anti-dis-establish-ment-ar-ian-ism

pseudo-pseudo-hypo-para-thyroid-ism

We will discuss morphemes in Volume 5.

---

[1] *Reading at the Speed of Sight* by Mark Seidenberg.

[2] For more information on how the brain learns to read, I recommend the books *Reading at the Speed of Sight* by Mark Seidenberg and *Reading in the Brain* by Stansilas Dehaene.

[3] *What's the Longest Word in the World?* by Kevin Kampwirth (Mental Floss)

Dictionary Entries

When you look at a dictionary entry, one of the first things you see is the word divided into parts.

pro · fes · sor	**aba · cus**
gi · raffe	**aban · don**

Those are syllable divisions, right?

Actually, they are not.

While the words **professor** and **giraffe** are divided correctly into syllables, **abacus** would be divided into syllables as **ab/a/cus** and **abandon** would be divided into syllables as **a/ban/don.**

The dictionary word divisions above (with the dots between them) are called "end-of-line division dots." Theses are divisions that dictionaries created for writers back in (recent) history when most correspondence and books were handwritten or typed on a typewriter. At that time, multi-syllable words were divided up if a person ran out of room at the edge of the paper, or to make the ends of lines in a printed book look more even.

Often these word/typing divisions were divided into syllables, which is probably what started the confusion about these being syllable divisions. However, dictionary editors also considered morphemes (units of meaning), spoken conventions, and other factors when they divided up the words. These divisions were all based on whatever the dictionary editors thought would be the most recognizable way to divide up a word when you reach the end of a line of print.

Someone typing a letter at that time would type:

> We went to the zoo, and we saw a gi-
> raffe. It was very tall.

It is puzzling why writers thought that the even spacing of the words on the page was more important than keeping whole words intact, but for some reason that was a priority for the people who were doing it. Some book publishers still use hyphenated word divisions when they are trying to "justify" or even up both sides of a paragraph. I used justification on this paragraph you are currently reading, so that you can see the difference. Most printed books have justified paragraphs.

Word processors can now even out the lines for us. Printed dictionaries still retain these word divisions, but several online dictionaries have given up listing these end-of-page divisions.

So that brings us back to syllables. If the dictionary dot divisions do not show us the syllables in a word, where are the syllables listed?

Dictionary editors consider syllables to be a *spoken* convention, not a *written* convention. Because of that, most dictionary editors will divide a word into syllables only in the dictionary pronunciation section. Hyphens or spaces will indicate syllable divisions.

prə-'fes- ər

jə 'raf

That is helpful if you want to look up a pronunciation, but it is not always helpful when it comes to dividing up the letters in a word into syllables for the purpose of reading and spelling.

This Orton-Gillingham Word Dictionary divides words by the traditional syllable division rules used by Orton-Gillingham practitioners. In general, those rules help students divide up words for easier reading and pronunciation. Because syllables are naturally a spoken convention and not a written convention, applying syllable division rules to print will still cause occasional confusion when it comes to pronunciation.

The most common complaint about syllable division is when double letters are divided. We say **kitt-en**, not "**kit-ten**." We do not make the **/t/** sound twice. The reason that the **T's** and other double letters are divided (and are even in the word in the first place), is to indicate that one of the syllables is closed, and therefor has a short vowel sound. If **kitten** were spelled **kiten**, it would be pronounced with a long / **ī** /sound.

Other problems with syllable division happen when two syllable division rules conflict with each other, or when a syllable division rule breaks up a phonogram. In these cases, I will provide an alternative way to divide up a word.

Alternative divisions will be marked with an asterisk (*).

For example, the word **sprinkle** is traditionally divided between consonants as

sprin-kle

This follows the traditional rule to "count back three" when you see a **CLE** syllable.

Unfortunately, when you divide a word like this, you split up the phonogram **INK**. The beginning of the word **sprinkle** then appears to be pronounced "**sprin**" with a short vowel **ĭ** sound.

The alternate division **sprink-le** keeps the phonogram **INK** together.

The entry for sprinkle will look like this:

sprinkle	**sprin-kle**
	***sprink-le**

Morphemes (units of meaning)

Some teachers prefer to have their students divide words by morphemes (units of meaning), instead of by syllables.

frac-tion (This division emphasizes the sounds within the word, **TION** is pronounced **/shun/)**

fract-ion (This division emphasizes the meaning of the word. We see that **fract** means to divide.)

There are both positives and negatives to dividing by morphemes, which I describe in detail later in this book.

Learning about ***both*** syllable division and morphology provide valuable tools for students to use in their reading. It is not necessary to focus on one to the exclusion of the other. This Volume 4 Word List Dictionary focuses on Syllables. Volume 5 will cover Morphology (word part meanings).

6 (or 7) Syllable Types

There are 6 syllable types. If you take a letter of each syllable type, you can spell the word **CLOVER**. (See the CLOVER template in the Resources section). If your program teaches 7 syllable types, see the note at the bottom of this page.[4]

C – Closed
L - CLE
O – Open
V – Vowel
E – Silent E
R – R-controllled

The 6 syllable types are:

Closed – a syllable that has a single vowel, followed by one or more consonants. The consonant "closes in" the vowel and makes it say its short sound.

whole words - **bat, duck**
syllables - **at** (attic), **hic** (hiccup)

Open – a syllable that ends in a vowel (no consonants). The vowel says its long sound.

whole words – **go**, **by**
syllables - **na** (navy), **pho** (photo)

VCE - a syllable that has the pattern **V**owel/ **C**onsonant/ **E**. The **E** at the end of the syllable/word causes the vowel to say its long sound.

whole words - **bike**, **cake**
syllables – **crobe** (microbe), **cede** (precede)

CLE - a syllable that follows the **C**onsonant- **L**-**E** pattern. The **CLE** pattern is a syllable only and never presents as a whole word.

syllables – **cle** (uncle), **ple** (triple)

Vowel team – a syllable that has two or more vowels that form a phonogram (letter team).

whole words – **paint, coat**
syllables **ie** (goalie), **hoo** (hooray)

R-controlled – a syllable that includes an **R-controlled** phonogram (letter team)

whole words – **car, bird**
syllables – **er** (flower), **or** (origami)

---

[4] Some programs teach 7 syllable types. The programs that teach seven syllable types typically divide the vowel teams into two groups, **vowel teams** and **dipthongs**. A **vowel team** in these programs would be a letter team that has two vowels that say only one of the vowel sounds (**AI** in **train**). A **dipthong** in these programs would be considered any vowel team that makes a new sound (such as **OO** in **boot**). This is not the correct usage of the word **dipthong**. A **dipthong** as defined by a linguist is a vowel team that begins with one vowel sound and glides into another sound (**OU** in **sour** or **OI** in **coin**). There are very few genuine dipthongs.

Syllable Patterns

Syllable patterns are often used as an aid for teaching students how to divide longer words into syllables. They are also helpful for dictionary category headings, so that you can find similar words.

One section of this Word List Dictionary arranges the word lists by syllable patterns (for example **VCCV**). Another section arranges word lists by syllable types (**O**pen, **C**losed, **CLE**, etc). These two sections lists are all two-syllable words. A third section divides words with 3 or more syllables by number of syllables.

In syllable patterns, the letter **V** represents vowels. The letter **C** represents consonants.

In formal syllable division, the vowels are underlined. The underlined vowels and the consonants between them are labeled either with a **V** for vowel or a **C** for consonant.

VCV bacon

VCCV happen

One consonant in between the vowels VCV

V**C**V
be**g**un

Two consonants in between the vowels VCCV

V**CC**V
pu**pp**et

Three consonants in between the vowels VCCCV

V**CCC**V
co**ntr**act

Four consonants in between the vowels VCCCCV

V**CCCC**V
su**bscr**ibe

The word is then divided into syllables by hash marks, hyphens, or spaces.

kit/ten **kit-ten** **kit ten**

In the word **kitten**, the **I** and **E** are vowels. Because **kitten** has two consonants between the vowels, it is labeled **VCCV**.

VCCV
kitten

There are two consonants between the vowels in the word kitten (**tt**). The slash mark indicates that kitten is divided into syllables between the two consonants. Kitten will be labeled **VC/CV**.

VC/CV
kit/ten

Vowel teams **(OA, IE)** are one vowel sound, and therefore in this book they are labeled by only one **V**. Below are two words that are both labeled **VCV**, because they both have a single consonant between the vowels.

V**C**V V**C**V
be**g**un coo**k**ie

For the purpose of syllable division, the entire word is not labeled. The focus is on the dividing the consonants between the vowels, so the other letters are unnecessary and distracting.

ki**tt**en V**CC**V not CVCCVC

How to Divide by Syllables

The best way to decode a multi-syllable word is to break the word down into smaller parts.

If you saw the following syllables written separately on index cards, you would probably find them easy to read, even though some of them are not real words.

pot hip a mus po

Those small syllables are much easier for a student to handle than reading a long word like

hippopotamus

By teaching students to break large multi-syllable words into syllables, we make it possible for them to read words that would otherwise be overwhelmingly difficult.

hip-po-pot-a-mus

Here is another example. Read the word below out loud:

pococurante – meaning "indifferent"

Think about how you sounded out the word pococurante. When you read the word out loud, did you find yourself slowing down?

Did you read each letter by itself?

p.....o.....c.....o.....c.....u.....r.....a.....n.....t.....e

or did you read the letters in groups like this?

po co cur an te

If you broke the word down into letter groups, you were informally breaking the word down into syllables.

Before teaching syllable division

Before you teach syllable division, it is important for students to know the difference between an open and closed vowel.

An open vowel has no consonant following the vowel. The open vowel has a long vowel sound.

he (open – long vowel **/ē/** sound - no consonant at the end of the syllable)

Open vowels can also have a schwa sound, which is extremely common in multi-syllable words. We will discuss schwa in a later section.

A closed vowel has a consonant following or "closing off" the vowel. The closed vowel has a short sound. Closed vowels can also have a schwa sound.

hen (closed – short vowel **/ĕ/** sound - consonant at the end of the syllable)

Here's another example of open and closed vowels:

go (open – no consonant at the end – long vowel **o** sound)

go<u>**t**</u> (closed – consonant at the end – short vowel **o** sound)

Some teachers use houses with doors to illustrate this concept. To the left is an example of one such product, sold by 180 Days of Reading on www.teacherspayteachers.com[5]. The closed word is written on the front, and the last letter is written on the door. When you open the door, you can see an open vowel sound. If you make these yourself, be sure that the door opens to the right of the letter and not to the left, or the door will cover up part of the word.

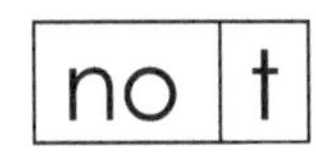

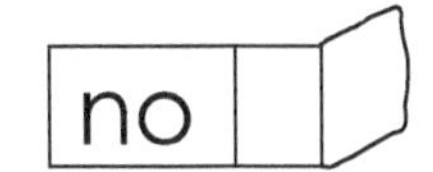

Formal syllable division

The traditional way to decode multi-syllable words is to teach formal syllable division. Formal syllable division teaches the common patterns of syllable division (such as VC/CV) and it teaches many rules to help divide those syllables. With this method, students are usually required to label the vowels and consonants above the word, and then to recognize the patterns to know where to divide the consonants. A good video describing this type of syllable division can be found in the video series *Breaking the Big Words* by Josh Morgan on You Tube.

Flexible syllable division

A more flexible method of syllable division does not teach students rules, but instead encourages the students to divide the syllables in the place that makes the most sense to them, or that "looks right." As they read the syllables, they try out different vowel sounds (long, short and schwa) to see which one is correct. Michael Hunter teaches this method in the video, *Lose the Rules: Reading and Spelling Multi-syllable Words Made Easy* by PaTTAN, which is available on YouTube.

Simple syllable division

Although all of the methods of syllable division are helpful, I prefer a middle ground between Formal syllable division, (which requires learning the patterns and/or a lot of rules), and Flexible syllable division, (which may not be explicit enough for some students). I call this method Simple Syllable Division. This is a method I distilled from several different methods I have seen other teachers using.

See next page for the steps to Simple Syllable Division.

---

[5] I do not receive compensation for any products that I recommend in this book.

Simple Syllable Division

Before beginning syllable division, students should know the difference between a long and short vowel sound. They should know that an open syllable makes a long vowel sound and a closed syllable makes a short vowel sound. They should also be familiar with blends and digraphs.

There are two main principles of Simple Syllable Division.

Simple Syllable Division

Principle #1 Divide the middle consonants equally as much as possible.

Principle #2 Keep letter teams together.

Here are the steps to follow. They include practice problems because the concepts are easier to understand when they are practiced.

1) **Underline all the vowels in a word.** (The **U** in **QU** does not count as a vowel for syllable division and should not be underlined)

kitten napkin aqua

Vowel teams are underlined together and are treated as one vowel.

mushroom painter

The **R** in R-controlled letter teams is not underlined, because it is not a vowel.

anchor ornate

VCE letter teams are treated as one vowel. In the word **mistake**, the **A** and the **E** are one vowel team. Students can draw a curve or **V** to show that the vowels go together, and therefore will not be split up, or students can underline the entire **VCE** part of the syllable. I prefer underlining the entire **VCE**, because it is the least visually distracting.

mistake mistake mistake

Practice (each step will have practice problems)

Answers to all practice problems are at the end of this section.

Underline the vowels in the following words. The first one is done for you. **Y** counts as a vowel, unless it is at the beginning of a word. Watch for **VCE** and vowel teams.

acorn	salute
doggy	email
motorcycle	hippopotamus
fourteen	snowflake

2) Look at the consonants between the vowels. Divide the consonants as evenly as possible. (One way to describe this is to talk about two friends dividing a cookie evenly).

VC/CV
kit / ten
nap / kin

Practice.

Underline the vowels in the following words. Divide the two consonants in the middle (evenly).

pen/cil	puffin
rattle	winter
happen	silver

3) Keep letter teams together. Do not divide the middle consonants evenly if there is a blend, digraph, or some other kind of letter team that needs to stay together. (One way to describe this is that when a group of children is divided into teams, best friends always stick together on the same team).

Some Orton-Gillingham training programs emphasize that you do not teach blends as a phonogram/letter team because blends retain their original two or three sounds (**BL, DR, ST**, etc). They do not make a new sound, like digraphs do (**SH, CH, TH**, etc). However, when students get to syllable division, recognizing blends is sometimes critical in knowing where to divide a word. Therefore, it is important to teach that blends go together as a letter team, even if they are not a pure phonogram.

Two consonants in the middle:

u**sh**/er	not	u**s**/**h**er	(Digraph **SH** stays together)
de/**fr**ost	not	de**f**/**r**ost	(Blend **FR** stays together)

Three consonants in the middle:

sou**th** / **w**est	not	sou**t** / **hw**est	(Digraph **TH** stays together)
co**n** / **cl**ude	not	co**nc** / **l**ude	(Blend **CL** stays together)

Four consonants in the middle:

o**b** / **str**uct	not	o**bst** / **r**uct	(Three letter blend **STR** stays together)
pa**m** / **ph**let	not	pa**mp** / **h**let	(Digraph **PH** stays together)

Practice

Underline the vowels in the following words. Draw a line between the consonants, but keep the blends and digraphs together. (Some programs teach that words with a **CLE** pattern are divided by counting back 3, but if you stick to principle #2 of not dividing up blends and digraphs, you do not have to teach **CLE** as a separate syllable division rule.

ar|cher	humble
sandwich	Jackson
Congress	conflict

4) If a word has only one consonant in between the vowels, you can divide it either before the consonant or after the consonant. The most common division is before the middle consonant, so try that first. After you divide, try saying the word. If it doesn't make sense, try dividing it after the middle consonant.

It is important for students to understand the difference between closed and open vowel sounds, before teaching this syllable division.

V/**C**V	**or**	V**C**/V
ti/**g**er		ro**b**/in

See next page for practice problems.

Practice

Underline the vowels in the following words. Divide either before or after the middle consonant. Try before the consonant first.

ruby	shiver	shovel	valor
yoga	zero	slogan	yodel

5) **A small number of words have two vowels that divide**. You can usually identify these vowels because you will see two vowels next to each other that do not make a vowel team. Students should be familiar with most of the vowel teams before learning this syllable division.

V/V
ne / on (**EO** is not a vowel team, so that gives us a clue that this is a **V/V** division)

vi / o / lin (**IO** is not a vowel team, so that gives us a clue that this is a **V/V** division)

Sometimes a word divides between two vowel teams.

v/v
joy / ous (**OY** is a vowel team and **OU** is a vowel team, so the division goes in between the two vowel teams.)

On rare occasions, what appears to be a vowel team, will instead be a divided vowel.

Noah looks like team **OA** but is divided **No/ah**.

Practice

Underline the vowels in the following words. Divide between the vowels. Keep any vowel teams together.

client	ruin
crayon	riot
layer	fluent

See next page for answers to practice problems.

After answers to practice problems are some notes and exceptions to the syllable dividing rules.

Answers to practice problems

1) Underline the vowels in the following words. Y counts as a vowel, unless it is at the beginning of a word. Watch for VCE and vowel teams.

acorn salute
doggy email
motorcycle hippopotamus
fourteen snowflake

2) Underline the vowels in the following words. Divide the two consonants in the middle.

pen/cil puf/fin
rat/tle win/ter
hap/pen sil/ver

3) Underline the vowels in the following words. Draw a line between the consonants, but keep the blends and digraphs together.

ar/cher hum/ble
sand/wich Jack/son
Con/gress con/flict

4) Underline the vowels in the following words. Divide either before or after the middle consonant. Try before the consonant first.

ru/by shiv/er shov/el val/or
yo/ga ze/ro slo/gan yo/del

5) Underline the vowels in the following words. Divide in between the vowels. Keep any vowel teams together.

cli/ent ru/in
cray/on ri/ot
lay/er flu/ent

Notes & Exceptions

- Some teachers prefer to have students take off prefixes and suffixes before they divide the rest of the word. After students take off the prefixes and suffixes, they divide the rest of the word into syllables. This only works for prefixes and suffixes that are familiar to the student.

  The Simple Syllable Division method works to separate the prefixes and suffixes from the root word, even if those prefixes and suffixes have not yet been learned. Therefore, separating prefixes and suffixes first is not necessary. However, some teachers find that separating the prefixes and suffixes first helps the students to focus on the meaning of the base or root word. This is up to the preference of the teacher.

complete syllable division	or	removing affixes first
dis/lo/ca/ting		**dis** lo/ca/t **ing**

- The traditional way to teach dividing syllables with a **-CLE** combination (-**BLE**, -**DLE**, etc), is by counting back 3 letters from the end of the word and dividing before those three letters. However, if you follow Simple Syllable Division, and follow principle #2 (keeping blends and digraphs together), the **-CLE** syllable will divide naturally and does not need special teaching.

  gar/gle

  thim/ble

  For -**CKLE** words, you traditionally divide between the **CK** and the **LE**. This also will divide naturally if you follow principle #2 of keeping blends and digraphs together.

  pick/le

  freck/le

- Sometimes, letters that appear to be a blend or digraph will instead be two sounds that are next to each other. This happens most often with compound words.

  be**d**/**r**oom (not **DR**)
  mu**sh**/**r**oom (not **SHR**)
  mi**s**/**h**ap (not **SH**)

- Some words are complicated and do not divide easily. The words that are the most tricky are the ones that have a lot of single or open vowels.

  hippopotamus

  hip/po/pot/a/mus

Suggested Sequence for Syllable Division

Syllable division is not something that can be taught in one lesson. This Suggested Sequence for Syllable Division starts with easy concepts and moves up to harder concepts. Each concept is practiced and reinforced before moving on to another concept.

1) Compound words, (both words/bases are already known to the student).

   baby/sit **wild/life**

1) Two middle consonants that are the same letter (twin/doubles) - **VC/CV**

   simple - **kit/ten**

2) Two middle consonants that are not the same (not twin/doubles) - **VC/CV**

   simple - **nap/kin**

3) Two middle consonants (looking for digraphs and blends). Teach this only after students are familiar with blends and digraphs. – **VCC/V, V/CCV**

   whisk/er **de/frost**

4) Three middle consonants (looking for digraphs and blends) - **VC/CCV** and **VCC/CV**

   or/chard **tick/le**

5) One middle consonant - **V/CV** and **VC/V**

   be/gun **rob/in**

6) No middle consonants - **V/V** (Look for two vowels together that are not a vowel team). Teach this syllable division only after students are familiar with most vowel teams.

   li/on **ne/on**

7) Four middle consonants (looking for trigraphs, complex letter teams & three letter blends) **– VCCC/CV and VC/CCCV.** Four middle consonants is a rare combination. Teach this only after students are familiar with three letter blends and trigraphs.

   health/ful **sub/scribe**

Accent/Stress and Schwa

Accent/Stress

Most multi-syllable words have one syllable that is emphasized. This syllable is spoken a little louder and a little clearer than the rest of the word. This syllable is called the ***stressed*** part of the word, or the ***accented*** part of the word. (Occasionally some words will have more than one stressed syllable).

In dictionaries, this accent/stress is marked by what is called an ***acute accent*** mark. (')

po ta' to

ham' bur ger

mi' cro wave

In this book, the accent/stress is marked by bold print

po **ta** to

ham bur ger

mi cro wave

Students with dyslexia often have trouble discerning which part of the word is stressed. One way to practice listening for stress is to say words with an exaggerated voice. I like to teach that it is like "pig calling" (sooEEEE). If you pretend you are calling a pig (or a dog) and you call out any word, you will naturally emphasize the part of the word that is stressed. Plus, it's fun!

frustration	frust raaaaa tion
beetle	beeeee tle

Long words may have more than one accent/stress. The most prominent stressed syllable is the primary accent and the one that is stressed slightly less is the secondary accent.

Schwa

Many people think of the schwa sound as mysterious or complicated. But it really isn't mysterious once you learn more about it.

Every time we say a multi-syllable word, there will be syllables that we say very clearly. Those are the **accented** or **stressed** parts of words. Then there will be syllables that we say less clearly. The way we pronounce those syllables is what I like to call "mush mouth."

In the parts of the words that we say less clearly, we often don't say the vowel sounds the way they are written. Instead, we make a sound that is similar to a short **u /uh/** sound. That "mush mouth" **/uh/** sound is the schwa sound. Any vowel letter can have a schwa sound.

Try saying the words below out loud the way you naturally do when you are speaking, and notice which parts of the word you say with the short **u** **/uh/** sound. Notice that those **/uh/** sounds are in the unstressed portion of the word. (**Bold** print indicates the stressed parts of the word).

about /ŭ **bowt/**

second **/sek** ŭnd/

police /pŭ **lees/**

In some dialects and some words, the schwa may sound like a short **i**, or sometimes it may have almost no sound at all, but in general the short **u** **/uh/** sound is considered the basic schwa sound.

Example:

The word pickle can be pronounced **/pikul/** or **/pikl/**, depending on your dialect.

An official schwa sound will never be in the accented/stressed syllable of a word. It will always be in the unaccented syllable of the word.

Dictionaries usually indicate the schwa sound with what looks like an upside down **e** symbol. I do not use that symbol with students who have dyslexia, because it can be confused with the letter **e**.

Schwa symbol - ə

Some dictionaries label all short **u** sounds with a schwa symbol, even the ones that in the accented/stressed syllables of a word. That can cause some confusion, because those are not true schwa. It is important to remember that the true schwa sound is *only* in the unaccented/unstressed syllable/s of a word.

Learning about accent/stress is not as important as learning phonograms (phoneme/graphemes), but understanding schwa is very helpful for reading and spelling multi-syllable words. Understanding about accent/stress and the schwa sound can help students to read more clearly and fluently. Learning about schwa can help students to understand why words are not always spelled the way they sound. Understanding schwa can also help students to be better spellers. When they hear the **/uh/** sound, they know that it could be spelled by a vowel other than the letter **U**.

Schwa and Stress Shift

When students read longer multi-syllable words, they will find that when words are changed (for example, when suffixes are added to a base word), the pronunciation of the words will sometimes change. That pronunciation change is usually based on the accent/stress in the word changing.

trans' port   trans por **ta'** tion

ex **plore'**   ex plor **a'** tion

When suffixes are added to a base word, the pronunciation and accent/stress may change, but the basic spelling of the original word will stay the same (with the exception of certain spelling rules, such as doubling a letter before adding **ing** or dropping the **e** when adding a vowel suffix).

This consistency of base word spelling can help students to know how to spell vowels that make the schwa ə **/uh/** sound.

For example:

biography   bi-**og**'-raph-y
biographical   bi-ə-**graph**'-ic-al

In the word **biographical**, The letter **o** makes the schwa **/uh/** sound. A student may not know what vowel letter/s to use for that **/uh/** sound. However, if the student can think about the connection between the base word **biography** and the word they want to spell, **biographical**, they will hear the short **o** sound in **biography**, and know to spell the **/uh/** sound with the letter **o**.

You see this again, with the words **productive** and **production**. The letter **o** in both words makes the schwa **/uh/** sound, but if the student thinks of the base word, **product**, they will hear the short **o** sound and know to spell the word with an **o**.

product   **prod'-**uct
productive   prə -**duc**'tive
production   prə -**duc'**-tion

Some students with dyslexia may find that it is too difficult to think of the base word, but other students with dyslexia may find that it is very helpful. Sometimes it just takes good demonstration and practice.

Students who grow up speaking English will naturally change the stress in a word when they are speaking, provided they have either heard that word before, or they have heard words that are similar.

Accent/Stress Rules

It would be difficult for students to learn or apply all the accent/stress rules, but it can be helpful for teachers to know some of the rules so that they can explain why words that are spelled similarly are pronounced differently (such as in the words we discussed in the last section - **biography** and **biographical**).

When students have a verbal knowledge of the vocabulary words they are reading, they should have no problem pronouncing those words correctly without learning the accent rules.

Note how many of these accent/stress rules have to do with placing the focus on the root/base word.

1) **Nouns** and **Adjectives** are usually stressed on the **first** syllable of a two-syllable word. **Verbs** are usually stressed on the **last** syllable of a two-syllable word.

There are exceptions to these rules and patterns, as there are with most English rules and patterns. English is a conglomeration of words that were adopted from other languages, so sometimes the pronunciation depends on the original language of the word.

Nouns	Adjectives	Verbs
Ro-bot	**hap**-py	dis-**cuss**
show-er	**or**-ange	be-**come**
ta-ble	**fuzz**-y	ar-**range**

You can see this shift also when you have a two-syllable word that can function as both a noun and a verb.

He is going into combat. **com-**bat (noun)
How do you combat the growing conflict? com**-bat** (verb)

I will give you a refund for your purchase. **re-**fund (noun)
Can you refund me the money for my purchase? re**-fund** (verb)

2) If you add a prefix or suffix to a word, the stress is often on the base/root word. That is because the base/root word is the most important part of the word.

break-a-ble

pre-**pare**

3) When a two-syllable word pattern is prefix-base, the accent/stress is usually on the base word.

pre-**pay**
en-**gage**

4) In a three-syllable word, the stress is often on the base/root word. For example, if the pattern is **root**-suffix-suffix, the stress is on the first syllable of a three-syllable word (the root), However, if the pattern is prefix-**root**-suffix, the stress is on the second syllable of a three-syllable word.

root-suffix-suffix	prefix-**root**-suffix
sweet-en-er	un-**sight**-ly
tal-ent-ed	re-**quire**-ment

5) Suffixes have a lot of power when it comes to changing the accent/stress of a word. Some suffixes have special rules that determine the stress in a word.

In the following words, the suffixes influence the location of the accent/stress. The stressed part of the word comes directly before these the suffixes. There are many suffixes that cause similar changes.

-ic (forms adjectives)	syn-**thet**-ic
-ery (forms nouns)	em-**broid**-er-y
-i-ous (forms adjectives)	hi-**lar**-i-ous

6) Some prefixes are not stressed. This keeps the focus on the base/root word. These are just examples. There are many prefixes that are not stressed.

de-	de-**ceive**
ex-	ex-**cel**
re-	re-**write**

7) When a word has a double letter before the suffix, the accent/stress is usually on the syllable that ends in the first double letter. This keeps the accent/stress on the base/root word.

shop-ping
o-**mit**-ted

8) British English and American English sometimes differ in where they put their stress.

American English	bro**chure**	ba**ton**	**de**tail	gar**age**
British English	**bro**chure	**bat**on	de**tail**	**gar**age

Multi-Sensory Syllable Spelling

The following is a sample lesson that demonstrates how to teach spelling of multi-syllable words using a multi-sensory approach.

Materials:

Small dry-erase boards, (slightly smaller than an index card). They are sold online under names like Dry Erase Index Cards and SyllaBoards. If you don't have these syllable boards, you can draw lines or boxes for each syllable on a regular dry erase board.

Dry-erase markers

A larger dry-erase board, or a notebook and pencil (optional)

Tiles or round discs (for beginners) You will need enough discs to cover all the sounds in the words that your student is spelling. I use blue discs for consonant sounds and red discs for vowel sounds, because it helps to emphasize the vowel patterns. Some teachers use stoplight colors for the discs - green for the beginning sounds, yellow for the middle sound, and red for the final sounds. Because this book is printed in black and white, I have chosen solid for the consonants and lined for the vowels.

Procedure:

The procedure below will need to be modeled several times before your students are ready to do them on their own. I recommend the "I do. We do. You do." method,

I do. The teacher models the entire procedure several times, including giving all the answers and explaining each part.

We do. The teacher models the procedure. The students copy the teacher's procedure and the students give the answers, either at the same time as the teacher, or with some help and cuing from the teacher.

You do. The teacher says the word and the students do both the procedure and answers on their own, with the teacher providing guidance if they make an error.

Two options for syllable spelling are given on the following pages. The first is the option using syllable boards and discs or tiles. The second option is using only fingers/hands and a large dry erase board.

Multi-Sensory Syllable Spelling

Option 1 – Syllable boards and discs/tiles

Start with 3-5 syllable boards at the bottom of the work area and the discs at the top of the work area.

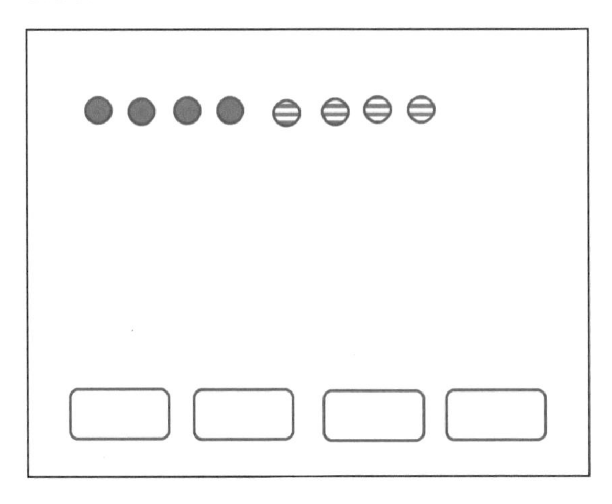

1) Teacher says each word out loud, one at a time.

   Teacher says, "Repeat the word I say: **gravity**."

   Student repeats "**gravity**."

2) Student pushes up one syllable board for each syllable, while saying the syllable out loud,

   /grav/ /i/ /ty/

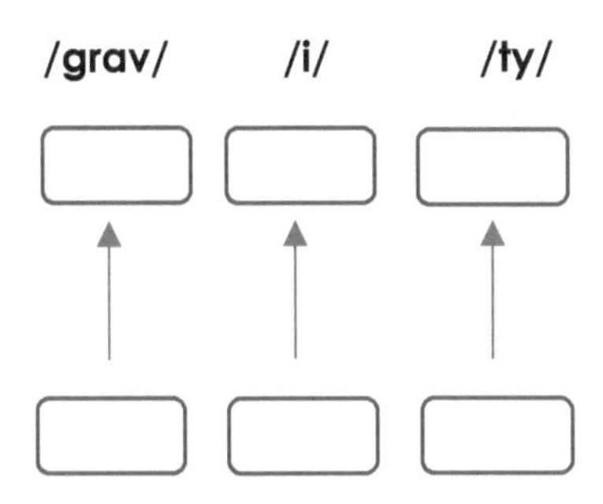

3) Student says the first syllable **/grăv/** and points to the first syllable board.

4) Student pulls down one disc for each sound in the syllable, while saying each *separate* sound out loud. (This is for beginning spellers. More advanced spellers may skip the sound discs.)

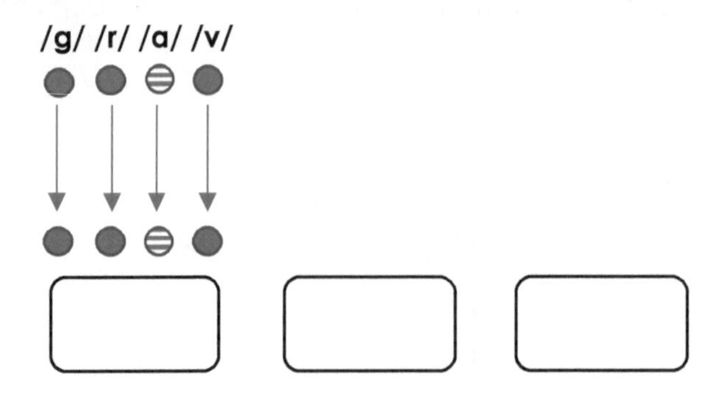

5) Student writes "**grav**" on the syllable board, while sounding out & blending the letter sounds as they write.

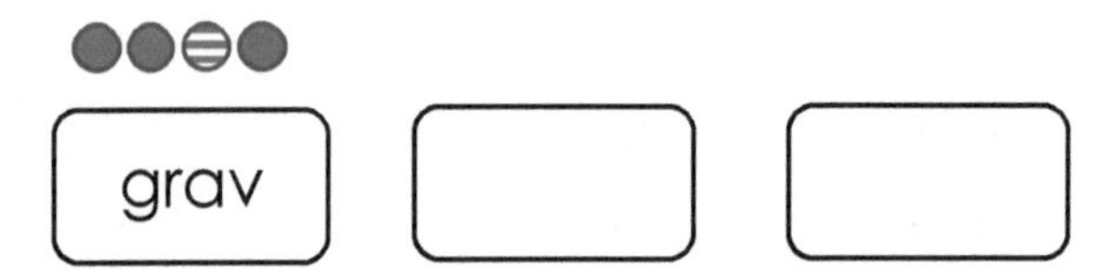

6) Next syllable (repeat same procedure):

Student says **/ ĭ /** and points to the second board.

Student pulls down one disc for each sound in the syllable, while saying each sound out loud.

Student writes "**i**" on the syllable board, while sounding out the letter/s sounds as they write.

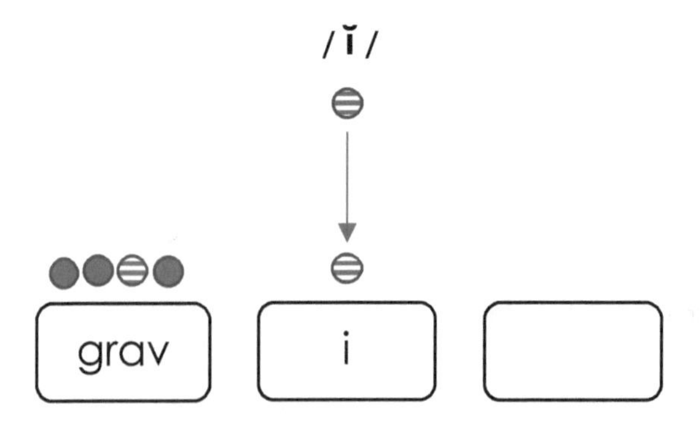

7) Final syllable (repeat same procedure):

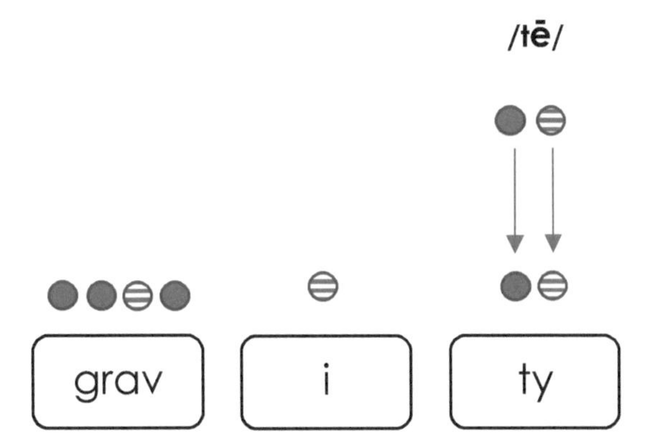

You may need to give guidance for some spelling. For example, in the word **gravity**, the **y** makes the long **e** sound.

8) Student reads the syllables they have written, while tapping under each syllable board.

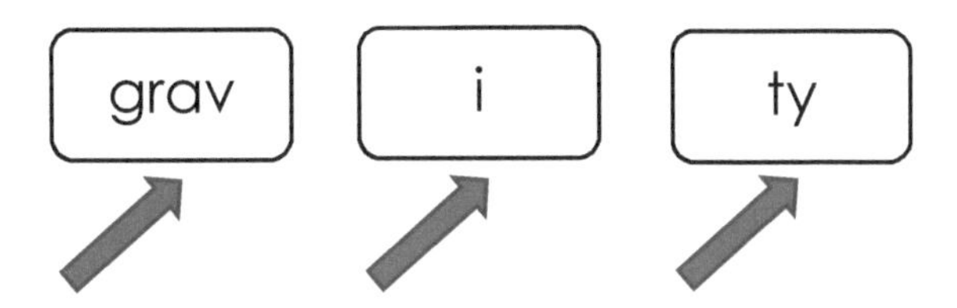

9) Student slides their finger under the word as a whole and reads the word more quickly, blending the whole word together.

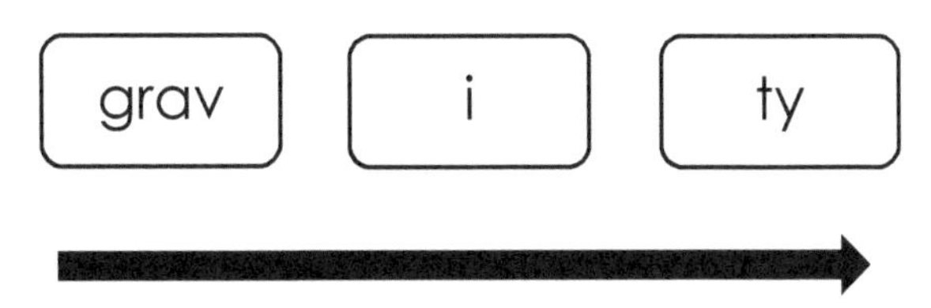

10) Optional: After writing the word with syllables, the student writes the word (as a whole) on the dry erase board, or in a notebook.

Once students become more proficient, they can write the words without using the syllable boards.

Some sounds will have more than one letter. For example, in the word **choppy**, the first syllable **chop** has three sounds, and will therefore have three sound discs. The **/ch/** sound will be spelled with two letters – **CH,** so the syllable will have four letters.

Multi-Sensory Syllable Spelling

Option 2 – Dry Erase Board

Materials: Large personal dry erase board and a dry erase marker.

Procedure:

1) Teacher says each word out loud, one at a time.

   Teacher says, "**Repeat the word I say: gravity**. "

   Student repeats "**gravity**."

2) Student pounds on the table three times, while saying out loud, **/grav – i – ty/**. They can also snap or clap the syllables.

3) Student draws three lines on the dry erase board.

   ________ ________ ________

4) Beginning spellers will tap out the *sounds* in each syllable. Experienced spellers may not need to tap each sound.

   Student says **/grăv/** and points to the first line.

   ________ ________ ________

5) Student taps out the sounds with fingers, while saying each sound out loud. Students can tap fingers on the table, or tap fingers to thumb.

   /g/ /r/ /a/ /v/

   tap-tap-tap-tap

Alternatively, instead of tapping they can make dots under syllable lines, one dot for each sound. Students should do one syllable at a time.

________ ________ ________

• • • •

6) Student writes **"grav"** on the first line, while sounding it out.

grav_

7) Next syllable: Student says **/ ĭ /** and points to the second line.

________ ________ ________

Student taps fingers or makes dots, while saying each sound.

/ ĭ /

tap

Student writes **"i,"** while saying the sound.

grav _i_

8) Last syllable: Student says **/tē/** and points to the third line.

________ ________ ________

Student taps fingers while saying sounds.

/t/ /ē/

tap-tap

Student writes "**ty**," while saying the sounds.

grav i ty

9) You may need to give guidance for some spelling. For example, in the word **gravity**, the **y** makes the long **e** sound.

Student reads the syllables they have written, while tapping under each syllable line.

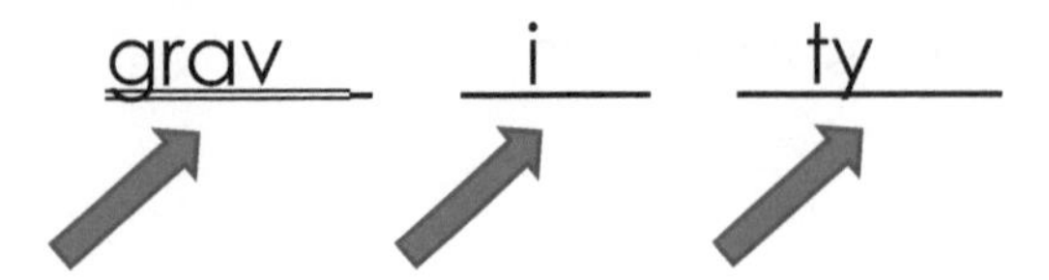

10) Student slides their finger under the word as a whole and reads the word quickly, blending the whole word together.

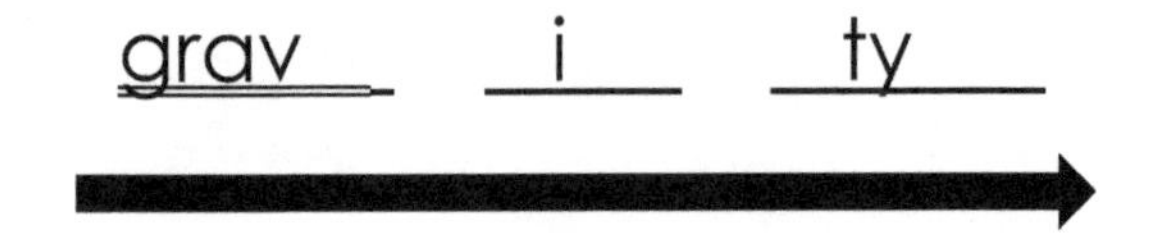

11) Optional: After writing the word with syllables, the student writes the word (as a whole) on the larger dry erase board, or in a notebook.

Once students become more proficient, they can write the words on the lines without tapping, and eventually they can spell without drawing the lines.

Practicing Multi-Syllable Words:

Word Patterns

The following is a sample lesson of one way to provide practice in reading multi-syllable words.

Teacher preparation: Find a word list that you would like to practice and choose 5-10 words. The teacher in this example has decided to practice the **VC/CV** (twin) word pattern.

Day one preparation: Type a word list in large font with the words you have chosen, with plenty of space both above and below each word.

kitten
happen
muffin
button
lesson
bottom
hidden

Day two preparation: Prepare a "cut out" table, such as the one below. The font below is 20, but you may want to use a larger font, such as 36. There is a template in the resources section if you want to hand-write the table.

Syllable types lesson – VC/CV (twin) example

Teacher List	Word Cards	Syllables	
kitten	kitten	kit	ten
muffin	muffin	muf	fin
button	button	but	ton
lesson	lesson	les	son
bottom	bottom	bot	tom
hidden	hidden	hid	den
happen	happen	hap	pen

The left column is left intact. That column is for the teacher to reference during the lesson.

The second column is cut on the lines into mini word cards.

The last section is cut into syllables. For example, the word **kitten** will be cut into:

kit

ten

If you are doing this activity with more than one student, you can have the students cut apart the table. Cut-outs are needed for day 2 of this lesson.

See next page.

Day 1 – Dividing words

Students should understand the terms "vowel" and "consonant" and should also be familiar with the difference between closed and open vowel sounds before beginning this lesson.

Teacher demonstrates everything for the first few words, then gradually transitions students to doing the procedure and the answers.

1) Teacher says, "**Today we are going to learn how to make longer words easier to read by dividing those words into syllables. Syllables are word parts that have one vowel sound each. Place your hand underneath your chin. We are going to say the word butterfly together, and feel how many times our chin drops as we speak.**"

   Teacher demonstrates by placing a hand under his/her chin. "**Say butterfly.**"

   Students place their hands under their chin and say "**butterfly.**"

   Teacher says, "**How many times did you feel your jaw drop?**"

   Students reply "**three times**".

   Teacher says, "**That means that the word butterfly has three syllables.**"

   If students are unfamiliar with syllables, the teacher should practice with several other words so that they become more familiar with the concept.

2) Teacher gives students the word list paper.

   kitten

   happen

   muffin

2) Teacher says "Now I am going to show you how to divide a longer word into syllables to make it easier to read. **Point to the first word. We are going to underline the vowels.**" Teacher demonstrates how to underline the vowels in the word.

3) Teacher asks "**How many consonants are in between the vowels?**" Teacher demonstrates by counting the consonants.

4) Teacher asks, **"If we could divide these consonants evenly, like we were sharing cookies with a friend, how many consonants would each person get ?"** Teacher shows students how to divide the word kitten between the two T's.

kit/ten

Some teachers have students label the consonants and vowels. This is not necessary if you are using the principles of Simple Syllable Division.

VCCV	VC/CV
kitten	kit/ten

5) Teacher covers up the second syllable (ten) in kitten and demonstrates how to sound out **kit.** Teacher reminds students that closed syllables have short vowel sounds.

Next, teacher covers up the first syllable in kitten (kit) and demonstrates how to sound out the second syllable, **ten**.

Finally, teacher displays the whole word kitten, places a finger under the word, and swipes from left right, while sounding out the whole word.

Repeat with the other words. As students become more comfortable with this procedure, they should transition to dividing the words on their own, and reading them on their own.

For more information on how to divide different types of words, see the section, "How to Divide by Syllables"

Some students may need more intensive work in dividing, reading and spelling multi-syllable words. If you have a student who is really struggling, I highly recommend the syllable materials from 95% Group[6].

See next page for Day 2

[6] I receive no compensation for any of the materials I recommend in this book.

Day 2

Step 1: Phonemic awareness

Step 1 is an auditory/phonemic awareness activity and the words should not be shown to the students at this time.

Teacher says each word one at a time.

Student/s repeat each word out loud.

Students verbally divide the words into syllables by using their hands or using manipulatives (choose one option below).

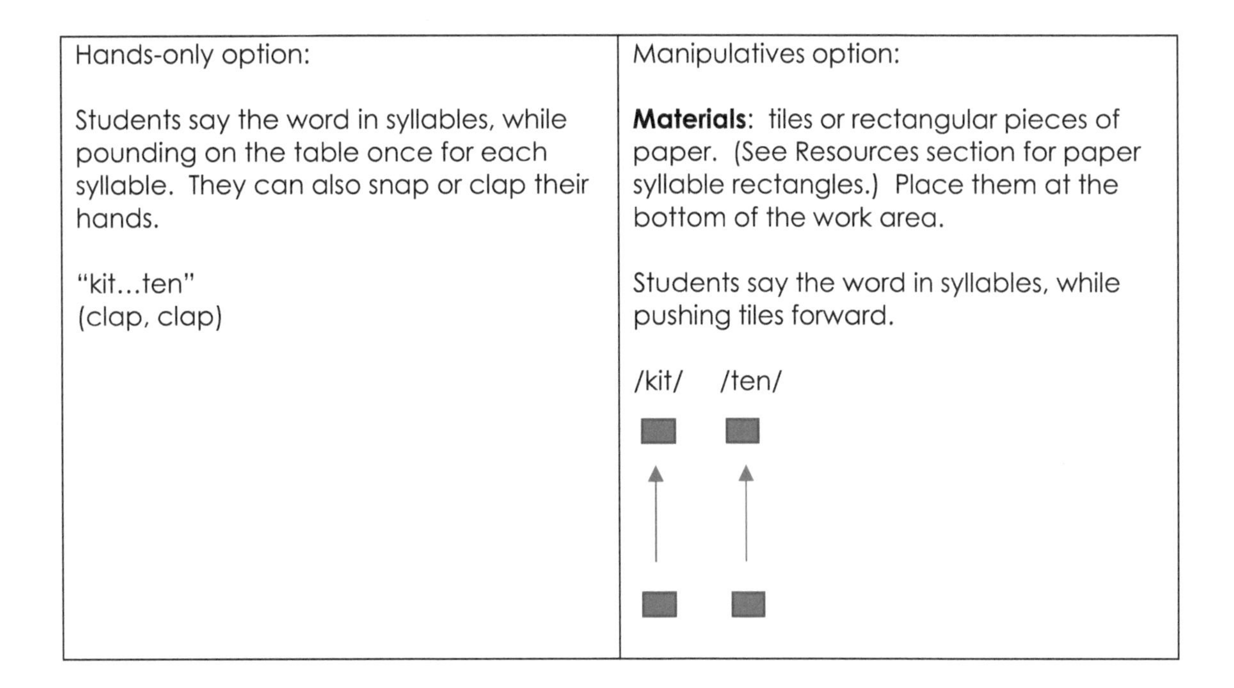

Hands-only option:	Manipulatives option:
Students say the word in syllables, while pounding on the table once for each syllable. They can also snap or clap their hands. "kit...ten" (clap, clap)	**Materials**: tiles or rectangular pieces of paper. (See Resources section for paper syllable rectangles.) Place them at the bottom of the work area. Students say the word in syllables, while pushing tiles forward. /kit/ /ten/

Repeat for each of the words.

See next page.

Step 2: Build words

Students mix up all their syllable slips of paper and place them face up on top of their work area.

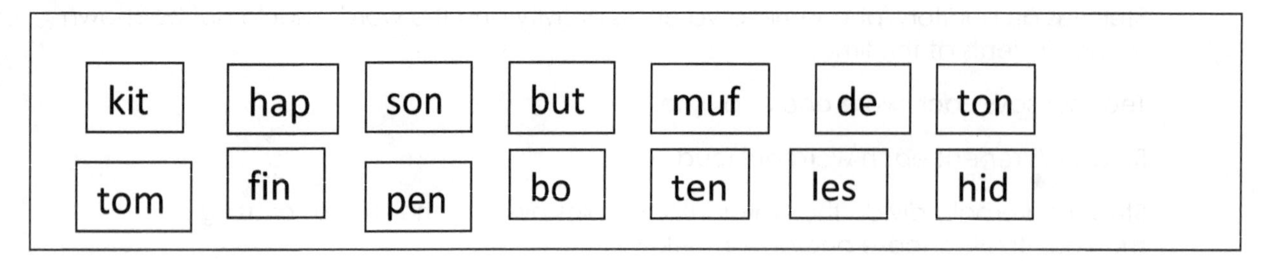

Check to see if all of the syllable slips are facing upright so that they can be easily read.

Teacher says the words one at a time, and students spell each word with the syllable slips. For example, teacher says "kitten" and the students pull down the paper slips to spell:

kit ten

After the first few times of doing this activity, some students enjoy figuring out the words on their own, without the teacher saying the words. I call this "word puzzles." After they have built as many words as they can figure out on their own,the teacher can tell them any words that are left.

Sometimes when students are doing word puzzles on their own, they will make words that are not in the word list. If they do this, you can tell them, "That is a great word that you made. That word is not on our list today, so we will use these syllable cards to make other words." Some teachers like to have a list on the board called "bonus words," so they can write down any extra words that students discover.

Step 3: Read words out loud by syllable

In an individual tutoring setting, you can have the students read the words that they made out loud. Help them to correct any errors. In a group setting, you can write the words on the board (divided into syllables). Then you can switch between having the class read the words chorally and having students take turns reading the words out loud.

Clean up the syllable slips. You will want to have students save them in a baggie if you are going to be using them again for extra activities.

Step 4: Read whole words out loud

Teacher gives students the slips of paper that are whole words one at a time. Students read the words. If students have trouble with this, have them divide the words into syllables using the procedure you taught on the first day.

See next page.

Step 5: Write the words into a notebook (optional)

After your students have spelled each word with paper slips, you may have them write the words in a notebook. (This is optional)

If students have trouble copying, have them follow the copying procedure detailed below:

1) Student says each syllable part out loud
   Student says: **/mes/**

2) Student spells (says the letters) for each syllable out loud.
   Student says "**M-E-S**"

3) Student writes the syllable in their notebooks, while spelling the syllable out loud.

   Student says "**M-E-S**" while writing "**mes**" in their notebook.

This continues through the rest of the word, one syllable at a time.

Student says: **/en/...E-N**

Student says "**E-N**" while writing **en** in their notebook.

Student says **/ger/...G-E-R**

Student says "**G-E-R**" while writing **ger** in their notebook.

4) Student looks at the word they just wrote and reads the whole word, /**messenger**/. This is a chance for the student to see if the word looks like it is spelled correctly.

Step 6: Review words.

If possible, continue to review the words over the next couple of days. Here are some ideas:

Students spell the words on Syllable Boards (See Multi-Sensory Syllable Spelling).

Students read the words in sentences or paragraphs.

Students keep the whole word cards in an envelope or plastic bag and practice reading them alone or with partners.

In teams, one student reads the whole word cards, and the other student makes the words with the syllable slips of paper.

Teacher gives students a sheet of paper with the words written on it and students divide the words into syllables. Students can divide by drawing lines or drawing scoops under each syllable.

Students take the whole word cards and cut them apart into syllables with scissors.

Practicing Multi-syllable words: Content Passages

When your students become proficient enough to read multi-syllable words, they are often given texts that are no longer "decodable readers." In addition, while students may be using decodable readers in their tutoring time, they may be presented with non-controlled reading materials in their school classes, especially in science or social studies.

You may also find if you are a teacher in the older grades, that your students were not taught phonics well in the earlier grades, and they are not prepared to read the harder texts and the harder words that you are required to teach them.

In these cases, your students are presented with words that are not easy for them to decode, or words that do not follow the rules and patterns that they have been taught. The lesson below is an example of one way to help students practice these longer words. This lesson gives students practice both in reading individual syllables and in developing their reading comprehension of content area texts and higher-level fiction texts.

The following is an example of a tutoring session that will teach multi-syllable words, while at the same time preparing the students to read the content passage for their class.

Teacher preparation: read the student's text and write down the words that you think your student will find challenging. The number of words that you write down will depend on your student's ability level and needs. A typical amount would be 5-10 words.

Below is the sample passage.

"A ribosome is a cellular particle made of RNA and protein that serves as the site for protein synthesis in the cell. The ribosome reads the sequence of the messenger RNA (mRNA) and, using the genetic code, translates the sequence of RNA bases into a sequence of amino acids." (Genome.gov)

The teacher considers the student's skills and ability levels and chooses the following words:

ribosome

cellular

particle

genetic

amino

messenger

synthesis

(Lesson continues on next page).

To prepare for the lesson, the teacher prepares a "cut out" table, such as the one below. The font below is 20, but you may want to use a larger font, such as 36. There is a template in the resources section if you want to hand-write the table.

ribosome cellular particle genetic amino messenger synthesis	ribosome	ri	bo	some
	cellular	cel	lu	lar
	particle	par	ti	cle
	genetic	ge	net	ic
	amino	a	mi	no
	messenger	mes	sen	ger
	synthesis	syn	the	sis

The left column is left intact. That column is for the teacher to reference during the lesson.

The second column is cut on the lines into mini word cards.

The last section is cut into syllables. For example, the word **particle** will be cut into:

par

ti

cle

If you are doing this activity with more than one student, you can have the students cut apart the table.

There are two websites I recommend that will divide words into syllables for you - howmanysyllables.com and www.syllablecount.com. I would not recommend using a regular dictionary. The divisions in dictionaries are not real syllable divisions; they are typing conventions (see section on Dictionary Entries for more info).

Procedure:

Step 1: Phonemic awareness

This is solely an auditory/phonemic awareness activity and the words should not be shown to the students at this time.

Teacher says each word one at a time.

Student/s repeat the word out loud.

Choose one of the options below:

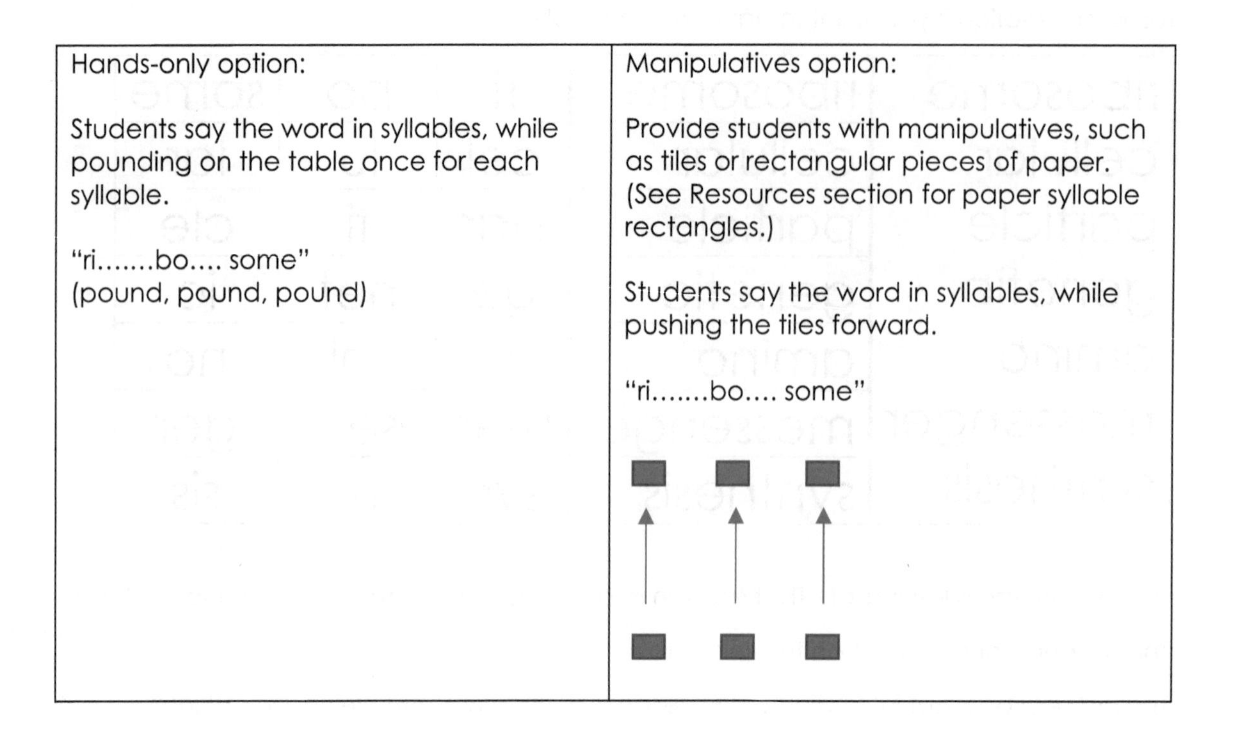

Hands-only option:	Manipulatives option:
Students say the word in syllables, while pounding on the table once for each syllable. "ri.......bo.... some" (pound, pound, pound)	Provide students with manipulatives, such as tiles or rectangular pieces of paper. (See Resources section for paper syllable rectangles.) Students say the word in syllables, while pushing the tiles forward. "ri.......bo.... some"

Repeat for each of the words.

Step 2: Build words

Students mix up their syllable cards (slips of paper) and place them face up on top of their work surface.

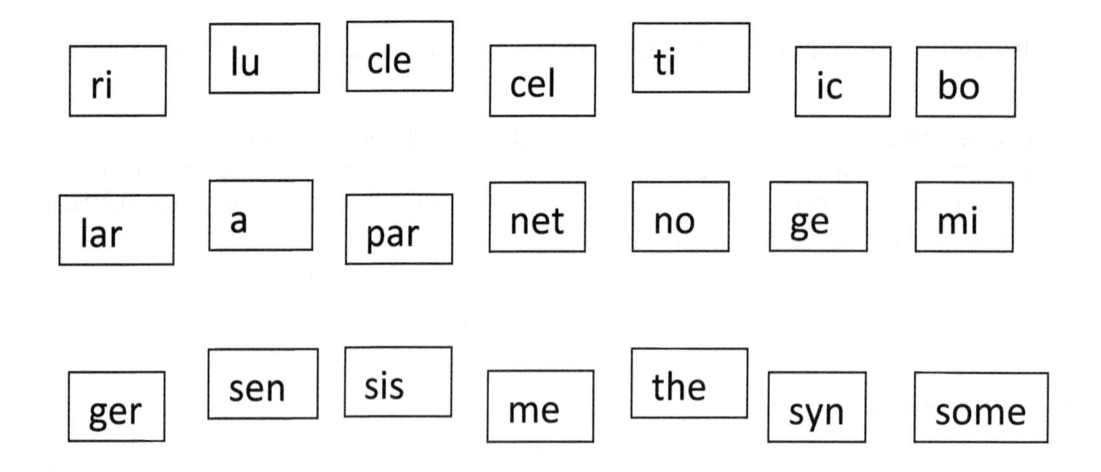

Teacher checks to see that all the syllable slips are facing upright so that they can be easily read.

Teacher says the words one at a time, and the students spell each word with the syllable slips. For example, teacher says "ribosome" the students find the paper slips to spell:

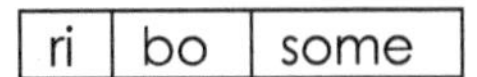

This is a good time to teach and review phonograms and spelling patterns. For example, in the word **ribosome**, you can discuss open syllables and the fact that **s** is often pronounced **/z/.** For the word **messenger**, you could discuss closed syllables and the concept that **g** followed by the letter **e** makes **g** say its soft sound.

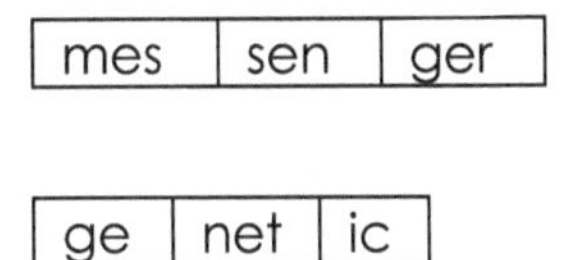

Step 3: Read words out loud by syllable

In a tutoring setting, you can have the students read the words that they made out loud. Help them to correct any errors. In a group setting, you can pair up students who are sitting next to each other. The first student reads one of their words out loud, while the second student finds that word on their work surface. Once the second student has located that word, both students remove those slips of paper. Then the second student takes a turn reading a word, while the first student looks for the word. Turns continue until all of the slips of paper have been removed.

Students clean up the syllable slips.

Step 5: Read whole words out loud

Teacher gives students the slips of paper that are whole words. Students read the words one at a time. In a group setting, you can have students read the words to each other.

Step 6: Write the words into a notebook (optional)

As an option, after your students have spelled each word with paper slips, you may have them write the words in a notebook. Those words can be read at a later time.

If students have trouble copying, follow the copying procedure detailed below:

The word is **ribosome**.

Student sounds out each syllable part out loud
Student says: **/ri/**

Student spells (says the letters) for each syllable out loud.
Student says "**R-I**"

Student writes the syllable in their notebooks, while spelling the syllable out loud.

Student says "**R-I**" while writing "**ri**" in their notebook.

This continues through the rest of the word, one syllable at a time.

Student says: **/bo/...B-O**

Student says "**B-O**" while writing **"bo"** in their notebook.

Student says **/zom/...S-O-M-E**

Student says "**S-O-M-E**" while writing **"some"** in their notebook.

5) Student looks at the word they just wrote and reads the whole word, "**ribosome**". This is a chance for the student to see if the word looks like it is spelled correctly.

Step 6: Read words in the original text.

Students now read the original text that includes the words that they practiced. This is the opportunity to discuss the meaning/comprehension of the vocabulary words and the passage.

Step 7: Review new words.

If possible, continue to work on the words and the passage over the next couple of days. Here are some ideas:

Students re-read the text.

Students keep the whole word cards in an envelope or plastic bag and practice reading them over the next few days.

Teacher says words out loud and students spell them on a dry-erase board, or with syllable boards (See Multi-Sensory Syllable Spelling).

In pairs, one student reads a word card, and the other student makes the word with the syllable slips of paper (to do this, the students need to save their syllable slips and word slips in a baggie for use the next day).

Teacher gives students a sheet of paper with the practiced words written on it and students divide the words into syllables. Students can divide by drawing lines, drawing scoops under each syllable, or cutting apart the words with scissors.

Students spell the words using the Multi-Sensory Syllable Spelling method.

Compound Words

Compound Words

- There are three types of compound words – **connected, hyphenated** and **separated**.
  - **Connected** compound words are made up of two or more words that together form a new word. This is the most common kind of compound word.

    arrowhead

    airport

  - **Hyphenated** compound words are made up of two or more words/bases that have a hyphen connecting them.

    hide-and-seek

    part-time

  - **Separated** compound words are made up of two or more words/bases that are appear to be separated as two words, but they make a new "word" when they are together.

    chicken pox – The compound word **chicken pox** is not simply the combination of a **chicken** and a **pox** (disease). It's not a chicken disease. It's a new concept.

    green thumb – The compound word **green thumb** is not simply a **thumb** that is **green**. It's a new concept.

compound

connnected

- **Connected** compound words are made up of two or more words that together form a new word. This is the most common kind of compound word.

  arrowhead

  airport

- Two-base compounds (this list) generally consist of two nouns, or an adjective and a noun.

  Airbag – Noun-Noun
  Blackboard – Adjective-Noun

afterlife	af-ter life	anywhere	an-y where
aftermath	af-ter math	applesauce	ap-ple sauce
afternoon	af-ter noon	armchair	arm chair
aftershock	af-ter shock	armpit	arm pit
afterthought	af-ter thought	arrowhead	ar-row head
airbag	air bag	babyproof	ba-by proof
aircraft	air craft	babysat	ba-by sat
airfare	air fare	babysit	ba-by sit
airline	air line	babysitter	ba-by sitter
airplane	air plane	backboard	back board
airport	air port	backbone	back bone
airship	air ship	backfire	back fire
airtight	air tight	backflip	back flip
alongside	a-long side	background	back ground
anybody	an-y body	backhand	back hand
anyhow	an-y how	backpack	back pack
anymore	an-y more	backstroke	back stroke
anyone	an-y one	backtrack	back track
anyplace	an-y place	backup	back up
anything	an-y thing	backyard	back yard
anytime	an-y time	bagpipe	bag pipe
anyway	an-y way	ballroom	ball room

barcode	bar code
bareback	bare back
barnyard	barn yard
baseball	base ball
basketball	bas-ket ball
bathrobe	bath robe
bathroom	bath room
bathtub	bath tub
battlefield	battle field
battleground	bat-tle ground
battleship	bat-tle ship
bedrock	bed rock
bedroom	bed room
bedspread	bed spread
beehive	bee hive
beeline	bee line
beeswax	bees wax
beforehand	be-fore hand
beheld	be held
behold	be hold
bellybutton	bel-ly but-ton
betray	be tray
bewitch	be witch
billboard	bill board
birthday	birth day
birthmark	birth mark
birthplace	birth place
birthright	birth right
blackberry	black ber-ry
blackbird	black bird
blackboard	black board
blackmail	black mail
blackout	black out
blacksmith	black smith
blacktop	black top
blindfold	blind fold
bloodhound	blood hound
bloodshed	blood shed
bloodshot	blood shot
bloodstream	blood stream
blowtorch	blow torch
blueberry	blue ber-ry
bluebird	blue bird
bluegrass	blue grass
blueprint	blue print
bobcat	bob cat
bobsled	bob sled
bookbag	book bag
bookcase	book case
bookend	book end
bookkeeping	book keep-ing
booklet	book let
bookmark	book mark
boomtown	boom town
bottleneck	bot-tle neck
boyfriend	boy friend
boyhood	boy hood
brainstorm	brain storm
brainwash	brain wash
breakdown	break down
breakfast	break fast
breakthrough	break through
breathless	breath less
breathtaking	breath tak-ing
bricklayer	brick layer
briefcase	brief case
broadband	broad band
broadcast	broad cast
brotherhood	broth-er hood
buckwheat	buck wheat

bulldozer	bull doz-er
bullfrog	bull frog
bullpen	bull pen
bumblebee	bum-ble bee
burdensome	bur-den some
busybody	bus-y body
busywork	bus-y work
buttercup	but-ter cup
butterfly	but-ter fly
buttermilk	but-ter milk
butterscotch	but-ter cup
buttonhole	but-ton hole
bygone	by gone
bypass	by pass
byproduct	by prod-uct
bystander	by stand-er
candlestick	can-dle stick
cardboard	card board
carefree	care free
careless	care less
caretaker	care tak-er
cartwheel	cart wheel
catbird	cat bird
catnap	cat nap
catnip	cat nip
cellphone	cell phone
centerpiece	cen-ter piece
chainsaw	chain saw
chairman	chair man
chairperson	chair per-son
chairwoman	chair wom-an
chalkboard	chalk board
chatroom	chat room
checkerboard	check-er board
checkup	check up
cheerleader	cheer lead-er
cheeseburger	cheese bur-ger
chickpea	chick pea
studentbirth	student birth
studenthood	student hood
studentlike	student like
studentproof	student proof
chopsticks	chop sticks
churchyard	church yard
clambake	clam bake
classmate	class mate
classroom	class room
clockwork	clock work
clothesline	clothes line
clothespin	clothes pin
coastline	coast line
cobblestone	cob-ble stone
cockroach	cock roach
cocktail	cock tail
coleslaw	cole slaw
collarbone	col-lar bone
colorblind	col-or blind
congressman	con-gress man
congresswoman	con-gress woman
cookbook	cook book
cookout	cook out
copyright	cop-y right
corkscrew	cork screw
cornstarch	corn starch
cottonmouth	cot-ton mouth
cottontail	cot-ton tail
cottonwood	cot-ton wood
countdown	count down
counterpart	count-er part
countless	count less

countryman	coun-try man
countryside	coun-try side
countrywoman	coun-try woman
courthouse	court house
courtroom	court room
courtship	court ship
courtyard	court yard
crabapple	crab ap-ple
crawfish	craw fish
crisscross	criss cross
crossbow	cross bow
crossroads	cross roads
crosswalk	cross walk
crowbar	crow bar
cubbyhole	cub-by hole
cupboard	cup board
cupcake	cup cake
daredevil	dare devil
dashboard	dash board
database	da-ta base
daybreak	day break
daycare	day care
daydream	day dream
daylight	day light
daytime	day time
deadline	dead line
desktop	desk top
dodgeball	dodge ball
dogwood	dog wood
doorbell	door bell
doorknob	door knob
doorstep	door step
doorway	door way
doubtless	doubt less
doughnut	dough nut
downcast	down cast
downfall	down fall
downhill	down hill
download	down load
downpour	down pour
downright	down right
downstairs	down stairs
downstream	down stream
downtown	down town
downward	down ward
dragonfly	drag-on fly
drawback	draw back
drawbridge	draw bridge
driveway	drive way
drugstore	drug store
drumroll	drum roll
drumstick	drum stick
dumbbell	dumb bell
eardrum	ear drum
earlobe	ear lobe
earmuffs	ear muffs
earphones	ear phones
earthquake	earth quake
earthworm	earth worm
eastward	east ward
eavesdrop	eaves drop
eggnog	egg nog
eggplant	egg plant
elsewhere	else where
evergreen	ever green
everybody	eve-ry body
everyday	eve-ry day
everyone	eve-ry one
everything	eve-ry thing
everywhere	eve-ry where

eyeball	eye ball
eyebrow	eye brow
eyeglasses	eye glass-es
eyelash	eye lash
eyelid	eye lid
eyepiece	eye piece
eyesight	eye sight
eyesore	eye sore
eyewitness	eye wit-ness
fairway	fair way
fallout	fall out
falsehood	false hood
farewell	fare well
fearless	fear less
fearsome	fear some
feedback	feed back
figurehead	fig-ure head
fingerprint	fin-ger print
firecracker	fire crack-er
firefighter	fire fight-er
firefly	fire fly
firehouse	fire house
fireman	fire man
fireplace	fire place
fireproof	fire proof
fireside	fire side
firewood	fire wood
fireworks	fire works
firsthand	first hand
fisherman	fish-er man
fishhook	fish hook
flagpole	flag pole
flapjack	flap jack
flashback	flash back
flashlight	flash light

flightless	flight less
floodlight	flood light
foghorn	fog horn
folklore	folk lore
folktale	folk tale
foolhardy	fool har-dy
foolproof	fool proof
football	foot ball
foothill	foot hill
foothold	foot hold
footnote	foot note
footprint	foot print
footstep	foot step
footstool	foot stool
forklift	fork lift
foursquare	four square
foxhound	fox hound
framework	frame work
freestyle	free style
freeway	free way
freshman	fresh man
freshwater	fresh wa-ter
frostbite	frost bit
fullback	full back
furthermore	fur-ther more
gangplank	gang plank
gangway	gang way
gateway	gate way
gingerbread	gin-ger bread
glowworm	glow worm
godfather	god fa-ther
godmother	god moth-er
goldenrod	gold-en rod
goldfinch	gold finch
goldfish	gold fish

Goldsmith	Gold smith	handcuff	hand cuff
goodbye	good bye	handkerchief	hand ker-chief
Goodman	Good man	handlebars	han-dle bars
goodwill	good will	handmade	hand made
grandchildren	grand chil-dren	handout	hand out
granddaughter	grand daugh-ter	handrail	hand rail
grandfather	grand fa-ther	handshake	hand shake
grandmother	grand moth-er	handsome	hand some
grandparent	grand par-ent	handspring	hand spring
grandson	grand son	handstand	hand stand
grandstand	grand stand	handwriting	hand writ-ing
grapefruit	grape fruit	hangnail	hang nail
grapevine	grape vine	hardship	hard ship
grasshopper	grass hop-per	hardware	hard ware
grassland	grass land	hardwood	hard wood
greenhouse	green house	harmless	harm less
greyhound	grey hound	hashtag	hash tag
grindstone	grind stone	hayloft	hay loft
groundhog	ground hog	hayride	hay ride
grownup	grown up	haystack	hay stack
guideline	guide line	haywire	hay wire
guideword	guide word	headache	head ache
gumdrop	gum drop	headband	head band
hairdresser	hair dress-er	headdress	head dress
hairpin	hair pin	headfirst	head first
hairstyle	hair style	headland	head land
halfback	half back	headlight	head light
halfhearted	half heart-ed	headline	head line
halfpipe	half pipe	headlong	head long
halfway	half way	headphones	head phones
hallway	hall way	headrest	head rest
hammerhead	ham-mer head	headstrong	head strong
handbag	hand bag	headwaters	head wa-ters
handball	hand ball	headway	head way
handbook	hand book	hearsay	hear say

heartbeat	heart beat	horsehair	horse hair
heartbroken	heart bro-ken	horseplay	horse play
heartwarming	heart warm-ing	horsepower	horse pow-er
hedgehog	hedge hog	horseshoe	horse shoe
helpless	help less	hotheaded	hot head-ed
herself	her self	hourglass	hour glass
highland	high land	houseboat	house boat
highlight	high light	housefly	house fly
highway	high way	housekeeper	house keep-er
hillside	hill side	houseplant	house plant
hilltop	hill top	housewarming	house warm-ing
himself	him self	housework	house work
hitchhike	hitch hike	huckleberry	huck-le ber-ry
holdup	hold up	humankind	hu-man kind
homegrown	home grown	iceberg	ice berg
homeland	home land	icebreaker	ice break-er
homeless	home less	icecap	ice cap
homemade	home made	inchworm	inch worm
homepage	home page	income	in come
homeroom	home room	indeed	in deed
homeschool	home school	indent	in dent
homesick	home sick	indirect	in di-rect
homespun	home spun	indoor	in door
homestead	home stead	induct	in duct
homestretch	home stretch	infamous	in fa-mous
hometown	home town	infield	in field
homeward	home ward	inflame	in flame
homework	home work	inform	in form
honeybee	honey bee	inhabit	in hab-it
honeycomb	honey comb	inland	in land
honeymoon	honey moon	inlet	in let
hopeless	hope less	input	in put
hopscotch	hop scotch	inscribe	in scribe
horseback	horse back	insight	in sight
horsefly	horse fly	install	in stall

instead	in stead
instep	in step
instill	in still
intake	in take
intend	in tend
intent	in tent
intercom	in-ter com
jackknife	jack knife
jackpot	jack pot
jackrabbit	jack rab-bit
jaywalk	jay walk
jellyfish	jel-ly fish
jigsaw	jig saw
joystick	joy stick
keepsake	keep sake
keyboard	key board
keyhole	key hole
keypad	key pad
keystone	key stone
keyword	key word
kinship	kin ship
knapsack	knap sack
kneecap	knee cap
knickknack	knick knack
knighthood	knight hood
ladybug	la-dy bug
Lakewood	Lake wood
landlady	land la-dy
landlord	land lord
landmark	land mark
landscape	land scape
landslide	land slide
laptop	lap top
lawsuit	law suit
leadership	lead-er ship

leapfrog	leap frog
leftover	left o-ver
lengthwise	length wise
lifeboat	life boat
lifeguard	life guard
lifeless	life less
lifelike	life like
lifelong	life long
lifesaving	life sav-ing
lifespan	life span
lifestyle	life style
lifetime	life time
liftoff	lift off
lighthouse	light house
limestone	lime stone
linebacker	line back-er
lineman	line man
lipstick	lip stick
livestock	live stock
locksmith	lock smith
lonesome	lone some
Longfellow	Long fel-low
longhorn	long horn
lookout	look out
loudspeaker	loud speak-er
lowercase	low-er case
lumberjack	lum-ber jack
madcap	mad cap
mailbox	mail box
mailman	mail man
mainland	main land
mainstream	main stream
makeshift	make shift
makeup	make up
manhole	man hole

manhood	man hood	nighthawk	night hawk
mankind	man kind	nightmare	night mare
manmade	man made	nighttime	night time
Maryland	Mary land	northeast	north east
masterpiece	mas-ter piece	northwest	north west
meadowlark	mead-ow lark	nosebleed	nose bleed
meantime	mean time	notebook	note book
meanwhile	mean while	nowhere	no where
meatloaf	meat loaf	nutcracker	nut crack-er
midday	mid day	Oakland	Oak land
milestone	mile stone	oatmeal	oat meal
milkshake	milk shake	Oceanside	O-cean side
milkweed	milk weed	offshoot	off shoot
moonbeam	moon beam	offshore	off shore
moonlight	moon light	offside	off side
moonlit	moon lit	offspring	off spring
motherhood	moth-er hood	oilskin	oil skin
motorboat	mo-tor boat	oneself	one self
motorcade	mo-tor cade	ongoing	on go-ing
mouthpiece	mouth piece	online	on line
myself	my self	onset	on set
nearsighted	near sight-ed	onshore	on shore
necklace	neck lace	outbound	out bound
neckline	neck line	outbreak	out break
necktie	neck tie	outburst	out burst
needlework	nee-dle work	outcome	out come
network	net work	outcry	out cry
newborn	new born	outdid	out did
newcomer	new com-er	outdo	out do
newscast	news cast	outdone	out done
newspaper	news pa-per	outdoor	out door
newsstand	news stand	outdoors	out doors
nickname	nick name	outfield	out field
nightfall	night fall	outfielder	out field-er
nightgown	night gown	outgoing	out go-ing

outgrew	out grew
outgrow	out grow
outgrown	out grown
outlaw	out law
outlet	out let
outline	out line
outlook	out look
outnumber	out num-ber
outpost	out post
output	out put
outright	out right
outside	out side
outskirts	out skirts
outspoken	out spok-en
outstanding	out stand-ing
outweigh	out weight
outwit	out wit
overboard	o-ver board
overcame	o-ver came
overcast	o-ver cast
overcoat	o-ver coat
overcome	o-ver come
overdid	o-ver did
overdo	o-ver do
overdone	o-ver done
overdue	o-ver due
overflow	o-ver flow
overhand	o-ver hand
overhaul	o-ver haul
overhead	o-ver head
overhear	o-ver hear
overlap	o-ver lap
overlook	o-ver look
overnight	o-ver night
overpass	o-ver pass
overpower	o-ver pow-er
overrule	o-ver rule
overseas	o-ver seas
oversight	o-ver sight
overtake	o-ver take
overtaken	o-ver tak-en
overthrew	o-ver threw
overthrow	o-ver throw
overtime	o-ver time
overtook	o-ver look
overturn	o-ver turn
overweight	o-ver weight
pacemaker	pace mak-er
paddleboard	pad-dle board
painless	pain less
painstaking	pain stak-ing
paintbrush	paint brush
pancake	pan cake
panhandle	pan han-dle
paperback	pa-per back
parkway	park way
passageway	pas-sage way
Passover	Pass over
passport	pass port
password	pass word
patchwork	patch work
pavement	pave ment
payroll	pay roll
peacekeeping	peace keep-ing
peacock	pea cock
peanut	pea nut
penknife	pen knife
penlight	pen light
photocopy	pho-to copy
photograph	pho-to graph

pickax	pick ax	potluck	pot luck
pickaxe	pick axe	powwow	pow wow
pickup	pick up	priceless	price less
piggyback	pig-gy back	pronghorn	prong horn
pigheaded	pig head-ed	proofread	proof read
pigtail	pig tail	purebred	pure bred
pillowcase	pil-low case	pushup	push up
pinball	pin ball	quarterback	quar-ter back
pineapple	pine ap-ple	quicksand	quick sand
pinkeye	pink eye	racetrack	race track
pinpoint	pin point	racquetball	rac-quet ball
pinwheel	pin wheel	radioactive	ra-di-o ac-tive
pipeline	pipe line	radioactivity	ra-di-o ac-tiv-i-ty
pitchfork	pitch fork	railroad	rail road
pitfall	pit fall	railway	rail way
playground	play ground	rainbow	rain bow
playoff	play off	raincoat	rain coat
playwright	play wright	raindrop	rain drop
plywood	ply wood	rainfall	rain fall
pocketbook	pock-et book	rawhide	raw hide
pocketknife	pock-et knife	redwood	red wood
podcast	pod cast	restless	rest less
policeman	po-lice man	restroom	rest room
policewoman	po-lice wom-an	riverside	riv-er side
porthole	port hole	roommate	room mate
Portland	Port land	rosebush	rose bush
postcard	post card	rosemary	rose mar-y
postman	post man	Rosemary	Rose mar-y
postmark	post mark	roundtrip	round trip
postmaster	post mast-er	roundup	round up
postpone	post pone	rowboat	row boat
postscript	post script	runaway	run a-way
postseason	post sea-son	rundown	run down
potholder	pot hold-er	runway	run way
pothole	pot hole	safeguard	safe guard

sagebrush	sage brush
sailboat	sail boat
salesman	sales man
salesperson	sales per-son
saleswoman	sales wom-an
saltshaker	salt shak-er
saltwater	salt wa-ter
sandbar	sand bar
sandbox	sand box
sandpaper	sand pa-per
sandstone	sand stone
saucepan	sauce pan
sawdust	saw dust
sawmill	saw mill
scapegoat	scape goat
scarecrow	scare crow
schoolhouse	school house
schoolteacher	school teach-er
schoolwork	school work
schoolyard	school yard
scoreboard	score board
scrapbook	scrap book
screenplay	screen play
screwdriver	screw driv-er
seacoast	sea coast
seafood	sea food
seagoing	sea go-ing
seagull	sea gull
seahorse	sea horse
seaplane	sea plane
searchlight	search light
seashell	sea shell
seashore	sea shore
seasick	sea sick
seaweed	sea week
seesaw	see saw
shameless	shame less
sheepdog	sheep dog
shellfish	shell fish
shipshape	ship shape
shipwreck	ship wreck
shipyard	ship yard
shoelace	shoe lace
shoestring	shoe string
shoplift	shop lift
shortcut	short cut
shortsighted	short sight-ed
shortstop	short stop
showcase	show case
showoff	show off
Shreveport	Shreve port
shutdown	shut down
shuttlecock	shut-tle cock
sideburns	side burns
sideline	side line
sidestep	side step
sidetrack	side track
sidewalk	side walk
sideways	side ways
sightless	sight less
sightseeing	sight see-ing
signpost	sign post
silkworm	silk worm
silversmith	sil-ver smith
skateboard	skate board
skydiving	sky div-ing
skylight	sky light
skyline	sky line
skyrocket	sky rock-et
skyscraper	sky scrap-er

sleepover	sleep over	Springfield	Spring field
slingshot	sling shot	spyglass	spy glass
smallpox	small pox	stagecoach	stage coach
smokestack	smoke stack	stairway	stair way
snapdragon	snap dragon	stalemate	stale mate
snapshot	snap shot	standpoint	stand point
snowboard	snow board	standstill	stand still
snowfall	snow fall	starfish	star fish
snowflake	snow flake	statesman	states man
snowman	snow man	stateswoman	states wom-an
snowmobile	snow mo-bile	steamboat	steam boat
snowplow	snow plow	steamroller	steam roll-er
snowshoe	snow shoe	steamship	steam ship
snowstorm	snow storm	stepbrother	step broth-er
softball	soft ball	stepdaughter	step daugh-ter
someday	some day	stepfather	step fa-ther
somehow	some how	stepmother	step moth-er
someone	some one	stepparent	step par-ent
something	some thing	stepsister	step sis-ter
sometime	some time	stepson	step son
somewhat	some what	stingray	sting ray
somewhere	some where	stockpile	stock pile
songbird	song bird	stockyard	stock yard
soundproof	sound proof	stoplight	stop light
soundtrack	sound track	stopwatch	stop watch
southeast	south east	storehouse	store house
southwest	south west	stowaway	stow a-way
soybean	soy bean	streamlined	stream lined
spacecraft	space craft	streetlight	street light
spaceship	space ship	strikeout	strike out
speechless	speech less	stronghold	strong hold
spineless	spine less	sugarcane	sug-ar cane
spotless	spot less	sugarless	sug-ar less
spotlight	spot light	sunbathe	sun bathe
springboard	spring board	sunbeam	sun beam

sunburn	sun burn	thumbtack	thumb tack
Sunday	Sun day	thunderbolt	thun-der bolt
sundial	sun di-al	thundercloud	thun-der cloud
sunflower	sun flow-er	thunderstorm	thun-der storm
sunglasses	sun glass-es	thunderstruck	thun-der struck
sunlight	sun light	tightrope	tight rope
Sunnyvale	Sun-ny vale	timberline	tim-ber line
sunscreen	sun screen	timeless	time less
sunset	sun set	timeline	time line
sunshine	sun shine	timepiece	time piece
superhero	super hero	timetable	time ta-ble
superhuman	su-per human	tiptoe	tip toe
supermarket	su-per market	tireless	tire less
supernatural	su-per natural	tiresome	tire some
sweatshirt	sweat shirt	toadstool	toad stool
sweetheart	sweet heart	toenail	toe nail
swimsuit	swim suit	tombstone	tomb stone
swordfish	sword fish	tomcat	tom cat
tablecloth	ta-ble cloth	toothache	tooth ache
tablespoon	ta-ble spoon	toothbrush	tooth brush
tapeworm	tape worm	toothpaste	tooth paste
tattletale	tat-tle tale	toothpick	tooth pick
taxicab	tax-i cab	topsoil	top soil
teakettle	tea ket-tle	touchdown	touch down
teammate	team mate	townhouse	town house
teamwork	team work	township	town ship
teapot	tea pot	trademark	trade mark
teardrop	tear drop	treadmill	tread mill
teaspoon	tea spoon	trustworthy	trust wor-thy
textbook	text book	tryout	try out
thankless	thank less	tugboat	tug boat
themselves	them selves	tumbleweed	tum-ble week
thereby	there by	turnout	turn out
threadbare	thread bare	turnover	turn o-ver
throughout	through out	turnpike	turn pike

turnstile	turn stile	upkeep	up keep
turntable	turn ta-ble	upload	up load
turtleneck	tur-tle neck	upright	up right
typewriter	type writ-er	uprising	up ris-ing
underarm	un-der arm	uproar	up roar
underbrush	un-der brush	uproot	up root
underclothes	un-der clothes	upset	up set
undercover	un-der cov-er	upshot	up shot
underdog	un-der dog	upstream	up stream
underfoot	un-der foot	useful	use ful
undergarment	un-der gar-ment	videotape	vid-e-o tape
undergone	un-der gone	viewpoint	view point
underground	un-der ground	voicemail	voice mail
undergrowth	un-der growth	volleyball	vol-ley ball
underhand	un-der hand	walkway	walk a-way
underhanded	un-der hand-ed	wallpaper	wall pa-per
underline	un-der line	warehouse	ware house
underpass	un-der pass	warfare	war fare
undersea	un-der sea	warlike	war like
undershirt	un-der shirt	warship	war ship
underside	un-der side	wastebasket	waste bas-ket
understood	un-der stood	wasteland	waste land
undertake	un-der take	watchdog	watch dog
undertone	un-der tone	watchman	watch man
undertook	un-der took	waterbird	wa-ter bird
undertow	un-der tow	watercolor	wa-ter col-or
underwater	un-der wa-ter	waterfall	wa-ter fall
underwear	un-der wear	waterfront	wa-ter front
underweight	un-der weight	waterpower	wa-ter pow-er
underwent	un-der went	watershed	wa-ter shed
update	up date	waterway	wa-ter way
upgrade	up grade	wayside	way side
upheld	up held	weathervane	weath-er vane
uphill	up hill	webcam	web cam
uphold	up hold	webpage	web page

website	web site
wedlock	wed lock
weekday	week day
weekend	week end
weightless	weight less
whatever	what ever
wheelbarrow	wheel bar-row
wheelchair	wheel chair
whenever	when ev-er
whichever	which ev-er
whirlpool	whirl pool
whirlwind	whirl wind
whiteboard	white board
whitecap	white cap
whitewash	white wash
whoever	who ev-er
wholesale	whole sale
wholesome	whole some
whomever	whom ev-er
widespread	wide spread
wildcat	wild cat
wildflower	wall flow-er
wildlife	wild life
willpower	will pow-er
windmill	wind mill
windowpane	win-dow pane
windpipe	wind pipe
windshield	wind shield
windstorm	wind storm
windsurf	wind surf
wintergreen	win-ter green

wireless	wire less
wishbone	wish bone
withdraw	with draw
withdrawn	with drawn
withdrew	with drew
withheld	with held
withhold	with hold
within	with in
withstand	with stand
withstood	with stood
womanhood	wom-an hood
womankind	wom-an kind
woodchuck	wood chuck
woodland	wood land
woodpecker	wood peck-er
woodwind	wood wind
woodwork	wood work
woodworking	wood work-ing
workbench	work bench
workbook	work book
workman	work man
workout	work out
worldwide	world wide
worthless	worth less
worthwhile	worth while
wristwatch	wrist watch
wrongdoing	wrong do-ing
yardstick	yard stick
yourself	your self
yourselves	your selves
zigzag	zig zag

compound

hyphenated

- **Hyphenated** compound words are made up of two or more words/bases that have a hyphen connecting them.

  hide-and-seek
  part-time

absent-minded
broken-down
brother-in-law
built-in
bull's-eye
chin-up
cover-up
cold-blooded
cold-hearted
court-martial
cross-country
cross-country skiing
cross-reference
crow's-nest
cul-de-sac
double-cross
double-header
drive-through
dry-clean
eagle-eyed
e-mail/email
face-off
father-in-law
first-class
first-rate
flip-flop
forget-me-not
good-bye/goodbye
great-grandfather
great-grandmother
great-grandparent
grown-up/grownup
half-mast
hand-me-down
happy-go-lucky
hard-boiled
head-on
hide-and-seek
high-rise
high-strung
hip-hop
ice-skate
jack-in-the-box
jack-o'-lantern
jump-start
know-how
know-it-all
lay-up
left-handed
life-size
lip-read
long-range
long-winded
loose-leaf
low-growing
made-up
make-believe
make-up/makeup
man-of-war
matter-of-fact
merry-go-round
middle-aged
mix-up
mother-in-law
narrow-minded
next-door
night-light
old-fashioned
one-way
open-minded
paper-maché
part-time
pell-mell
pitch-dark
pop-up

pull-up
quick-witted
red-handed
right-hand
right-handed
runner-up
second-class
self-addressed
self-confident
self-conscious
self-control
self-defense
self-government
self-portrait
self-reliance
self-righteous
short-lived
single-handed
sister-in-law
sit-up
soft-boiled
son-in-law
so-so
thick-skinned
three-dimensional
tic-tac-toe
tie-dye
time-out
tom-tom
topsy-turvy
T-shirt
two-dimensional
upside-down/upside down
up-to-date
U-turn
voice-over
walkie-talkie
warm-blooded
water-ski/water ski
well-balanced
well-behaved
well-being
well-known
x-axis
X-ray/x-ray
y-axis
yo-yo

compound

separated

- **Separated** compound words are made up of two or more words/bases that are appear to be separated as two words, but they make a new "word" when they are together.

  chicken pox – The compound word **chicken pox** is not simply the combination of a **chicken** and a **pox** (disease). It's not a chicken disease. It's a new concept.

  green thumb – The compound word **green thumb** is not simply a **thumb** that is **green**. It's a new concept.

- Separated compounds (this list) look very similar to phrases Linguists argue over the differences between compounds and phrases, but the issue is not completely clear. Dictionaries will usually include separated compounds as words but will not include phrases.

acid rain
action verb
active voice
acute angle
African American
African violet
Air Force
air pressure
alimentary canal
Alzheimer's disease
American Indian
amino acid
amusement park
Arabic numerals
area code
armed forces
Asian American
associative property
atomic energy
aurora borealis
baby boom
baby tooth
baking powder
balance beam
bald eagle
ball bearing
bar graph
bar mitzvah
barbed wire
base runner
bat mitzvah
bathing suit
battering ram
batting a rage
bighorn sheep
Bill of Rights
black hole
blood pressure
blood vessel
blow dryer
blue jay
blue whale

boa constrictor
boarding school
bobby pin
boll weevil
brass instrument
bronchial tube
brown recluse spider
brussels sprout
bulletin board
cable car
candy cane
capital punishment
carbon dioxide
cardinal number
cash crop
cast iron
CAT scan
cat's cradle
chain reaction
charley horse
charter school
chest of drawers
chewing gum
chicken pox/chickenpox
chop suey
chow mein
Christmas tree
circuit breaker
circulatory system
civil rights
civil service
civil war
coast guard
coat of arms
cocker spaniel
cold cuts
combination lock
comic book
comic strip
common denominator
common noun
common sense
commutative property
compact disc
coordinate plane
coordinating conjunction
coral snake
corned beef
corner kick
country music
covered wagon
cream cheese
credit card
crepe paper
cross section
crossword puzzle
CT scan
daddy longlegs
dead end
decimal point
declarative sentence
definite article
Democratic Party
department store
diamondback rattlesnake
digestive system
dining room
direct current
direct object
distributive property

diving board
Doberman pinscher
dog paddle
double bass
Down syndrome
downhill skiing
drum major
drum majorette
dump truck
dwarf planet
each other
egg roll
Emancipation Proclamation
en route
English horn
English muffin
equilateral triangle
fairy tale
family name
fast food
fax machine
Ferris wheel
field goal
field hockey
field house
field trip
figure of speech
figure skating
fire alarm
fire drill
fire engine
fire escape
fire extinguisher
fire station
first name
fish stick
fishing rod
flight attendant
flutter kick
flying fish
folk dance
folk music
folk song
food chain
food web
fossil fuel
foul line
Fourth of July
French fries
French horn
French toast
frog kick
frying pan
future tense
garage sale
garter snake
gas station
German shepherd
ghost town
Gila monster
ginger ale
given name
glee club
global warming
glove compartment
goal line
gold rush
goose bumps
gospel music
grade school

graham cracker
grammar school
grand jury
grandfather clock
green bean
green card
green thumb
greenhouse effect
greenhouse gas
grizzly bear
grocery store
ground ball
half brother
half sister
hang glider
hard copy
hard drive
hash browns
hay fever
head start
health care
health food
hearing aid
heart attack
hermit crab
high jump
high school
high seas
high tide
home plate
homing pigeon
honeydew melon
horseshoe crab
hot dog
hot plate
hot spring
hot tub
House of Representatives
human being
human race
ice age
ice cream
ice hockey
ice pack
ice skate
immune system
improper fraction
Independence Day
index finger
indirect object
inline skate
instant message
jelly roll
jet engine
jet stream
jigsaw puzzle
jump rope
jump shot
jumping jack
jungle gym
junior high school
junior varsity
junk food
kidney bean
killer whale
kung fu
Labor Day
labor union
last name
Latin American

launch pad
lawn mower
leap year
learning disability
letter carrier
lie detector
life jacket
life preserver
life raft
light bulb
light year
lily of the valley
lily pad
lima bean
line drive
line of scrimmage
linking verb
lip gloss
litmus paper
litmus test
Little Dipper
living room
locker room
long jump
long shot
low tide
lower class
luna moth
Lyme disease
lymphatic system
machine gun
magnetic field
magnetic pole
magnifying glass
maiden name
mail carrier
malted milk
Marine Corps
martial art
mass production
Memorial Day
metric system
microwave oven
Middle Ages
middle name
middle school
migrant worker
Milky Way
mill wheel
mixed number
mobile home
monkey wrench
motion picture
mountain goat
mountain lion
music box
music hall
musical chairs
National Guard
Native American
natural gas
nervous system
New Testament
New Year's Day
next door
no one
North American
North Pole
North Star
northern lights

nuclear reactor
nursery rhyme
nursery school
nursing home
oblique angle
obtuse angle
Old Testament
one another
ordinal number
outer space
ozone layer
paddle wheel
paper clip
Parmesan cheese
part of speech
passenger pigeon
passive voice
past tense
patent leather
peanut butter
pen name
pep talk
perfect tense
piggy bank
pit bull
pitcher plant
plastic wrap
point of view
poison ivy
polar bear
pole vault
police officer
polka dot
pony express
pop music
post office
pot pie
power play
practical joke
prairie dog
prairie schooner
praying mantis
prepositional phrase
present tense
prickly pear
primary color
primary school
primary stress
prime meridian
prime minister
prime number
printing press
proper noun
public school
Puerto Rico
punctuation mark
pussy willow
Queen Anne's lace
question mark
quotation mark
real estate
red blood cell
registered nurse
relay race
relief map
relief pitcher
remote controlled
report card
Republican Party
right angle

right triangle
rock music
rocking chair
rocking horse
role model
roll call
roller coaster
roller skate
rolling pin
Roman numeral
Romance language
root beer
Rosh Hashanah
rubber band
running back
safety pin
Saint Bernard
science fiction
scuba diving
sea anemone
sea level
sea lion
sea turtle
sea urchin
search engine
seat belt
secondary school
secondary stress
senior citizen
service station
shooting star
short circuit
shot put
shoulder blade
sign language
simple sentence
skate park
skim milk
sleeping bag
small intestine
smoke detector
snapping turtle
snare drum
social studies
solar system
sour cream
South American
South Pole
soy sauce
space shuttle
space station
space suit
Spanish moss
spe<u>cial</u> needs
spider web
spinal column
spinal cord
spinning wheel
square dance
Stars and Stripes
static electricity
steam engine
stock market
strep throat
string bean
stringed instrument
subordinating conjunction
sugar beet
Supreme Court
sweet potato

swimming pool
swing set
Swiss cheese
table tennis
tall tale
tape measure
tape recorder
tartar sauce
teacher's aide
teddy bear
test tube
text message
tissue paper
totem pole
track and field
trading post
traffic circle
tree nut
ultraviolet light
umbilical cord
United Nations
upper class
upper hand
upside down
vacuum cleaner
Venus flytrap
Veteran's Day
vice president
vice versa
video game
vocal cords
wagon train
waiting room
walking stick
washing machine
water buffalo
water lily
water moccasin
water polo
water ski
water wheel
white blood cell
White House
whole number
whooping cough
whooping crane
wind instrument
word processor
World Wide Web
yellow jacket
Yom Kippur
ZIP code

One

Consonant

V/CV

VC/V

V/CV

- When a word has only one consonant between the vowels, it is necessary to separate it either before the consonant or after the consonant. The division before the consonant **(V/CV)** is more common than the division after the consonant **(VC/V).**

- The **V/CV** division usually results in an open vowel (unless it's a vowel team). The open vowel makes either the long vowel sound, or it makes the schwa sound.

around	a round	became	be came
Asian	A sian	because	be cause
aside	a side	become	be come
atone	a tone	before	be fore
atop	a top	began	be gan
avert	a vert	begin	be gin
avoid	a void	begun	be gun
await	a wait	behalf	be half
awake	a wake	behave	be have
award	a ward	behead	be head
aware	a ware	beheld	be held
awoke	a woke	behind	be hind
Babar	Ba bar	behold	be hold
Babel	Ba bel	Beijing	Bei jing
baby	ba by	Beirut	Bei rut
bacon	ba con	belie	be lie
Baden	Ba den	belief	be lief
bagel	ba gel	Belize	Be lize
basic	ba sic	belong	be long
basil	ba sil	below	be low
basin	ba sin	beneath	be neath
basis	ba sis	benign	be nign
Baylor	Bay lor	berate	be rate
bazaar	ba zaar	beret	be ret
Beacon	Bea con	beseech	be seech
beaver	bea ver	beset	be set

beside	be side	cozy	co zy
besides	be sides	Cramer	Cra mer
besiege	be siege	crater	cra ter
Cabul	Ca bul	crazy	cra zy
cadet	ca det	creature	crea ture
café	ca fé	crisis	cri sis
Cairo	Cai ro	croquet	cro quet
Calah	Ca lah	crouton	crou ton
Cana	Ca na	crucial	cru cial
Canaan	Ca naan	crusade	cru sade
canal	ca nal	Cuba	Cu ba
canine	ca nine	Cuban	Cu ban
canoe	ca noe	cubic	cu bic
caper	ca per	cuisine	cui sine
career	ca reer	deacon	dea con
cater	ca ter	debut	de but
caution	cau tion	decay	de cay
cautious	cau tious	deceit	de ceit
Cecil	Ce cil	deceive	de ceive
cedar	ce dar	decent	de cent
cement	ce ment	decide	de cide
cheetah	chee tah	decode	de code
Chico	Chi co	decoy	de coy
China	Chi na	deduce	de duce
Chinese	Chi nese	deduct	de duct
chlorine	chlo rine	deface	de face
chorus	cho rus	defeat	de feat
chosen	cho sen	defect	de fect
cider	ci der	defend	de fend
climate	cli mate	defense	de fense
climax	cli max	defer	de fer
cobalt	co balt	define	de fine
cocoa	co coa	deform	de form
cocoon	co coon	defy	de fy
Cody	Co dy	delay	de lay

delete	de lete
delight	de light
deluxe	de luxe
demand	de mand
demote	de mote
denote	de note
deny	de ny
depart	de part
depend	de pend
depict	de pict
deport	de port
depot	de pot
derive	de rive
desert	de sert
deserve	de serve
design	de sign
desire	de sire
detach	de tach
detail	de tail
detain	de tain
detect	de tect
deter	de ter
detest	de test
detour	de tour
device	de vice
devise	de vise
devout	de vout
DeWitt	De Witt
diesel	die sel
digest	di gest
dilute	di lute
direct	di rect
feline	fe line
female	fe male
fever	fe ver
fiber	fi ber
Fiji	Fi ji
final	fi nal
finance	fi nance
finite	fi nite
flavor	fla vor
focal	fo cal
focus	fo cus
freedom	free dom
Fremont	Fre mont
frequent	fre quent
Friday	Fri day
frozen	fro zen
frugal	fru gal
fury	fu ry
fusion	fu sion
futile	fu tile
future	fu ture
Gabon	Ga bon
gala	ga la
galore	ga lore
garage	ga rage
gazelle	ga zelle
genie	ge nie
genome	ge nome
genus	ge nus
geyser	gey ser
Ghana	Gha na
Gigi	Gi gi
Gino	Gi no
giraffe	gi raffe
Giselle	Gi selle
glacier	gla cier
gleeful	glee ful
glucose	glu cose

gluten	glu ten	Iraq	I raq
gracious	gra cious	irate	I rate
Grady	Gra dy	Irish	I rish
gravy	gra vy	iron	i ron
Grayson	Gra son	item	i tem
Greeley	Gree ley	ivy	i vy
grenade	gre nade	Jacob	Ja cob
grocer	gro cer	Jafar	Ja far
Grover	Gro ver	Jamar	Ja mar
guava	gua va	Jamie	Ja mie
guitar	gui tar	Japan	Ja pan
guru	gu ru	Jesus	Je sus
haiku	hai ku	Jody	Jo dy
Haiti	Hai ti	Jonah	Jo nah
halo	ha lo	Joseph	Jo seph
harass	ha rass	Judah	Ju dah
haven	ha ven	Judith	Ju dith
Hayward	Hay ward	judo	ju do
hazel	ha zel	Julie	Ju lie
hazy	ha zy	July	Ju ly
hijack	hi jack	juror	ju ror
hobo	ho bo	jury	ju ry
holy	ho ly	kazoo	ka zoo
homer	ho mer	Keaton	Kea ton
Homer	Ho mer	kebab	ke bab
hooray	hoo ray	kiwi	ki wi
human	hu man	Koran	Ko ran
humane	hu mane	Kuwait	Ku wait
humid	hu mid	label	la bel
humor	hu mor	labor	la bor
hygiene	hy giene	Lacy	La cy
icon	i con	lady	la dy
icy	i cy	lagoon	la goon
idol	i dol	Lagos	La gos
Iran	I ran	Lahore	La hore

lapel	la pel	mature	ma ture
latex	la tex	maybe	may be
Laurel	Lau rel	meager	mea ger
lazy	la zy	melee	me lee
legal	le gal	mellow	mel low
legion	le gion	mesa	me sa
Lehi	Le hi	meter	me ter
leisure	lei sure	Micah	Mi cah
Leland	Le land	minor	mi nor
lemur	le mur	minus	mi nus
LeRoy	Le Roy	miser	mi ser
levy	lev y	mobile	mo bile
license	li cense	modem	mo dem
lilac	li lac	molar	mo lar
liter	li ter	moment	mo ment
llama	lla ma	Moses	Mo ses
local	lo cal	motel	mo tel
locate	lo cate	motion	mo tion
locust	lo cust	motive	mo tive
loiter	loi ter	motor	mo tor
lotion	lo tion	mural	mu ral
lotus	lo tus	music	mu sic
Lucille	Lu cille	mutant	mu tant
Lucy	Lu cy	mutate	mu tate
lunar	lu nar	Nahor	Na hor
Macon	Ma con	Nahum	Na hum
Macy	Ma cy	naked	na ked
major	ma jor	nasal	na sal
Mali	Ma li	nation	na tion
malign	ma lign	native	na tive
manure	ma nure	nature	na ture
Marie	Ma rie	naval	na val
marine	ma rine	Navy	Na vy
maroon	ma roon	navy	na vy
mason	ma son	Nepal	Ne pal

Niger	Ni ger	polish	pol ish
nomad	no mad	Polish	Po lish
notion	no tion	polite	po lite
open	o pen	pony	po ny
oral	o ral	potion	po tion
oval	o val	prairie	prai rie
pagan	pa gan	precede	pre cede
papa	pa pa	precinct	pre cinct
paper	pa per	Precious	Pre cious
parade	pa rade	precious	pre cious
parole	pa role	precise	pre cise
patient	pa tient	predict	pre dict
pauper	pau per	prefer	pre fer
payment	pay ment	premiere	pre miere
peacock	pea cock	prepare	pre pare
peanut	pea nut	preserve	pre serve
Peru	Pe ru	preside	pre side
peso	pe so	presume	pre sume
Peter	Pe ter	pretend	pre tend
Phoenix	Phoe nix	pretext	pre text
phony	pho ny	prevail	pre vail
photo	pho to	prevent	pre vent
physique	phy sique	preview	pre view
pigeon	pi geon	primate	pri mate
pilot	pi lot	primer	pri mer
pita	pi ta	private	pri vate
Plato	Pla to	proceed	pro ceed
platoon	pla toon	procure	pro cure
playful	play ful	produce	pro duce
plaza	pla za	profess	pro fess
Pluto	Plu to	profile	pro file
poison	poi son	profound	pro found
Poland	Po land	profuse	pro fuse
polar	po lar	prolong	pro long
police	po lice	promote	pro mote

pronoun	pro noun	recede	re cede
pronounce	pro nounce	receipt	re ceipt
propel	pro pel	receive	re ceive
protect	pro tect	recent	re cent
protein	pro tein	recess	re cess
protest	pro test	recite	re cite
proton	pro ton	recoil	re coil
provide	pro vide	recount	re count
Provo	Pro vo	recur	re cur
provoke	pro voke	redeem	re deem
Prudence	Pru dence	reduce	re duce
prudent	pru dent	refer	re fer
pupa	pu pa	refill	re fill
pupil	pu pil	refine	re fine
Qatar	Qa tar	reform	re form
quasar	qua sar	refund	re fund
quaver	qua ver	regain	re gain
query	que ry	regal	re gal
quota	quo ta	regard	re gard
quotient	quo tient	rehearse	re hearse
racial	ra cial	reject	re ject
radar	ra dar	rejoice	re joice
raisin	rai sin	result	re sult
Raleigh	Ra leigh	retail	re tail
raucous	rau cous	retain	re tain
raven	ra ven	retire	re tire
ravine	ra vine	return	re turn
razor	ra zor	reveal	re veal
Reagan	Rea gan	review	re view
reason	rea son	revise	re vise
rebate	re bate	revive	re vive
rebound	re bound	revoke	re voke
rebuff	re buff	revolt	re volt
rebuild	re build	reward	re ward
recall	re call	rhubarb	rhu barb

Riley	Ri ley
rival	ri val
robot	ro bot
robust	ro bust
rodent	ro dent
Roma	Ro ma
Roman	Ro man
romance	ro mance
Romans	Ro mans
Rosa	Ro sa
Roseville	Rose ville
rotate	ro tate
rotor	ro tor
Ruby	Ru by
ruby	ru by
Rudolf	Ru dolf
rumor	ru mor
rural	ru ral
saber	sa ber
saga	sa ga
Salem	Sa lem
saline	sa line
salute	sa lute
saucer	sau cer
sausage	sau sage
savor	sa vor
scenic	sce nic
season	sea son
secede	se cede
secure	se cure
sedan	se dan
seizure	sei zure
select	se lect
sepal	se pal
sequel	se quel
sequence	se quence
sequin	se quin
serene	se rene
series	se ries
serum	se rum
Shalom	Sha lom
Sheila	Shei la
Sidon	Si don
silence	si lence
silent	si lent
silo	si lo
Sinai	Si nai
sinus	si nus
siren	si ren
Skyler	Sky ler
slogan	slo gan
sober	so ber
social	so cial
soda	so da
sofa	so fa
solar	so lar
solo	so lo
sonar	so nar
spacious	spa cious
special	spe cial
species	spe cies
spider	spi der
spinal	spi nal
spiral	spi ral
Spokane	Spo kane
spoken	spo ken
Stacy	Sta cy
stamen	sta men
station	sta tion
status	sta tus

stolen	sto len
stupid	stu pid
Sudan	Su dan
sumac	su mac
Sumer	Su mer
super	su per
Sweden	Swe den
tailor	tai lor
Taiwan	Tai wan
taper	ta per
tapir	ta pir
Taylor	Tay lor
teepee	tee pee
Thailand	Thai land
thyroid	thy roid
Tibet	Ti bet
tidal	ti dal
tiger	ti ger
Titus	Ti tus
Toby	To by
today	to day
tofu	to fu
Togo	To go
toilet	toi let
token	to ken
tonight	to night
topaz	to paz
total	to tal
totem	to tem
toucan	tou can
toupee	tou pee
toward	to ward
Tracy	Tra cy
trauma	trau ma
Travon	Tra von
treason	trea son
treaty	trea ty
tripod	tri pod
trousers	trou sers
Trudy	Tru dy
truly	tru ly
Truman	Tru man
tuba	tu ba
tuber	tu ber
tumor	tu mor
tumult	tu mult
tuna	tu na
tunic	tu nic
tutor	tu tor
Tutu	Tu tu
Twyla	Twy la
tycoon	ty coon
Tyler	Ty ler
tyrant	ty rant
unit	u nit
unite	u nite
Uruk	U ruk
vacant	va cant
vacate	va cate
vapor	va por
vegan	ve gan
Venus	Ve nus
veto	ve to
Viking	Vi king
vinyl	vi nyl
viper	vi per
viral	vi ral
virus	vi rus
visor	vi sor
vital	vi tal

vocal	vo cal	yoga	yo ga
Waco	Wa co	yogurt	yo gurt
wafer	wa fer	Yupik	Yu pik
wager	wa ger	zany	za ny
water	wa ter	zebu	ze bu
waver	wa ver	zenith	ze nith
weasel	wea sel	zero	ze ro
weevil	wee vil	Zorah	Zo rah
yodel	yo del		

VC/V

- When a word has only one consonant between the vowels, it is necessary to separate it either before the consonant or after the consonant. The division before the consonant **(V/CV)** is more common than the division after the consonant **(VC/V).**
- The **VC/V** division usually results in a closed vowel, unless the **V** is a vowel team, or **R-controlled**. The closed vowel usually either says the short vowel sound, or it makes a schwa sound.

atoll	at oll
atom	at om
avid	av id
axis	ax is
bailiff	bail iff
baker	bak er
Baker	Bak er
balance	bal ance
banish	ban ish
Boris	Bor is
cabin	cab in
carob	car ob
carol	car ol
Carol	Car ol
cashew	cash ew
ceiling	ceil ing
chapel	chap el
cheery	cheer y
chemist	chem ist
cherish	cher ish
Chevy	chev y
chewy	chew y
Chile	Chil e
chili	chil i
chisel	chis el
chronic	chron ic
civic	civ ic
civil	civ il
clamor	clam or
Clara	Clar a
Clarence	Clar ence
Claudette	Claud ette
cleaner	clean er
clearance	clear ance
clearing	clear ing
cleaver	cleav er
Clement	Clem ent
clever	clev er
closet	clos et
cloudy	cloud y
color	col or
column	col umn
comet	com et
comic	com ic
cookie	cook ie
Cooper	Coop er
coral	cor al
Corey	Cor ey
Corinth	Cor inth
Cory	Cor y
courage	cour age
cousin	cous in

cover	cov er
covet	cov et
Cowan	Cow an
coward	cow ard
cower	cow er
craving	crav ing
creamy	cream y
credit	cred it
creepy	creep y
crevice	crev ice
crooked	crook ed
Cyril	Cyr il
dairy	dair y
Daniel	Dan iel
daring	dar ing
deade	dead en
deafen	deaf en
decade	dec ade
deluge	de luge
denim	den im
Dhaka	Dhak a
digit	dig it
disarm	dis arm
feta	fet a
figure	fig ure
finish	fin ish
flaxen	flax en
fleeting	fleet ing
Fleming	Flem ing
Florence	Flor ence
flourish	flour ish
flower	flow er
fluoride	fluor ide
foolish	fool ish
footer	foot er
footing	foot ing
foreign	for eign
forest	for est
fragile	frag ile
frigid	frig id
frolic	frol ic
Gareth	Gar eth
Gary	Gar y
gaudy	gaud y
gavel	gav el
genius	gen ius
Gerald	Ger ald
given	giv en
Gladys	Glad ys
glamour	glam our
global	glob al
gloomy	gloom y
glossy	gloss y
goalie	goal ie
goatee	goat ee
govern	gov ern
grader	grad er
granite	gran ite
grater	grat er
gravel	grav el
greasy	greas y
greedy	greed y
Gretel	Gret el
grimace	grim ace
grimy	grim y
grovel	grov el
habit	hab it
hairy	hair y
havoc	hav oc
hazard	haz ard

header	head er
heater	heat er
Heaven	Heav en
heaven	heav en
heavy	heav y
heifer	heif er
heiress	heir ess
heron	her on
homey	hom ey
honest	hon est
honey	hon ey
honor	hon or
Horace	Hor ace
hover	hov er
Howard	How ard
image	im age
inert	in ert
jaguar	jag uar
jealous	jeal ous
Jerash	Jer ash
Jewel	Jew el
Jewish	Jew ish
juicy	juic y
junior	jun ior
keeping	keep ing
Kenya	Ken ya
khaki	khak i
Latin	Lat in
lavish	lav ish
leaden	lead en
leader	lead er
leafy	leaf y
leaven	leav en
legume	leg ume
lemon	lem on
leopard	leop ard
levee	lev ee
level	lev el
lever	lev er
Lewis	Lew is
liken	lik en
Lily	Lil y
lily	lil y
limit	lim it
linen	lin en
liquid	liq uid
	*li quid
liven	liv en
liver	liv er
livid	liv id
lizard	liz ard
logic	log ic
loosen	loos en
lousy	lous y
Lowell	Low ell
magic	mag ic
maiden	maid en
malice	mal ice
manage	man age
manor	man or
many	man y
Mary	Mar y
meadow	mead ow
mealy	meal y
melon	mel on
memo	mem o
memoir	mem oir
menace	men ace
menu	men u
merit	mer it

metal	met al	peril	per il
minute	min ute	perish	per ish
misuse	mis use	petal	pet al
mixer	mix er	pharaoh	phar aoh
model	mod el	pharynx	phar ynx
modern	mod ern	pheasant	pheas ant
modest	mod est	Philip	Phil ip
module	mod ule	phonics	phon ics
movie	mov ie	physics	phys ics
needy	need y	Pithom	Pith om
never	nev er	pity	pit y
Newark	New ark	pixel	pix el
noisy	nois y	placid	plac id
nosy	nos y	planet	plan et
nourish	nour ish	pleasure	pleas ure
novel	nov el	polyp	pol yp
novice	nov ice	Powell	Pow ell
orange	or ange	preface	pref ace
outage	out age	premise	prem ise
outer	out er	presence	pres ence
oven	ov en	present	pres ent
package	pack age	prison	pris on
packet	pack et	promise	prom ise
pageant	pag eant	proper	prop er
palace	pal ace	proven	prov en
palate	pal ate	proverb	prov erb
palette	pal ette	province	prov ince
panel	pan el	punish	pun ish
panic	pan ic	quiver	quiv er
parent	par ent	racer	rac er
Paris	Par is	radish	rad ish
parish	par ish	rainy	rain y
patent	pat ent	rapid	rap id
peasant	peas ant	rapids	rap ids
pedal	ped al	ravage	rav age

reader	read er
ready	read y
reaper	reap er
rebel	reb el
record	rec ord
refuge	ref uge
refuse	ref use
rider	rid er
rigid	rig id
ripen	rip en
risen	ris en
river	riv er
rivet	riv et
Robert	Rob ert
robin	rob in
Roger	Rog er
Ronald	Ron ald
rookie	rook ie
roomy	room y
rosy	ros y
router	rout er
ruler	rul er
sailor	sail or
satin	sat in
satire	sat ire
Saturn	Sat urn
Savior	Sav ior
savior	sav ior
scaly	scal y
scary	scar y
schedule	sched ule
scholar	schol ar
schooner	schoon er
sealant	seal ant
second	sec ond
senate	sen ate
senior	sen ior
seventh	sev enth
sewage	sew age
sewer	sew er
shadow	shad ow
shady	shad y
Sharon	Shar on
shaven	shav en
sheriff	sher iff
shiver	shiv er
shovel	shov el
shower	show er
showy	show y
shrivel	shriv el
sinew	sin ew
skewer	skew er
sleepy	sleep y
smoky	smok y
sneaker	sneak er
sneaky	sneak y
snowy	snow y
soapy	soap y
solemn	sol emn
solid	sol id
Spaniard	Span iard
spaniel	span iel
Spanish	Span ish
speaker	speak er
speedy	speed y
spicy	spic y
spigot	spig ot
spinach	spin ach
spiny	spin y
spirit	spir it

squeaky	squeak y
static	stat ic
statue	stat ue
steady	stead y
sterile	ster ile
steward	stew ard
Stewart	Stew art
storage	stor age
streamer	stream er
striven	striv en
study	stud y
suburb	sub urb
sugar	sug ar
suitor	suit or
sweater	sweat er
sweeten	sweet en
swivel	swiv el
syrup	syr up
taken	tak en
talent	tal ent
talon	tal on
tariff	tar iff
tenant	ten ant
tenor	ten or
tepid	tep id
Texas	Tex as
Thomas	Thom as
thorough	thor ough
threaten	threat en
timid	tim id
towel	tow el
tower	tow er
toxic	tox ic
tragic	trag ic
travel	trav el
Travis	Trav is
treasure	treas ure
tremor	trem or
Trevor	Tre vor
tribute	trib ute
Trixie	Trix ie
trooper	troop er
tropic	trop ic
trowel	trow el
valiant	val iant
valid	val id
valor	val or
value	val ue
vanish	van ish
venom	ven om
very	ver y
visit	vis it
vivid	viv id
volume	vol ume
vomit	vom it
vowel	vow el
wagon	wag on
waiter	wait er
wary	war y
weaken	weak en
weapon	weap on
weaver	weav er
Weaver	Weav er
weedy	weed y
whaler	whal er
Wheaton	Wheat on
Wheeler	wheel er
whiten	whit en
widen	wid en
widow	wid ow

wizard	wiz ard	woolen	wool en
woman	wom an	wooly	wool y
women	wom en	writer	writ er
wooden	wood en	Yemen	Yem en
woody	wood y	zealous	zeal ous

Two Consonants

VC/CV

VCC/V

V/CCV

VC/CV

twin doubles

simple

- The **VC/CV** words in this word list all have twin/double letters for the consonants. This pattern is usually one of the first ones that is taught, because it is easy to identify double letters and divide between them.
- The **VC/CV** words in this list were chosen because they have closed vowel syllables, and are therefore the easiest of the **VC/CV** words to read. For more advanced words, see the **VC/CV** advanced list.

Allen	Al len	mussel	mus sel
attic	at tic	mutton	mut ton
cannon	can non	pallid	pal lid
cannot	can not	pellet	pel let
coffin	cof fin	pollen	pol len
commit	com mit	possum	pos sum
common	com mon	puffin	puf fin
cotton	cot ton	pummel	pum mel
fossil	fos sil	puppet	pup pet
funnel	fun nel	ridden	rid den
gallon	gal lon	rotten	rot ten
gallop	gal lop	rugged	rug ged
gibbon	gib bon	sadden	sad den
happen	hap pen	sodden	sod den
hiccup	hic cup	sonnet	son net
hidden	hid den	sudden	sud den
hummus	hum mus	suffix	suf fix
kitten	kit ten	Sukkot	Suk kot
lesson	les son	sullen	sul len
maggot	mag got	tassel	tas sel
mallet	mal let	tennis	ten nis
mammal	mam mal	tunnel	tun nel
millet	mil let	vassal	vas sal
mitten	mit ten	vessel	ves sel
muffin	muf fin	Willis	Wil lis

VC/CV

twin doubles

advanced

- The **VC/CV** words in this list have double letters for the middle consonants, but they are more complex than the **VC/CV** twin simple word list. These words have schwa sounds for open vowels, more advanced vowel teams, or more complex letter teams.

abbey	ab bey	attach	at tach
Abbey	Ab bey	attack	at tack
Abby	Ab by	attain	at tain
accent	ac cent	attempt	at tempt
accept	ac cept	attend	at tend
access	ac cess	attest	at test
accord	ac cord	attire	at tire
account	ac count	baggy	bag gy
accuse	ac cuse	ballad	bal lad
addend	ad dend	ballast	bal last
affect	af fect	ballet	bal let
affirm	af firm	balloon	bal loon
affix	af fix	banner	ban ner
afford	af ford	barracks	bar racks
Akko	Ak ko	barrage	bar rage
allege	al lege	barrel	bar rel
alley	al ley	barren	bar ren
allow	al low	barrette	bar rette
alloy	al loy	Barry	Bar ry
allure	al lure	bellow	bel low
ally	al ly	berry	ber ry
Ammon	Am mon	Betty	bet ty
annex	an nex	Billie	Bil lie
annoy	an noy	Billings	Bil lings
appoint	ap point	Billy	Bil ly

Blossom	Blos som	commence	com mense
bunny	bun ny	commend	com mend
cabbage	cab bage	comment	com ment
caffeine	caf feine	commerce	com merce
callous	cal lous	commute	com mute
carrot	car rot	connect	con nect
carry	car ry	Connor	Con nor
Cassie	Cas sie	copper	cop per
cellar	cel lar	corral	cor ral
cello	cel lo	correct	cor rect
challenge	chal lenge	corrode	cor rode
channel	chan nel	corrupt	cor rupt
Channing	Chan ning	cottage	cot tage
chassis	chas sis	cranny	cran ny
chatter	chat ter	cunning	cun ning
chatty	chat ty	currant	cur rant
cherry	cher ry	current	cur rent
chubby	chub by	curry	cur ry
clammy	clam my	daddy	dad dy
clapper	clap per	dagger	dag ger
classic	clas sic	Dallas	Dal las
Clifford	Clif ford	Darrow	Dar row
clipper	clip per	Derrick	Der rick
clutter	clut ter	dinner	din ner
coffee	cof fee	fellow	fel low
collage	col lage	ferret	fer ret
collapse	col lapse	ferry	fer ry
collar	col lar	fillet	fil let
collards	col lards	flannel	flan nel
collect	col lect	flatten	flat ten
college	col lege	flatter	flat ter
collide	col lide	flipper	flip per
collie	col lie	floppy	flop py
Collins	Col lins	Flossie	Flos sie
comma	com ma	flurry	flur r

flutter	flut ter	Hassan	Has san
fodder	fod der	hello	hel lo
foggy	fog gy	hippo	hip po
follow	fol low	hollow	hol low
folly	fol ly	Holly	Hol ly
fritter	frit ter	holly	hol ly
fully	ful ly	hopper	hop per
funny	fun ny	horrid	hor rid
furrow	fur row	hummus	hum mus
furry	fur ry	hurrah	hur rah
gallant	gal lant	hurray	hur ray
galley	gal ley	hurried	hur ried
garret	gar ret	immense	im mense
Gerry	Ger ry	immerse	im merse
giddy	gid dy	immune	im mune
gimmick	gim mick	inner	in ner
Ginny	Gin ny	issue	is sue
gizzard	giz zard	Jaffa	Jaf fa
glimmer	glim mer	jagged	jag ged
glitter	glit ter	jelly	jel ly
glutton	glut ton	Jenny	Jen ny
grammar	gram mar	Jerry	Jer ry
Griffin	Grif fin	Jesse	Jes se
Griffith	Grif fith	jetty	jet ty
groggy	grog gy	jolly	jol ly
gunner	gun ner	Kellah	Kel lah
guppy	gup py	Kelly	Kel ly
gutter	gut ter	Kenneth	Ken neth
haddock	had dock	Kenny	Ken ny
Haggai	Hag gai	Kerry	Ker ry
hammer	ham mer	kitten	kit ten
Hannah	Han nah	kitty	kit ty
happy	hap py	knotty	knot ty
harrow	har row	ladder	lad der
Harry	Har ry	lasso	las so

latter	lat ter	mummy	mum my
letter	let ter	Murray	Mur ray
lettuce	let tuce	mutter	mut ter
Libby	Lib by	muzzle	muz zle
litter	lit ter	nanny	nan ny
little	lit tle	narrate	nar rate
lobby	lob by	narrow	nar row
logger	log ger	Nissan	Nis san
Lubbock	Lub bock	Norris	Nor ris
luggage	lug gage	oppose	op pose
mallard	mal lard	otter	ot ter
mammoth	mam moth	parrot	par rot
manner	man ner	passage	pas sage
manners	man ners	passion	pas sion
marriage	mar riage	passive	pas sive
marrow	mar row	patter	pat ter
marry	mar ry	pattern	pat tern
massage	mas sage	Patty	Pat ty
massive	mas sive	patty	pat ty
matter	mat ter	pennant	pen nant
merry	mer ry	Penny	Pen ny
message	mes sage	penny	pen ny
midday	mid day	pepper	pep per
million	mil lion	Perry	Per ry
mirror	mir ror	petty	pet ty
missile	mis sile	pillage	pil lage
mission	mis sion	pillar	pil lar
mollusk	mol lusk	pillow	pil low
Molly	Mol ly	pizza	piz za
mommy	mom my	platter	plat ter
Mommy	Mom my	plummet	plum met
Morris	Mor ris	pollute	pol lute
motto	mot to	Polly	Pol ly
muddy	mud dy	Poppy	Pop py
muggy	mug gy	poppy	pop py

porridge	por ridge
possess	pos sess
potter	pot ter
pressure	pres sure
pudding	pud ding
pulley	pul ley
puppy	pup py
putty	put ty
quarrel	quar rel
quarry	quar ry
rabbi	rab bi
raccoon	rac coon
ragged	rag ged
rally	ral ly
rapport	rap port
rigging	rig ging
rubber	rub ber
rubbish	rub bish
rudder	rud der
ruddy	rud dy
rummage	rum mage
runner	run ner
Russell	Rus sell
Russian	Rus sian
Sabbath	Sab bath
sallow	sal low
Sally	Sal ly
scabbard	scab bard
scaffold	scaf fold
scallop	scal lop
scanner	scan ner
scatter	scat ter
scissors	scis sors
Scottish	Scot tish
scrimmage	scrim age
scurry	scur ry
session	ses sion
setter	set ter
Shabbat	Shab bat
shabby	shab by
shaggy	shag gy
Shannon	Shan non
shatter	shat ter
shellac	shel lac
Sherri	Sher ri
Sherry	Sher ry
shimmer	shim mer
shipping	ship ping
shoddy	shod dy
shudder	shud der
shutter	shut ter
silly	sil ly
simmer	sim mer
skillet	skil let
Skinner	Skin ner
skinny	skin ny
skipper	skip per
skittish	skit tish
slipper	slip per
sloppy	slop py
sluggish	slug gish
snippet	snip pet
soccer	soc cer
soggy	sog gy
Sonny	Son ny
sorrow	sor row
sorry	sor ry
sparrow	spar row
spatter	spat ter
sputter	sput ter

squirrel	squir rel	thinner	thin ner
Stafford	Staf ford	tissue	tis sue
stagger	stag ger	Torrance	Tor rance
stallion	stal lion	torrent	tor rent
stammer	stam mer	totter	tot ter
starry	star ry	traffic	traf fic
stiffen	stif fen	trapper	trap per
stirrup	stir rup	trigger	trig ger
Stoddard	Stod dard	trillion	tril lion
stopper	stop per	trodden	trod den
strapping	strap ping	trolley	trol ley
stubborn	stub born	tummy	tum my
stutter	stut ter	turret	tur ret
succeed	suc ceed	twitter	twit ter
success	suc cess	udder	ud der
suffer	suf fer	Umma	Um ma
suggest	sug gest	upper	up per
summer	sum mer	utter	ut ter
supper	sup per	vaccine	vac cine
support	sup port	valley	val ley
suppose	sup pose	village	vil lage
surround	sur round	villain	vil lain
swagger	swag ger	wallet	wal let
swallow	swal low	wallop	wal lop
swollen	swol len	wallow	wal low
tabby	tab by	Wally	Wal ly
tallow	tal low	warrant	war rant
tally	tal ly	Warren	War ren
tatter	tat ter	wedding	wed ding
tattoo	tat too	whinny	whin ny
terrace	ter race	wholly	whol ly
terrain	ter rain	William	Wil liam
Terrell	Ter rel	Willie	Wil lie
terror	ter ror	Willis	Wil lis
Terry	Ter ry	Willow	Wil low

willow	wil low	written	writ ten
winner	win ner	yellow	yel low
witty	wit ty	Yiddish	Yid dish
worry	wor ry	yucca	yuc ca
wrapper	wrap per	zipper	zip per

VC/CV

non-twin

simple

- The **VC/CV** words in this list divide between the middle consonants, but they are not twin/doubles. The words in this list are chosen because they have closed syllables, which makes them easier to read. For more advanced **VC/CV** words, see the non-twin advanced word list.

admit	ad mit	fungus	fun gus
Akron	Ak ron	gambol	gam bol
album	al bum	Gildad	Gil dad
anvil	an vil	hectic	hec tic
atlas	at las	helmet	hel met
bandit	ban dit	Hilton	Hil ton
basket	bas ket	hostel	hos tel
Boston	Bos ton	impel	im pel
cactus	cac tus	inlet	in let
Calvin	Cal vin	input	in put
cancel	can cel	Islam	Is lam
candid	can did	Justin	Jus tin
canvas	can vas	Kansas	Kan sas
casket	cas ket	kidnap	kid nap
census	cen sus	Landon	Lan don
combat	com bat	lentil	len til
compel	com pel	limpid	lim pid
consul	con sul	London	Lon don
convex	con vex	Ludwig	Lud wig
cosmic	cos mic	magnet	mag net
cosmos	cos mos	mantel	man tel
cutlet	cut let	mascot	mas cot
Felton	Fel ton	mental	men tal
fitful	fit ful	metric	met ric
		mishap	mis hap

misled	mis led	pulpit	pul pit
musket	mus ket	random	ran dom
Muslim	Mus lim	ransom	ran som
muslin	mus lin	rascal	ras cal
napkin	nap kin	seldom	sel dom
Nelson	Nel son	signal	sig nal
pencil	pen cil	sitcom	sit com
picnic	pic nic	sublet	sub let
pistil	pis til	submit	sub mit
pistol	pis tol	sultan	sul tan
piston	pis ton	tablet	tab let
public	pub lic	tendon	ten don

VC/CV

non-twin

advanced

- The **VC/CV** words in this list have non-twin consonant letters for the middle consonants, but they are more complex than the simple **VC/CV** non-twin words. They have schwa sounds for open vowels, more advanced vowel teams, **VCE** syllables, or more complex letter teams.

abduct	ab duct	alcove	al cove
absence	ab sence	Alden	Al den
absent	ab sent	algae	al gae
absorb	ab sorb	almond	al mond
absurd	ab surd	almost	al most
acquit	ac quit	alpine	al pine
action	ac tion	also	al so
active	ac tive	altar	al tar
actor	ac tor	alter	al ter
adhere	ad here	alto	al to
adjoin	ad join	always	al ways
adjourn	ad journ	amber	am ber
adjust	ad just	ambush	am bush
admire	ad mire	ancient	an cient
advance	ad vance	angel	an gel
advent	ad vent	anger	an ger
Advent	Ad vent	anguish	an guish
adverb	ad verb	Angus	An gus
adverse	ad verse	antic	an tic
advice	ad vice	antique	an tique
advise	ad vise	Atwood	At wood
after	af ter	augment	aug ment
ailment	ail ment	austere	aus tere
Albert	Al bert	Austin	Aus tin

axle	ax le
badly	bad ly
Bahrain	Bah rain
balsa	bal sa
balsam	bal sam
bamboo	bam boo
bandage	ban dage
banjo	ban jo
banquet	ban quet
banter	ban ter
baptism	bap tism
baptize	bap tize
barber	bar ber
Barney	Bar ney
barter	bar ter
Baxter	Bax ter
Belgium	Bel gium
Bernard	Ber nard
Bernice	Ber nice
Betsy	Bet sy
Bingo	bin go
Bosworth	Bos worth
Boulder	Boul der
Bradburn	Brad burn
Bradford	Brad ford
Bradley	Brad ley
Brandon	Bran don
Brandy	Bran dy
Branson	Bran son
Bridget	Brid get
Bromwell	Brom well
Burbank	Bur bank
Burnett	Bur nett
Buster	Bus ter
cacti	cac ti
Calney	Cal ney
cancer	can cer
Candice	Can dice
candid	can did
candy	can dy
canteen	can teen
canter	can ter
canyon	can yon
capsize	cap size
capsule	cap sule
captain	cap tain
caption	cap tion
captive	cap tive
capture	cap ture
carbon	car bon
carcass	car cass
cargo	car go
Carlee	Car lee
Carlow	Car low
Carly	Car ly
carpet	car pet
carton	car ton
cartoon	car toon
cascade	cas cade
Caspar	Cas par
catsup	cat sup
censor	cen sor
centaur	cen taur
center	cen ter
certain	cer tain
Chadwick	Chad wick
chamber	cham ber
chaplain	chap lain
Chaplin	Chap lin
Chapman	Chap man

chapter	chap ter
charcoal	char coal
Charlie	Char lie
Charlotte	Char lotte
charter	char ter
cheerful	cheer ful
Chelsey	Chel sey
Chester	Ches ter
chiefly	chief ly
chieftain	chief tain
chimney	chim ney
christen	chris ten
Christian	Chris tian
Christie	Chris tie
Christy	Chris ty
chunky	chun ky
cinder	cin der
Cindy	Cin dy
circa	cir ca
circuit	cir cuit
circus	cir cus
citrus	cit rus
clamber	clam ber
clatter	clat ter
Claxton	Clax ton
clergy	cler gy
Clifton	Clif ton
Clinton	Clin ton
clumsy	clum sy
cluster	clus ter
Colby	Col by
Colter	Col ter
Colton	Col ton
combine	com bine
compact	com pact
compare	com pare
compass	com pass
compete	com pete
compile	com pile
compose	com pose
compost	com post
compute	com pute
conceal	con ceal
concede	con cede
conceive	con ceive
concept	con cept
concern	con cern
concert	con cert
concise	con cise
concoct	con coct
concord	con cord
Concord	Con cord
concur	con cur
condemn	con demn
condense	con dense
condo	con do
conduct	con duct
confer	con fer
confess	con fess
confide	con fide
confirm	con firm
conform	con form
confuse	con fuse
Congo	Con go
conquer	con quer
conquest	con quest
Conroy	Con roy
consent	con sent
conserve	con serve
consist	con sist

console	con sole
consult	con sult
consume	con sume
contact	con tact
contain	con tain
contempt	con tempt
contend	con tend
content	con tent
contest	con test
contour	con tour
convent	con vent
converse	con verse
convert	con vert
convey	con vey
convict	con vict
convince	con vince
convoy	con voy
Conway	Con way
Corbin	Cor bin
Cordell	Cor dell
Cornell	Cor nell
corner	cor ner
cornet	cor net
costume	cos tume
council	coun cil
counsel	coun sel
counter	coun ter
county	coun ty
crescent	cres cent
crimson	crim son
Cromwell	Crom well
cryptic	cryp tic
crystal	crys tal
Crystal	Crys tal
culture	cul ture
culvert	cul vert
curfew	cur few
cursive	cur sive
cursor	cur sor
curtail	cur tail
curtain	cur tain
custard	cus tard
custom	cus tom
customs	cus toms
cutlass	cut lass
cymbal	cym bal
dainty	dain ty
Dalton	Dal ton
danger	dan ger
Darby	Dar by
Darcie	Dar cie
Darcy	Dar cy
darling	dar ling
Darnell	Dar nell
deadly	dead ly
dearly	dear ly
Delhi	Del hi
Delroy	Del roy
Denmark	Den mark
dental	den tal
dentist	den tist
Denton	Den ton
Denver	Den ver
Desmond	Des mond
dingy	din gy
disband	dis band
ferment	fer ment
fertile	fer tile
festive	fes tive
fiction	fic tion

fifty	fif ty	fulfill	ful fill
filter	fil ter	Fulton	Ful ton
Finland	Fin land	fungi	fun gi
fitness	fit ness	furlough	fur lough
fixture	fix ture	furnace	fur nace
flimsy	flim sy	furnish	fur nish
flounder	floun der	furtive	fur tive
fluster	flus ter	Gainesville	Gaines ville
folder	fol der	garbage	gar bage
forbid	for bid	garden	gar den
forceps	for ceps	gargoyle	gar goyle
forebear	for bear	garland	gar land
forgive	for give	garlic	gar lic
forgot	for got	garment	gar ment
forlorn	for lorn	garnet	gar net
formal	for mal	garnish	gar nish
format	for mat	garter	gar ter
fortune	for tune	gender	gen der
forty	for ty	genre	gen re
forward	for ward	genteel	gen teel
foster	fos ter	Gentile	Gen tile
fraction	frac tion	Georgia	Geor gia
fracture	frac ture	gerbil	ger bil
fragment	frag ment	German	Ger man
Francene	Fran cene	gesture	ges ture
Frances	Fran ces	giblets	gib lets
Francis	Fran cis	Gilbert	Gil bert
frantic	fran tic	Gilroy	Gil roy
frenzy	fren zy	ginger	gin ger
Fresno	Fres no	ginseng	gin seng
friction	fric tion	Glenda	Glen da
Frisco	Fris co	Glendale	Glen dale
frontier	fron tier	glisten	glis ten
fructose	fruc tose	goblet	gob let
fruitful	fruit ful	goblin	gob lin

Gospel	Gos pel
gourmet	gour met
gymnast	gym nast
halter	hal ter
hamlet	ham let
Hamlet	Ham let
hamper	ham per
Harding	Har ding
hardy	har dy
Harford	Har ford
Harley	Har ley
Harlow	Har low
harness	har ness
Harper	Har per
harpoon	har poon
harvest	har vest
Harvey	Har vey
Haskel	Has kel
hasten	has ten
hectic	hec tic
Hector	Hec tor
hemlock	hem lock
Henry	Hen ry
Herbert	Her bert
hermit	her mit
Hester	Hes ter
hinder	hin der
hormone	hor mone
hornet	hor net
hostage	hos tage
hostile	hos tile
hourly	hour ly
Houston	Hous ton
hunger	hun ger
Hunter	Hun ter
hunter	hun ter
husband	hus band
igloo	ig loo
ignite	ig nite
impact	im pact
impair	im pair
impeach	im peach
impede	im pede
import	im port
impose	im pose
impulse	im pulse
impure	im pure
inborn	in born
incense	in cense
incite	in cite
income	in come
indeed	in deed
indent	in dent
indoor	in door
induce	in duce
induct	in duct
indulge	in dulge
infant	in fant
infect	in fect
infer	in fer
infest	in fest
inform	in form
ingot	in got
inhale	in hale
inject	in ject
injure	in jure
inland	in land
inquire	in quire
insane	in sane
insert	in sert

inside	in side	Kremlin	Krem lin
insight	in sight	Kwanzaa	Kwan zaa
insist	in sist	lacquer	lac quer
insult	in sult	lactose	lac tose
insure	in sure	language	lan guage
intact	in tact	Lansing	Lan sing
intent	in tent	lantern	lan tern
intern	in tern	larva	lar va
into	in to	larvae	lar vae
invade	in vade	launder	laun der
invent	in vent	lawful	law ful
invert	in vert	leaflet	leaf let
invest	in vest	lecture	lec ture
invite	in vite	Leslie	Les lie
involve	in volve	Lester	Les ter
inward	in ward	Lincoln	Lin coln
Irving	Ir ving	Linda	Lin da
island	is land	listen	lis ten
itself	it self	Lizbeth	Liz beth
jargon	jar gon	Ludlow	Lud low
Jasmine	Jas mine	lumber	lum ber
jasmine	jas mine	luster	lus ter
Jasper	Jas per	Lyndon	Lyn don
jas per	jas per	magma	mag ma
Jersey	Jer sey	magpie	mag pie
jersey	jer sey	mainly	main ly
jester	jes ter	maintain	main tain
Jordan	Jor dan	Malcolm	Mal colm
journal	jour nal	Maldives	Mal dives
jumbo	jum bo	Malta	Mal ta
justice	jus tice	Mandy	Man dy
Kelsey	Kel sey	manger	man ger
Kendall	Ken dall	mango	man go
kernel	ker nel	mansion	man sion
kidney	kid ney	margin	mar gin

market	mar ket
martial	mar tial
Martian	Mar tian
Martin	Mar tin
martyr	mar tyr
marvel	mar vel
master	mas ter
matzoh	mat zoh
Maxwell	Max well
Medford	Med ford
medley	med ley
member	mem ber
mention	men tion
Mercy	Mer cy
mercy	mer cy
Merlin	Mer lin
mermaid	mer maid
mesquite	mes quite
midland	mid land
midnight	mid night
Milburn	Mil burn
mildew	mil dew
Milton	Mil ton
miscount	mis count
mislaid	mis laid
mislead	mis lead
mistake	mis take
mister	mis ter
mixture	mix ture
moisten	mois ten
moisture	mois ture
molten	mol ten
mongoose	mon goose
monkey	mon key
Monroe	Mon roe
monsoon	mon soon
Morgan	Mor gan
morsel	mor sel
mortal	mor tal
mortar	mor tar
Morton	Mor ton
Moscow	Mos cow
mountain	moun tain
moustache	mous tache
Mumbai	Mum bai
mundane	mun dane
mustache	mus tache
mustang	mus tang
mustard	mus tard
muster	mus ter
Nancy	Nan cy
nasty	nas ty
nearby	near by
nearly	near ly
nectar	nec tar
Neptune	Nep tune
newly	new ly
Newman	New man
Norfolk	Nor folk
Norman	Nor man
Norton	Nor ton
Norwalk	Nor walk
Norway	Nor way
option	op tion
ordain	or dain
ordeal	or deal
Ordell	Or dell
order	or der
organ	or gan
Orson	Or son

Orville	Or ville	person	per son
Orwell	Or well	persuade	per suade
Oscar	Os car	pertain	per tain
Osten	Os ten	perturb	per turb
Oswald	Os wald	pervade	per vade
outward	out ward	perverse	per verse
Oxford	Ox ford	Petra	Pet ra
Oxnard	Ox nard	pewter	pew ter
oyster	oys ter	phantom	phan tom
Pablo	Pab lo	Phyllis	Phyl lis
pamper	pam per	picture	pic ture
pansy	pan sy	pigment	pig ment
parcel	par cel	pilfer	pil fer
pardon	par don	pinto	pin to
parlor	par lor	plaintiff	plain tiff
parson	par son	plantain	plan tian
partial	par tial	plasma	plas ma
pasta	pas ta	plaster	plas ter
Pasteur	Pas teur	plastic	plas tic
pastor	pas tor	platform	plat form
pasture	pas ture	plenty	plen ty
Pearland	Pear land	plunder	plun der
penguin	pen guin	polka	pol ka
pension	pen sion	ponder	pon der
perceive	per ceive	pontoon	pon toon
percent	per cent	poplar	pop lar
Percy	Per cy	porpoise	por poise
perfect	per fect	Portage	Por tage
perform	per form	portage	por tage
perfume	per fume	portal	por tal
Perga	Per ga	porter	por ter
perhaps	per haps	portion	por tion
permit	per mit	powder	pow der
Persian	Per sian	practice	prac tice
persist	per sist	pregnant	preg nant

Prentice Pren tice
Prescott Pres cott
Presley Pres ley
prestige pres tige
Preston Pres ton
pretzel pret zel
Primrose *Prim rose*
primrose *prim rose*
Princess Prin cess
pristine pris tine
problem prob lem
Proctor Proc tor
progress prog ress
pronto pron to
prospect pros pect
prosper pros per
publish pub lish
Pueblo Pueb lo
purpose pur pose
pursue pur sue
pursuit pur suit
quagmire quag mire
quarter quar ter
quartet quar tet
question ques tion
Quimby Quim by
Quincy Quin cy
Radburn Rad burn
rampart ram part
Randolf Ran dolf
Randy Ran dy
ransack ran sack
ransom ran som
rapture rap ture
Redford *Red ford*
reindeer *rein deer*
rhombus rhom bus
Roscoe Ros coe
roster ros ter
rowdy row dy
Rugby Rug by
rupture rup ture
salsa sal sa
salvage sal vage
sandal san dal
Sanford San ford
sapling sap ling
sarcasm sar casm
sardine sar dine
Sardis Sar dis
saunter saun ter
scandal scan dal
scepter scep ter
scripture scrip ture
section sec tion
seedling seed ling
segment seg ment
sensor sen sor
sentence sen tence
sergeant ser geant
sermon ser mon
serpent ser pent
service ser vice
shampoo sham poo
shamrock sham rock
Shasta Shas ta
Shawnee Shaw nee
shepherd shep herd
sherbet sher bet
Sherlock Sher lock

Sherwin	Sher win	stanza	stan za
Sherwood	Sher wood	starling	star ling
Shirley	Shir ley	stencil	sten cil
sibling	sib ling	Sterling	Ster ling
Sidney	Sid ney	Stetson	Stet son
Sigmund	Sig mund	stingy	stin gy
silver	sil ver	stranger	stran ger
sister	sis ter	structure	struc ture
sixteen	six teen	sturdy	stur dy
sixteenth	six teenth	Sturgeon	Stur geon
sixty	six ty	subdue	sub due
skirmish	skir mish	subject	sub ject
slander	slan der	submerge	sub merge
slender	slen der	subside	sub side
slumber	slum ber	*subway*	*sub way*
smolder	smol der	suction	suc tion
snorkel	snor kel	sulfur	sul fur
soldier	sol dier	sundae	sun dae
somber	som ber	*Sunday*	*Sun day*
Spencer	Spen cer	surface	sur face
splendid	splen did	surgeon	sur geon
splendor	splen dor	surly	sur ly
splinter	splin ter	surpass	sur pass
spongy	spon gy	survey	sur vey
sponsor	spon sor	survive	sur vive
squadron	squad ron	suspect	sus pect
squander	squan der	sustain	sus tain
stagnant	stag nant	symbol	sym bol
Stamford	Stam ford	system	sys tem
stampede	stam pede	Tampa	Tam pa
standard	stan dard	tamper	tam per
Standish	Stan dish	tardy	tar dy
Stanford	Stan ford	target	tar get
Stanley	Stan ley	tarnish	tar nish
Stanton	Stan ton	tartan	tar tan

tartar	tar tar
Tempe	Tem pe
temper	tem per
tempest	tem pest
tempo	tem po
tender	ten der
tendril	ten dril
tension	ten sion
termite	ter mite
textile	tex tile
texture	tex ture
Thelma	Thel ma
thermal	ther mal
thermos	ther mos
thirteen	thir teen
thirteenth	thir teenth
thirty	thir ty
thunder	thun der
Thurgood	Thur good
Thurman	Thur man
Tianjin	Tian jin
timber	tim ber
tinker	tin ker
	*tink er
Tomkins	Tom kins
Tonga	Ton ga
	*Tong a
torment	tor ment
torso	tor so
torture	tor ture
tractor	trac tor
tranquil	tran quil
transit	tran sit
Trenton	Tren ton
trespass	tres pass
triplet	trip let
Tristan	Tris tan
Truesdale	Trues dale
trumpet	trum pet
Tuesday	Tues day
Tulsa	Tul sa
turban	tur ban
turbine	tur bine
Turkey	Tur key
turkey	tur key
turmoil	tur moil
turnip	tur nip
turquoise	tur quoise
twenty	twen ty
ugly	ug ly
umpire	um pire
under	un der
undo	un do
unfair	un fair
unfold	un fold
unfurl	un furl
unhook	un hook
unjust	un just
unkempt	un kempt
unkind	un kind
unless	un less
unlike	un like
unload	un load
unlock	un lock
unpack	un pack
unrest	un rest
unsound	un sound
untie	un tie
untold	un told
upright	up right

uproar	up roar
uproot	up root
upward	up ward
urban	ur ban
Urdu	Ur du
urgent	ur gent
varnish	var nish
velvet	vel vet
vendor	ven dor
venture	ven ture
verbal	ver bal
verdict	ver dict
vermin	ver min
Vermont	Ver mont
Verna	Ver na
Vernon	Ver non
versus	ver sus
Victor	Vic tor
victor	vic tor
Vincent	Vin cent
vintage	vin tage
virgin	vir gin
virtue	vir tue
voltage	vol tage
vulgar	vul gar
vulture	vul ture
waitress	wait ress
Walden	Wal den
Waldo	Wal do
Waldorf	Wal dorf
walnut	wal nut
walrus	wal rus
Walton	Wal ton
Wanda	Wan da
wander	wan der
warden	war den
warfare	war fare
weakly	weak ly
weekly	week ly
welcome	wel come
welfare	wel fare
Wendell	Wen dell
Wendy	Wen dy
Wharton	Whar ton
whimper	whim per
whimsy	whim sy
whisper	whis per
Whitcomb	Whit comb
Whitney	Whit ney
Wilbur	Wil bur
Wilmer	Wil mer
Wilson	Wil son
window	win dow
winter	win ter
wisdom	wis dom
witness	wit ness
wombat	wom bat
Woodrow	Wood row
worsen	wor sen
Xander	Xan der
Yahweh	Yah weh
yearling	year ling
yearly	year ly
yonder	yon der
Yonkers	Yon kers
Zander	Zan der
zombie	zom bie

VCC/V

- The words in this **VCC/V** list have two middle consonants. In general, when student see two middle consonants, they will separate the word evenly between the consonants. However, some words have two consonants that form a digraph, blend, or other letter team that needs to stay together to help with pronunciation. Consider the following words:

  cloth – ing **crank – y**

  If you divided it evenly between the consonants, you would get:

  clot – hing **cran – ky**

  When students look for letter teams, they can make better decisions about where to divide between syllables.

- The **VCC/V** pattern primarily divides into base and suffix.

ashen	ash en	dampen	damp en
Asher	Ash er	dancer	danc er
Athens	Ath ens		*dan cer
banker	bank er	darken	dark en
beckon	beck on	dashing	dash ing
Bethel	Beth el	debtor	debt or
bishop	bish op	dirty	dirt y
cashier	cash ier	fencing	fenc ing
Cathy	Cath y		fen cing
checkers	check ers	fender	fend er
chicken	chick en	fidget	fidg et
clothing	cloth ing	filling	fill ing
coastal	coast al	filthy	filth y
cocky	cock y	fishy	fish y
cracker	crack er	flicker	flick er
cranky	crank y	Fowler	Fowl er
Crockett	Crock ett	Frankie	Frank ie
curly	curl y	freshen	fresh en
cushion	cush ion	frisky	frisk y

frosting	frost ing
fussy	fuss y
gadget	gadg et
gather	gath er
gawky	gawk y
gecko	geck o
girder	gird er
girlish	girl ish
golden	gold en
Gresham	Gresh am
grouchy	grouch y
grumpy	grump y
guilty	guilt y
handy	hand y
hanger	hang er
harden	hard en
hasty	hast y
hearty	heart y
Heather	Heath er
heather	heath er
helping	help ing
hilly	hill y
holder	hold er
hostess	host ess
husky	husk y
jackal	jack al
jacket	jack et
jerky	jerk y
jockey	jock ey
Judges	Judg es
judges	judg es
jumper	jump er
jumpy	jump y
Kathy	Kath y
knickers	knick ers

knocker	knock er
Kurdish	Kurd ish
landing	land ing
lather	lath er
leather	leath er
lessen	less en
lesser	less er
locker	lock er
locket	lock et
lodger	lodg er
lodging	lodg ing
lofty	loft y
lucky	luck y
marker	mark er
messy	mess y
methane	meth ane
method	meth od
Mickey	Mick ey
milky	milk y
Miller	Mill er
miller	mill er
missing	miss ing
misty	mist y
molding	mold ing
moldy	mold y
mossy	moss y
mother	moth er
mourning	mourn ing
murky	murk y
mushy	mush y
nephew	neph ew
nervous	nerv ous
nickel	nick el
nothing	noth ing
painter	paint er

Parker	Park er	Rusty	Rust y
pendant	pend ant	rusty	rust y
perky	perk y	salmon	salm on
picket	pick et	salty	salt y
picky	pick y	Sandy	Sand y
pinkie	pink ie	sandy	sand y
pinky	pink y	scamper	scamp er
planter	plant er	scanty	scant y
plucky	pluck y	scrawny	scrawn y
plumbing	plumb ing	selfie	self ie
plunger	plung er	selfish	self ish
	*plun ger	Sellers	Sell ers
pocket	pock et	servant	serv ant
pointer	point er	sharpen	sharp en
pompous	pomp ous	shocking	shock ing
postage	post age	shortage	short age
postal	post al	shorten	short en
poster	post er	sicken	sick en
preacher	preach er	silken	silk en
prophet	proph et	silky	silk y
pucker	puck er	singer	sing er
puffy	puff y	slacken	slack en
quicken	quick en	slither	slith er
racket	rack et	smelly	smell y
rafter	raft er	smother	smooth er
ranger	rang er	snicker	snick er
raspy	rasp y	socket	sock et
rather	rath er	soften	soft en
Richard	Rich ard	speller	spell er
riches	rich es	Springer	Spring er
risky	risk y	sticker	stick er
rocker	rock er	sticky	stick y
rocket	rock et	stinger	sting er
roller	roll er	stockade	stock ade
rooster	roost er	stocking	stock ing

stocky	stock y	twister	twist er
stricken	strick en	usher	ush er
stroller	stroll er	Vicky	Vick y
stuffy	stuff y	voucher	vouch er
sucker	suck er	Walker	Walk er
tasty	tast y	washer	wash er
teacher	teach er	whether	wheth er
teller	tell er	whisker	whisk er
tether	teth er	wicked	wick ed
thicken	thick en	wicker	wick er
thicket	thick et	wicket	wick et
thorny	thorn y	windy	wind y
thresher	thresh er	wither	with er
thrifty	thrift y	wordy	word y
ticket	tick et	worker	work er
tiller	till er	Zephi	Zeph i
toaster	toast er	Zephyr	Zeph yr
trawler	trawl er	zither	zith er
trusty	trust y		

V/CCV

- The words in this **V/CCV** list have two middle consonants. In general, when student see two middle consonants, they will separate the word evenly between the consonants. However, some words have two consonants that form a digraph, blend, or other letter team that needs to stay together to help with pronunciation. Consider the following words:

  be - tray **su - shi**

  If you divided it evenly between the consonants, you would get:

  bet - ray **sus - hi**

  When students look for letter teams, they can make better decisions about where to divide between syllables.

- This **V/CCV** division results in open vowels and vowel teams for the first syllable. The open vowels can say their long sound, or they can say a schwa sound.

ablaze	a blaze	Aubrey	Au brey
able	a ble	author	au thor
abreast	a breast	awry	a wry
abridge	a bridge	beagle	bea gle
abroad	a broad	beetle	bee tle
acre	a cre	befriend	be friend
across	a cross	bestow	be stow
adrift	a drift	betray	be tray
afloat	a float	Bible	Bi ble
afraid	a fraid	Cedric	Ce dric
afresh	a fresh	Cephas	Ce phas
aghast	a ghast	cliché	cli ché
agree	a gree	cobra	co bra
aground	a ground	couple	cou ple
aphid	a phid	couplet	cou plet
April	A pril	cradle	cra dle
apron	a pron	crochet	cro chet
ashore	a shore	cycle	cy cle
askew	a skew	cyclone	cy clone

cypress	cy press	maple	ma ple
Cyprus	Cy prus	matron	ma tron
debris	de bris	measles	mea sles
declare	de clare	microbe	mi crobe
decline	de cline	migrant	mi grant
decree	de cree	migrate	mi grate
deflect	de flect	mocha	mo cha
defrost	de frost	nachos	na chos
degree	de gree	needle	nee dle
deplete	de plete	neglect	ne glect
depress	de press	neither	nei ther
deprive	de prive	neutral	neu tral
descend	de scend	neutron	neu tron
descent	de scent	noble	no ble
despair	de spair	noodle	noo dle
despise	de spise	Ophir	O phir
despite	de spite	patrol	pa trol
detract	de tract	patron	pa tron
Detroit	De troit	people	peo ple
fragrance	fra grance	poodle	poo dle
fragrant	fra grant	preschool	pre school
gopher	go pher	proclaim	pro claim
Goshen	Go shen	program	pro gram
hatred	ha tred	protract	pro tract
Hebrew	He brew	python	py thon
Hebron	He bron	reclaim	re claim
hybrid	hy brid	recline	re cline
hyphen	hy phen	recruit	re cruit
idle	i dle	reflect	re flect
Keisha	Kei sha	reflex	re flex
kosher	ko sher	refrain	re frain
lacrosse	la crosse	refresh	re fresh
ladle	la dle	regret	re gret
Luther	Lu ther	respect	re spect
machine	ma chine	respond	re spond

response	re sponse	stifle	sti fle
restore	re store	sucrose	su crose
retreat	re treat	supreme	su preme
retrieve	re trieve	sushi	su shi
sable	sa ble	table	ta ble
sacred	sa cred	title	ti tle
Sasha	Sa sha	trifle	tri fle
scruple	scru ple	trophy	tro phy
secret	se cret	trouble	trou ble
secrete	se crete	typhoon	ty phoon
siphon	si phon	Ukraine	U kraine
stable	sta ble	wheedle	whee dle
staple	sta ple	zebra	ze bra
steeple	stee ple		

Three Consonants

VC/CCV

VCC/CV

VCCC/V

VC/CCV

- The words in this **VC/CCV** list have three middle consonants. Each word has a digraph, blend or other letter team (**OR, ANK**, etc) that needs to stay together. Keeping those letter teams together helps in pronunciation. Consider the following word:

  ar - cher

  If you divided it without considering letter teams, you would get:

  arc – her

  When students look for letter teams, they can make better decisions about where to divide between syllables.

- When a word has three middle consonants (such as the words in this list), it makes finding the digraphs, blends and letter teams harder. For example, in the word **asphalt**, the **SP** could be a blend and the **PH** could be a digraph. In cases like this, the student needs to try both divisions and see which one results in a word that makes sense.

  as - phault

  asp - hault

abscess	ab scess	apple	ap ple
abstain	ab stain	apply	ap ply
acclaim	ac claim	appraise	ap praise
address	ad dress	approach	ap proach
afflict	af flict	approve	ap prove
affront	af front	archer	ar cher
Alfred	Al fred	Arthur	Ar thur
amble	am ble	asphalt	as phalt
ample	am ple	astride	as tride
anchor	an chor	attract	at tract
Andrew	An drew	babble	bab ble
answer	an swer	baffle	baf fle
anthem	an them	Bancroft	Ban croft
anther	an ther	battle	bat tle
applaud	ap plaud	belfry	bel fry
applause	ap plause	Bertha	Ber tha

Bertrand Ber trand
Brewster Brew ster
Cambridge Cam bridge
candle can dle
cartridge car tridge
castle cas tle
Castro Cas tro
cattle cat tle
cauldron caul dron
central cen tral
chortle chor tle
circle cir cle
cobbler cob bler
coddle cod dle
complain com plain
complaint com plaint
complete com plete
complex com plex
comply com ply
compress com press
comprise com prise
conclude con clude
concrete con crete
conflict con flict
conflict con flict
congress con gress
Congress Con gress
conscience con science
conscious con scious
conspire con spire
constant con stant
contract con tract
contract con tract
contrast con trast
contrite con trite

contrive con trive
control con trol
Cranston Cran ston
crinkle crin kle
*crink le
cripple crip ple
crumble crum ble
crumple crum ple
cuddle cud dle
culprit cul prit
dabble dab ble
dandruff dan druff
dangle dan gle
dappled dap pled
dawdle daw dle
dazzle daz zle
diddle did dle
dimple dim ple
dinghy din ghy
fiddle fid dle
franchise fran chise
frustrate frus trate
fulcrum ful crum
fumble fum ble
further fur ther
furthest fur thest
Gandhi Gan dhi
gargle gar gle
gentle gen tle
gently gen tly
Gertrude Ger trude
giggle gig gle
gobble gob ble
Gretchen Gret chen
griddle grid dle

gristle	gris tle
grumble	grum ble
gurgle	gur gle
guzzle	guz zle
haggle	hag gle
hamster	ham ster
handle	han dle
hassle	has sle
Hawthorn	Haw thorn
hobble	hob ble
holster	hol ster
huddle	hud dle
humble	hum ble
hundred	hun dred
hurdle	hur dle
hurtle	hur tle
hustle	hus tle
implant	im plant
implore	im plore
imply	im ply
impress	im press
imprint	im print
improve	im prove
instinct	in stinct
include	in clude
increase	in crease
inflate	in flate
inflict	in flict
inspect	in spect
inspire	in spire
install	in stall
instance	in stance
instant	in stant
instead	in stead
instinct	in stinct

intrigue	in trigue
intrude	in trude
jangle	jan gle
	*jang le
Jeffrey	Jef frey
jiggle	jig gle
jingle	jin gle
	*jing le
jostle	jos tle
juggle	jug gle
juggler	jug gler
jumble	jum ble
jungle	jun gle
Kendrick	Ken drick
kerchief	ker chief
kettle	ket tle
kinship	kin ship
laundry	laun dry
lobster	lob ster
maltreat	mal treat
mangle	man gle
mantle	man tle
marble	mar ble
marshal	mar shal
Martha	Mar tha
Matthew	Mat thew
mattress	mat tress
meddle	med dle
membrane	mem brane
Memphis	Mem phis
merchant	mer chant
middle	mid dle
mingle	min gle
misplace	mis place
misprint	mis print

misspell	mis spell
mistreat	mis treat
mistrust	mis trust
mongrel	mon grel
monster	mon ster
mottled	mot tled
muddle	mud dle
muffle	muf fle
muffler	muf fler
mumble	mum ble
musty	mus ty
nestle	nes tle
nettle	net tle
nibble	nib ble
nimble	nim ble
nonstop	non stop
nozzle	noz zle
oppress	op press
orchard	or chard
orchid	or chid
orphan	or phan
osprey	os prey
paddle	pad dle
paltry	pal try
panther	pan ther
pantry	pan try
pastry	pas try
pebble	peb ble
peddle	ped dle
peddler	ped dler
perplex	per plex
perspire	per spire
pestle	pes tle
pilgrim	pil grim
pimple	pim ple

poncho	pon cho
portrait	por trait
portray	por tray
poultry	poul try
puddle	pud dle
purchase	pur chase
puzzle	puz zle
quibble	quib ble
raffle	raf fle
ramble	ram ble
rattle	rat tle
riddle	rid dle
ripple	rip ple
rubble	rub ble
ruffle	ruf fle
rumble	rum ble
rustle	rus tle
saddle	sad dle
saffron	saf fron
sample	sam ple
sapphire	sap phire
scoundrel	scoun drel
scramble	scram ble
scribble	scrib ble
scuffle	scuf fle
scuttle	scut tle
sentry	sen try
settle	set tle
settler	set tler
shingle	shin gle
	*shing le
shuffle	shuf fle
shuttle	shut tle
simple	sim ple
simply	sim ply

single	sin gle
sizzle	siz zle
smuggle	smug gle
sniffle	snif fle
snuggle	snug gle
solstice	sol stice
spangled	span gled
sparkle	spar kle
spectrum	spec trum
spindle	spin dle
sprinkle	sprin kle
sprinkler	sprin kler
squabble	squab ble
startle	star tle
straggle	strag gle
struggle	strug gle
stubble	stub ble
stumble	stum ble
substance	sub stance
subtle	sub tle
subtract	sub tract
suffrage	suf frage
sultry	sul try
supple	sup ple
supply	sup ply
suppress	sup press
surplus	sur plus
surprise	sur prise
suspense	sus pence
swindle	swin dle
syndrome	syn drome
tantrum	tan trum
tattle	tat tle
temple	tem ple
thimble	thim ble

thistle	this tle
throttle	throt tle
tingle	tin gle
	*ting le
tinkle	tin kle
	*tink le
toddler	tod dler
Tolstoy	Tol stoy
topple	top ple
trample	tram ple
tremble	trem ble
trestle	tres tle
Trowbridge	Trow bridge
tumble	tum ble
tumbler	tum bler
tundra	tun dra
turtle	tur tle
uncle	un cle
undress	un dress
unknown	un known
unskilled	un skilled
waddle	wad dle
waffle	waf fle
Waltham	Wal tham
warble	war ble
warbler	war bler
wardrobe	war drobe
whistle	whis tle
whittle	whit tle
wiggle	wig gle
Winsted	Win sted
Winston	Win ston
wintry	win try
wobble	wob ble
Woodstock	Wood stock

worship wor ship
worthy wor thy
wrestle wres tle
wrestler wres tler

wriggle wrig gle
wrinkle wrin kle
*wrink le

VCC/CV

- The words in this **VCC/CV** list have three middle consonants. Each word has a digraph, blend or letter team (**OR, ANK**, etc) that needs to stay together. Keeping these letter teams together helps in pronunciation. Consider the following words:

  Shang hai **thank ful**

  If you divided it without considering the letter teams, you would get:

  Shan ghai **than kful**

  When students look for letter teams, they can make better decisions about where to divide between syllables.

- When a word has three middle consonants (such as the words in this list), it makes finding the digraphs, blends and letter teams harder. For example, in the word **Shanghai** the **ANG** could be a letter team, but the **GH** could be a digraph. In cases like this, the student needs to try both divisions and see which one results in a word that makes sense.

  Shang - hai

  Shan - ghai

antler	ant ler
arctic	arc tic
cackle	cack le
plankton	plank ton
Portland	*Port land*
postpone	post pone
prickle	prick le
pumpkin	pump kin
puncture	punc ture
rhythmic	rhyth mic
Richmond	Rich mond
Rockford	Rock ford
ruthless	ruth less
sanction	sanc tion
sandwich	sand wich
scornful	scorn ful
sculpture	sculp ture
Shanghai	Shang hai
shortly	short ly
shortness	short ness
sickle	sick le
sickly	sick ly
sickness	sick ness
skillful	skill ful
slaughter	slaugh ter
speckled	speck led
Stillman	*Still man*
Stockton	Stock ton
Strickland	Strick land
symptom	symp tom
thankful	thank ful

Thorndike	Thorn dike	transport	trans port
Thornton	Thorn ton	trickle	trick le
Thursday	Thurs day	truthful	truth ful
tickle	tick le	Wadsworth	Wads worth
Townsend	Town send	Westcot	West cot
transfer	trans fer	willful	will ful
transform	trans form	Windsor	Wind sor
translate	trans late	wistful	wist ful
transmit	trans mit		

VCCC/V

- Words with the **VCCC/V** pattern are not common.
- Words with the **VCCC/V** pattern have a letter team that needs to stay together. Many of those letter teams will be trigraphs and three letter blends.
- Consider the following words:

  catch - er **wealth - y**

  If you divided it without considering the letter teams, you could end up with

  catc - her **wealt - hy**

- A knowledge of three letter blends, digraphs, and trigraphs is essential for understanding how to divide these words.

catcher	catch er	mighty	might y
Fletcher	Fletch er	Mitchell	Mitch ell
freighter	freight er	northern	north ern
frighten	fright en	pitcher	pitch er
hatchet	hatch et	righteous	right eous
healthy	health y	sketchy	sketch y
heighten	height en	stealthy	stealth y
itchy	itch y	straighten	straight en
ketchup	ketch up	stretcher	stretch er
kitchen	kitch en	Thatcher	Thatch er
lengthen	length en	thirsty	thirst y
lighten	light en	tighten	tight en
lighting	light ing	wealthy	wealth y
luncheon	lunch eon	weighty	weight y
		wretched	wretch ed

Four Consonants

VCCC/CV

VC/CCCV

VCCC/CV

- The **VCCC/CV** pattern is rare.
- Words with the **VCCC/CV** pattern have a letter team that needs to stay together. Consider the following words:

  health ful **month ly**

  If you divided it evenly without considering the letter teams, you could end up with

  healt hful **mont hly**

- A knowledge of three letter blends, trigraphs, and advanced letter teams is essential for understanding how to divide these words.

Carlsbad	Carls bad
healthful	health ful
Hitchcock	Hitch cock
Kingsley	Kings ley
Kingston	Kings ton
Knightly	knight ly
lengthwise	length wise
monthly	month ly
nightly	night ly
rightful	right ful
watchful	watch ful

VC/CCCV

- The **VC/CCCV** pattern is rare.
- Words with the **VC/CCCV** pattern usually have a three letter blend, digraph, or trigraph that needs to stay together. Consider the following words:

  pam phlet **sub scribe**

  If you divided it evenly without considering the letter teams, you could end up with

  pamp hlet **subs cribe**
- A knowledge of three letter blends, digraphs, trigraphs, and advanced letter teams is essential for understanding how to divide these words.

abstract	ab stract
constrict	con strict
construct	con struct
instruct	in struct
minstrel	min strel
monstrous	mon strous
pamphlet	pam phlet
subscribe	sub scribe

Two vowels

V/V

V/V

- The **V/V** syllable division is not common.
- Students can identify the **V/V** syllable division by looking for two vowels that do not form a known vowel letter team. Some examples of non-vowel team combinations are **neon** (no **EO** team), and **prior** (no **IO** team).

  There are occasionally vowels that are divided that *could* form a vowel team. In those cases, the students could practice reading the word both ways:

  NOAH with vowel team **OA** would be pronounced **/noh/**.

  NO-AH divided between the vowel teams would be pronounced **/no-ah/.**

- Sometimes more than two vowels are next to each other. In that case, there is usually a vowel team that needs to stay together during the syllable division.

  joy – ous

bayou	bay ou	luau	lu au
Boaz	Bo az	mayor	may or
Cheyenne	Chey enne	meow	me ow
Cleo	Cle o	Moab	Mo ab
client	cli ent	neon	ne on
coed	co ed	Noah	No ah
coerce	co erce	pious	pi ous
crayon	cray on	player	play er
fluent	flu ent	pliers	pli ers
fluid	flu id	poem	po em
flyer	fly er	poet	po et
giant	gi ant	prayer	pray er
joyous	joy ous	prior	pri or
kayak	kay ak	rayon	ray on
layer	lay er	react	re act
lion	li on	riot	ri ot
Louis	Lou is	royal	roy al
loyal	loy al	ruin	ru in

science	sci ence	triumph	tri umph
skier	ski er	truant	tru ant
Stuart	Stu art	via	vi a
Thea	The a	voyage	voy age
theist	the ist	Zion	Zi on
trial	tri al		

Syllable Types CLOVER

Closed

C**L**E

Open

Vowel Team

VC**E**

R-Controlled

CC

closed-closed

twin consonants

no schwa

- The words in this list have two closed syllables. The closed syllables will be pronounced with the short vowel sound.
- The words in this list all have twin/double consonants.
- For more advanced **CC** words with schwa sounds and more complex letter teams, see the list on the next page.

addend	ad dend
addict	ad dict
address	ad dress
affix	af fix
Allen	Al len
annex	an nex
attic	at tic
cannot	*can not*
comment	com ment
flatten	flat ten
gimmick	gim mick
Griffin	Grif fin
Griffith	Grif fith
hiccup	hic cup
kitten	kit ten
pallid	pal lid
possum	pos sum
puffin	puf fin
Scottish	Scot tish
skittish	skit tish
sluggish	slug gish
summit	sum mit
tennis	ten nis
trodden	trod den
Willis	Wil lis
withheld	with held
withhold	with hold
Yiddish	Yid dish

CC

closed-closed

twin consonants

advanced and schwa

- The words in this list have two closed syllables. At least one of the syllables will be pronounced with the schwa **/uh/** sound.
- The words in this list all have twin consonants.
-
- For more simple **CC** words with no schwa sounds, see the **CC** list on the previous page.

accept	ac cept	common	com mon
afflict	af flict	cotton	cot ton
Ammon	Am mon	Dallas	Dal las
appall	ap pall	fillet	fil let
assent	as sent	flannel	flan nel
assess	as sess	funnel	fun nel
asset	as set	gallant	gal lant
assist	as sist	gallon	gal lon
attach	at tach	gallop	gal lop
attack	at tack	gladden	glad den
attempt	at tempt	glutton	glut ton
attend	at tend	haddock	had dock
attest	at test	Hannah	Han nah
ballad	bal lad	happen	hap pen
ballast	bal last	Hassan	Has san
ballet	bal let	hidden	hid den
ballot	bal lot	hummus	hum mus
Blossom	Blos som	Kenneth	Ken neth
cannon	can non	kitten	kit ten
channel	chan nel	lesson	les son
collect	col lect	maggot	mag got
commend	com mend	mammal	mam mal

mammoth	mam moth
millet	mil let
mitten	mit ten
mollusk	mol lusk
mottled	mot tled
muffin	muf fin
mussel	mus sel
mutton	mut ton
oppress	op press
paddock	pad dock
pellet	pel let
pennant	pen nant
plummet	plum met
pollen	pol len
possess	pos sess
pummel	pum mel
puppet	pup pet
rabbit	rab bit
ragged	rag ged
ribbon	rib bon
ridden	rid den
rotten	rot ten
rugged	rug ged
sabbath	sab bath
Sabbath	Sab bath

sadden	sad den
Saffron	Saf fron
scaffold	scaf fold
scallop	scal lop
Shabbat	Shab bat
Shannon	Shan non
shellac	shel lac
skillet	skil let
snippet	snip pet
stiffen	stif fen
success	suc cess
sudden	sud den
suffix	suf fix
suggest	sug gest
Sukkot	Suk kot
sullen	sul len
summon	sum mon
suppress	sup press
swollen	swol len
tassel	tas sel
tunnel	tun nel
wallet	wal let
wallop	wal lop
written	writ ten

CC

closed-closed

non-twin

simple, no schwa

- The **CC** words in this list are both closed. They are pronounced with the short vowel
- sounds.

- For more advanced **CC** words with schwa and more advanced letter teams, see the **CC** advanced list.

- Words in *italics* are compound words.

abscess	ab scess	bandit	ban dit
absent	ab sent	banish	ban ish
acrid	ac rid	baptism	bap tism
admit	ad mit	*bathtub*	*bath tub*
advent	ad vent	*bedrock*	*bed rock*
Advent	Ad vent	*blacksmith*	*black smith*
Alfred	Al fred	*blacktop*	*black top*
antic	an tic	*Blackwell*	*Black well*
Ash dod	Ash dad	*bobcat*	*bob cat*
aspect	as pect	*bobsled*	*bob sled*
Athens	Ath ens	*bullfrog*	*bull frog*
avid	av id	*bullpen*	*bull pen*
axis	ax is	cabin	cab in
backflip	*back flip*	cactus	cac tus
backhand	*back hand*	*catnap*	*cat nap*
backpack	*back pack*	*catnip*	*cat nip*
backtrack	*back track*	*Chadwick*	*Chad wick*
backup	*back up*	Chaplin	Chap lin

checkup	*check up*
chopsticks	*chop sticks*
chronic	chron ic
civic	civ ic
Clement	Clem ent
clinic	clin ic
clothespin	*clothes pin*
cockpit	*cock pit*
combat	com bat
comet	com et
comic	com ic
complex	com plex
concept	con cept
conduct	con duct
conquest	con quest
contact	con tact
content	con tent
contrast	con trast
convent	con vent
cosmic	cos mic
credit	cred it
Cresswell	Cress well
crisscross	*criss cross*
critic	crit ic
Crockett	Crock ett
crosswalk	*cross walk*
culprit	cul prit
cutlet	*cut let*
dampen	damp en
dentist	den tist
desktop	*desk top*
drumroll	*drum roll*
drumstick	*drum stick*
dumbbell	*dumb bell*
eggnog	*egg nog*
eggplant	*egg plant*
finish	fin ish
firsthand	*first hand*
flapjack	*flap jack*
flashback	*flash back*
Francis	Fran cis
frantic	fran tic
freshman	*fresh man*
fungus	fun gus
Gildad	Gil dad
goblet	gob let
goblin	gob lin
grandson	*grand son*
grandstand	*grand stand*
graphic	graph ic
grassland	*grass land*
gumdrop	*gum drop*
halfback	*half back*
handbag	*hand bag*
handcuff	*hand cuff*
handstand	*hand stand*
hatchback	*hatch back*
hectic	hec tic
Hedwig	Hed wig
helpless	*help less*
hemlock	hem lock
Hendrick	Hen drick
hilltop	*hill top*
himself	*him self*
hopscotch	*hop scotch*
in vent	in vent
in vest	in vest
indent	in dent
induct	in duct
inert	in ert

infect	in fect
infest	in fest
inflict	in flict
inject	in ject
inland	in land
insist	in sist
inspect	in spect
instep	*in step*
instill	in still
instruct	in struct
intend	in tend
intent	in tent
itself	*it self*
jackpot	*jack pot*
Kendrick	Ken drick
kidnap	kid nap
kinship	kin ship
knapsack	*knap sack*
knickknack	*knick knack*
laptop	*lap top*
lavish	lav ish
liftoff	*lift off*
limit	lim it
lipstick	*lip stick*
locksmith	*lock smith*
madcap	*mad cap*
mascot	mas cot
Maxwell	Max well
Memphis	Mem phis
metric	met ric
mimic	mim ic
mishap	mis hap
misled	mis led
misprint	mis print
misspell	mis spell

mistrust	mis trust
nonfat	non fat
nonstop	non stop
onset	on set
pamphlet	pam phlet
phonic	phon ic
pickax	*pick ax*
pickup	*pick up*
picnic	pic nic
podcast	*pod cast*
potluck	*pot luck*
Prescott	Pres cott
Princess	Prin cess
princess	prin cess
product	prod uct
profit	prof it
publish	pub lish
punish	pun ish
pushup	push up
quicksand	*quick sand*
ransack	ran sack
reckless	reck less
restless	rest less
robin	rob in
sandbox	*sand box*
sandwich	sand wich
segment	seg ment
selfish	self ish
shamrock	sham rock
shellfish	*shell fish*
shipwreck	*ship wreck*
shoplift	*shop lift*
sickness	sick ness
sitcom	sit com
snapshot	*snap shot*

solid	sol id	unkempt	un kempt
Spanish	Span ish	unless	un less
splendid	splen did	unlock	un lock
spotless	spot less	unpack	un pack
standstill	*stand still*	unrest	un rest
static	stat ic	until	un til
stepson	*step son*	upheld	up held
stopwatch	*stop watch*	uphill	up hill
subject	sub ject	upset	up set
sublet	sub let	upshot	up shot
sunset	*sun set*	valid	val id
tactic	tac tic	vanish	van ish
tantrum	tan trum	Vincent	Vin cent
thumbtack	*thumb tack*	visit	vis it
tidbit	tid bit	vivid	viv id
timid	tim id	vomit	vom it
tomcat	*tom cat*	*watchdog*	*watch dog*
Tomkins	Tom kins	watchful	watch ful
topic	top ic	*watchman*	*watch man*
toxic	tox ic	*webcam*	*web cam*
transit	tran sit	*wedlock*	*wed lock*
transmit	trans mit	*windmill*	*wind mill*
Travis	Trav is	*within*	*with in*
tropic	trop ic	*withstand*	*with stand*
undress	un dress	wombat	wom bat
unfit	un fit	*wristwatch*	*wrist watch*
unjust	un just	zigzag	zig zag

CC

closed-closed

non-twin

advanced & schwa

- The words in this list are the most complex of the **CC** words. They are closed, but they have advanced letter teams or schwa vowel sounds.
- Some of these syllables may appear to be **VCE** because they have an **E** at the end. However, they are not **VCE**. They are closed. The **E** there for a different job than to make the vowel say a long sound. For example, words that end in -**CE** or -**GE** , have the **E** at the end of the word to make the **C** or **G** say its soft sound instead of its hard sound. In words that end in -**SE**, the **E** is at the end of the word to show that the word is not plural.
- Some of the words in this list are closed syllable exceptions, instead of closed (**ALD, INK** etc.) These letter teams will have an alternative vowel sound and will not have a short vowel sound like most closed syllables.
- Words in *italics* are compound words.

absence	ab sence
acid	ac id
Adam	Ad am
adjust	ad just
advance	ad vance
Akron	Ak ron
album	al bum
almond	al mond
almost	al most
ambush	am bush
anthem	an them
anvil	an vil
ascend	as cend
ascent	as cent
ashen	ash en
Ashlynn	Ash lynn
Ashton	Ash ton
aspen	as pen
asphalt	as phalt
Aston	As ton
atlas	at las
atom	at om
balance	bal ance
Baldwin	Bald win
balsam	bal sam
bandage	band age
beckon	beck on
blindfold	*blind fold*
Boston	Bos ton
Brandon	Bran don
Branson	Bran son

Bridget	Brid get
Caldwell	Cald well
camel	cam el
cancel	can cel
canvas	can vas
canyon	can yon
Carlsbad	Carls bad
catsup	cat sup
Celtic	Celt ic
cement	ce ment
chapel	chap el
Chapman	Chap man
chemist	chem ist
chisel	chis el
christen	chris ten
Christmas	Christ mas
citrus	cit rus
civil	civ il
Claxton	Clax ton
Clifton	Clif ton
Clinton	Clin ton
closet	clos et
column	col umn
compact	com pact
compass	com pass
compel	com pel
compost	com post
compress	com press
concoct	con coct
condemn	con demn
condense	con dense
confess	con fess
confirm	con firm
conflict	con flict
confront	con front
consent	con sent
consist	con sist
constant	con stant
constrict	con strict
construct	con struct
consul	con sul
consult	con sult
contempt	con tempt
contend	con tend
contract	con tract
convex	con vex
convict	con vict
cosmos	cos mos
Crandall	Cran dall*
Cranston	Cran ston
crescent	cres cent
cricket	crick et
crimson	crim son
cryptic	cryp tic
crystal	crys tal
Crystal	Crys tal
custom	cus tom
customs	cus toms
cutlass	cut lass
Cybil	Cyb il
cymbal	cym bal
Cyril	Cyr il
Dalton	Dal ton
dandruff	dan druff
denim	den im
dental	den tal
Denton	Den ton
Desmond	Des mond
devil	dev il
digit	dig it

disband	dis band
Felton	Fel ton
fidget	fidg et
Finland	Fin land
fitful	fit ful
fitness	fit ness
flaxen	flax en
Frances	Fran ces
Franklin	Frank lin
freshen	fresh en
fulcrum	ful crum
fulfill	ful fill
fullback	full back
Fulton	Ful ton
gadget	gadg et
gangplank	*gang plank*
giblets	gib lets
gingham	ging ham
ginseng	gin seng
given	giv en
glisten	glis ten
godstudent	*god student*
golden	gold en
goldfinch	*gold finch*
goldfish	*gold fish*
Goldsmith	*Gold smith*
gravel	grav el
Gresham	Gresh am
Gretchen	Gret chen
Gretel	Gret el
gymnast	gym nast
habit	hab it
hamlet	ham let
Hampton	Hamp ton
handball	*hand ball*
handful	hand ful
Haskel	Has kel
hatchet	hatch et
havoc	ha voc
hedgehog	*hedge hog*
helmet	hel met
helpful	help ful
hidden	hid den
Hilton	Hil ton
Hitchcock	Hitch cock
holdup	*hold up*
honest	hon est
hostel	hos tel
hostess	host ess
hundred	hun dred
husband	hus band
illness	ill ness
impact	im pact
impel	im pel
implant	im plant
impress	im press
imprint	im print
induct	in duct
infant	in fant
ingot	in got
inland	in land
inlet	in let
input	in put
install	in stall
instant	in stant
instinct	in stinct
insult	in sult
Islam	Is lam
island	is land
jackal	jack al

jacket	jack et
Jackson	Jack son
Judges	judg es
judgment	judg ment
Justin	Jus tin
Kansas	Kan sas
Kendall	Ken dall
Kenneth	Ken neth
ketchup	ketch up
kindness	kind ness
kingdom	king dom
Kingston	Kings ton
kitchen	kitch en
Landon	Lan don
Latin	Lat in
legend	leg end
lemon	lem on
lengthen	length en
lentil	len til
level	lev el
Lincoln	Lin coln
Linda	Lin da
linen	lin en
listen	lis ten
Lizbeth	Liz beth
locket	lock et
logic	log ic
London	Lon don
Ludwig	Lud wig
Lyndon	Lyn don
magic	mag ic
magnet	mag net
Malcolm	Mal colm
mankind	man kind
mantel	man tel
matzoh	mat zoh
medal	med al
melon	mel on
mental	men tal
metal	met al
method	meth od
midland	mid land
Milton	Mil ton
mindful	mind ful
minstrel	min strel
Mitchell	Mitch ell
model	mod el
modest	mod est
mongrel	mon grel
musket	mus ket
muskrat	*musk rat*
Muslim	Mus lim
muslin	mus lin
mustang	mus tang
Nelson	Nel son
nickel	nick el
Nimrud	Nim rud
offspring	*off spring*
Osten	Os ten
Oswald	Os wald
oven	ov en
packet	pack et
panel	pan el
panic	pan ic
patent	pat ent
pedal	ped al
pencil	pen cil
pendant	pend ant
petal	pet al
Phyllis	Phyl lis

physics	phys ics
picket	pick et
pigment	pig ment
pilgrim	pil grim
pinball	*pin ball*
piston	pis ton
pitfall	pit fall
Pithom	Pith om
pivot	pi vot
pixel	pix el
placid	plac id
planet	plan et
plankton	plank ton
pollen	pol len
polyp	pol yp
postal	post al
postman	post man
postscript	post script
pregnant	preg nant
present	pres ent
Preston	Pres ton
pretzel	pret zel
prison	pris on
problem	prob lem
prophet	proph et
prospect	pros pect
proven	prov en
public	pub lic
pulpit	pul pit
pumpkin	pump kin
quicken	quick en
racket	rack et
Randolf	Ran dolf
random	ran dom
ransom	ran som

rapid	rap id
rapids	rap ids
rebel	reb el
reckon	reck on
rhombus	rhom bus
rhythmic	rhyth mic
riches	rich es
Richmond	Rich mond
rigid	rig id
rivet	riv et
rocket	rock et
salad	sal ad
salmon	salm on
sandal	san dal
satin	sat in
scandal	scan dal
second	sec ond
seldom	sel dom
seven	sev en
seventh	sev enth
shovel	shov el
shrivel	shriv el
shrunken	shrunk en
Sigmund	Sig mund
signal	sig nal
silken	silk en
skillful	skill ful
slacken	slack en
smallpox	*small pox*
socket	sock et
softball	*soft ball*
soften	soft en
solemn	sol emn
spangled	span gled
	*spang led

speckled	speck led	thicken	thick en
spectrum	spec trum	thicket	thick et
spigot	spig ot	Thomas	Thom as
spinach	spin ach	ticket	tick et
squadron	squad ron	tinsel	tin sel
Stanton	Stan ton	transplant	trans plant
Stetson	Stet son	travel	trav el
Stillman	*Still man*	Trenton	Tren ton
Stockton	Stock ton	trinket	trin ket
stomach	stom ach		*trink et
stricken	strick en	triplet	trip let
Strickland	Strick land	Tristan	Tris tan
striven	striv en	trumpet	trum pet
stronghold	*strong hold*	truthful	truth ful
substance	sub stance	unfold	un fold
subtract	sub tract	unkind	un kind
sultan	sul tan	untold	un told
sunken	sunk en	*uphold*	*up hold*
suspect	sus pect	vandal	van dal
swivel	swiv el	vassal	vas sal
symbol	sym bol	velvet	vel vet
symptom	symp tom	venom	ven om
syrup	syr up	victim	vic tim
system	sys tem	wagon	wag on
tablet	tab let	Walden	Wal den
talent	tal ent	walnut	wal nut
talon	tal on	walrus	wal rus
tassel	tas sel	Waltham	Wal tham
tempest	tem pest	Walton	Wal ton
tenant	ten ant	wanton	wan ton
tendon	ten don	Wendell	Wen dell
tendril	ten dril	Whitcomb	Whit comb
tepid	tep id	whiten	whit en
Texas	Tex as	wicket	wick et
thankless	thank less	wigwam	wig wam

wildcat	*wild cat*	wistful	wist ful
willful	will ful	witness	wit ness
Wilson	Wil son	woman	wom an
Wilton	Wil ton	women	wom en
Winsted	Win sted	wretched	wretch ed
Winston	Win ston	Yemen	Yem en
wisdom	wis dom		

CL

closed-CLE

- The words in this list have one closed vowel team syllable and one **CLE** syllable.
- The **CLE** syllable is always found at the end of a word. The only exception to this would be a compound word, where the **CLE** is at the end of the first base.
- Some of these words have closed syllable exceptions (ie **ANG**, **INK**). Traditional syllable division will divide up the closed syllable exception letter teams, because their goal is to keep the three letter **CLE** together. However, for pronunciation, they are better divided so that the closed syllable exception stays intact. In those cases, I have provided an alternative division that is marked with an asterisk.
- Words in *italics* are compound words.

amble	am ble	crinkle	crin kle
ample	am ple		*crink le
angle	an gle	cripple	crip ple
	*ang le	crumble	crum ble
ankle	an kle		*crumb le
	*ank le	crumple	crum ple
apple	ap ple	cuddle	cud dle
axle	ax le	dabble	dab ble
babble	bab ble	dangle	dan gle
baffle	baf fle		*dang le
bangle	ban gle	dazzle	daz zle
	*bang le	diddle	did dle
battle	bat tle	dimple	dim ple
candle	can dle	fiddle	fid dle
castle	cas tle	fumble	fum ble
cattle	cat tle	gentle	gen tle
chuckle	chuck le	giggle	gig gle
coddle	cod dle	gobble	gob ble
crackle	crack le	griddle	grid dle

gristle	gris tle
grumble	grum ble
guzzle	guz zle
haggle	hag gle
handle	han dle
	*hand le
hassle	has sle
heckle	heck le
hobble	hob ble
huddle	hud dle
humble	hum ble
hustle	hus tle
jangle	jan gle
	*jang le
jiggle	jig gle
jingle	jin gle
	*jing le
jostle	jos tle
juggle	jug gle
jumble	jum ble
jungle	jun gle
kettle	ket tle
kindle	kin dle
knuckle	knuck le
little	lit tle
mangle	man gle
	*mang le
mantle	man tle
middle	mid dle
mingle	min gle
	*ming le
muddle	mud dle
mumble	mum ble
muzzle	muz zle
nestle	nes tle
nettle	net tle
nibble	nib ble
nimble	nim ble
nipple	nip ple
paddle	pad dle
pebble	peb ble
peddle	ped dle
pestle	pes tle
pickle	pick le
pimple	pim ple
prickle	prick le
puddle	pud dle
puzzle	puz zle
quibble	quib ble
raffle	raf fle
ramble	ram ble
rattle	rat tle
riddle	rid dle
rifle	ri fle
ripple	rip ple
rubble	rub ble
ruffle	ruf fle
rumble	rum ble
rustle	rus tle
saddle	sad dle
sample	sam ple
scramble	scram ble
scribble	scrib ble
scuffle	scuf fle
scuttle	scut tle
settle	set tle
shingle	shin gle
	*shing le
shuffle	shuf fle
shuttle	shut tle

sickle	sick le
simple	sim ple
single	sin gle
	*sing le
sizzle	siz zle
smuggle	smug gle
snuggle	snug gle
spindle	spin dle
sprinkle	sprin kle
	*sprink le
squabble	squab ble
straggle	strag gle
strangle	stran gle
	*strang le
struggle	strug gle
stubble	stub ble
stumble	stum ble
subtle	sub tle
supple	sup ple
swindle	swin dle
tackle	tack le
tattle	tat tle
temple	tem ple
thimble	thim ble
thistle	this tle
throttle	throt tle
tickle	tick le
tingle	tin gle
	*ting le
tinkle	tin kle
	*tink le
topple	top ple
trample	tram ple
tremble	trem ble
trestle	tres tle
trickle	trick le
tumble	tum ble
uncle	un cle
waddle	wad dle
waffle	waf fle
whistle	whis tle
whittle	whit tle
wiggle	wig gle
wobble	wob ble
wrestle	wres tle
wriggle	wrig gle
wrinkle	wrin kle
	*wrink le

CO

closed-open

- Many words that end in **-A**, like pizza, follow the closed-open pattern, but the open syllable makes a schwa sound and not an open vowel long sound.
- Beginning students who are still learning open/closed should only be given words that make the long vowel sounds and not the schwa sound.
- A majority of the closed-open pattern words have suffixes, such as **-Y, -LY,** and **-EY**, but there are some that have other open syllables.
- Some of these words have closed syllable exceptions (ie **ANG**, **INK**). Traditional syllable division will divide up the closed syllable exception letter teams, because their goal is to keep the three letter **CLE** together. However, for pronunciation, they are better divided so that the closed syllable exception stays intact. In those cases, I have provided an alternative division that is marked with an asterisk.
- Words in *italics* are compound words.

Abby	Ab by		*bing o
Akko	Ak ko	Brandy	Bran dy
ally	al ly	Buffy	Buff-y
also	al so	bunny	bun ny
alto	al to	cacti	cac ti
angry	an gry	candy	can dy
	*ang ry	Candy	Can dy
apply	ap ply	Castro	Cas tro
Ashby	Ash by	Cathy	Cath y
badly	bad ly	cello	cel lo
baggy	bag gy	chatty	chat ty
balmy	balm y	Chile	Chil e
banjo	ban jo	chili	chil i
belfry	bel fry	chilly	chil ly
Betsy	Bet sy	Christy	Chris ty
Betty	bet ty	chunky	chunk y
Billy	Bil ly	Cindy	Cin dy
bingo	bin go	clammy	clam my

Clancy	Clan cy
clumsy	clum sy
cocky	cock y
comply	com ply
condo	con do
Congo	Con go
costly	cost ly
cranky	crank y
cranny	cran ny
daddy	dad dy
Daphne	Daph ne
Delhi	Del hi
Digby	Dig by
Dingo	Din go
	*Ding o
dingy	din gy
fifty	fif ty
filthy	filth y
fishy	fish y
floppy	flop py
fluffy	fluff y
foggy	fog gy
folly	fol ly
frenzy	fren zy
Fresno	Fres no
Frisco	Fris co
frisky	frisk y
fully	ful ly
fungi	fun gi
funny	fun ny
fussy	fuss y
Gandhi	Gan dhi
gecko	geck o
gently	gen tly
	*gent ly

ghastly	ghast ly
ghetto	ghet to
ghostly	ghost ly
giddy	gid dy
ginkgo	gink go
Ginny	Gin ny
glossy	gloss y
grassy	grass y
grimy	grim y
grumpy	grump y
guppy	gup py
handy	hand y
happy	hap py
hasty	hast y
healthy	health y
hearty	heart y
hefty	heft y
hello	hel lo
Henry	Hen ry
hilly	hill y
hippo	hip po
Holly	Hol ly
holly	hol ly
husky	husk y
imply	im ply
into	in to
itchy	itch y
jelly	jel ly
Jenny	Jen ny
Jesse	Jes se
Jethro	Jeth ro
jetty	jet ty
jolly	jol ly
jumbo	jum bo
jumpy	jump y

Kathy	Kath y
Kelly	Kel ly
Kenny	Ken ny
khaki	khak i
kindly	kind ly
kitty	kit ty
lasso	las so
lengthy	length y
levy	lev y
Libby	Lib by
Lily	Lil y
lily	lil y
lobby	lob by
lofty	loft y
lucky	luck y
Mandy	Man dy
mango	man go
	*mang o
many	man y
memo	mem o
menu	men u
messy	mess y
mighty	might y
milky	milk y
misty	mist y
moldy	mold y
Molly	Mol ly
mommy	mom my
Mommy	Mom my
mossy	moss y
motto	mot to
muddy	mud dy
muggy	mug gy
mummy	mum my
musty	mus ty
nasty	nas ty
pantry	pan try
pastry	pas try
patty	pat ty
Penny	Pen ny
penny	pen ny
petty	pet ty
picky	pick y
pinky	pink y
pinto	pin to
pity	pit y
plenty	plen ty
plucky	pluck y
Polly	Pol ly
poncho	pon cho
Poppy	Pop py
poppy	pop py
posse	pos se
pronto	pron to
puffy	puff y
puppy	pup py
putty	put ty
Quimby	Quim by
Quincy	Quin cy
rabbi	rab bi
rally	ral ly
Randy	Ran dy
raspy	rasp y
risky	risk y
rosy	ros y
ruddy	rud dy
Rugby	Rug by
Rusty	Rust y
rusty	rust y
Sally	Sal ly

salty	salt y
Sandy	Sand y
sandy	sand y
scanty	scant y
sentry	sen try
shabby	shab by
shady	shad y
shaggy	shag gy
Shelby	Shel by
Shelly	Shel ly
shiny	shin y
shoddy	shod dy
sickly	sick ly
Sidney	Sid ney
silky	silk y
silly	sil ly
simply	sim ply
sixty	six ty
sketchy	sketch y
skinny	skin ny
slimy	slim y
sloppy	slop py
smelly	smell y
soggy	sog gy
Sonny	Son ny
spiny	spin y
spongy	spon gy

starry	star ry
sticky	stick y
stocky	stock y
study	stud y
stuffy	stuff y
supply	sup ply
tabby	tab by
taffy	taf fy
tally	tal ly
Tempe	Tem pe
tempo	tem po
thirsty	thirst y
thirty	thir ty
thrifty	thrift y
trusty	trust y
ugly	ug ly
undo	un do
Vicky	Vick y
Waldo	Wal do
Wally	Wal ly
Wendy	Wen dy
whimsy	whim sy
whinny	whin ny
windy	wind y
wintry	win try
witty	wit ty
Zephi	Zeph i

CV

closed-vowel team

- Students should be familiar with the vowel teams before attempting these words.
- Words marked with *italics* are compound words.

abstain	ab stain
acclaim	ac claim
account	ac count
adjoin	ad join
adjourn	ad journ
Aleut	Al eut
alley	al ley
allow	al low
alloy	al loy
always	al ways
ancient	an cient
Andrew	An drew
annoy	an noy
appeal	ap peal
appear	ap pear
appease	ap pease
applaud	ap plaud
applause	ap plause
appoint	ap point
appraise	ap praise
approach	ap proach
Ashley	Ash ley
asleep	a sleep
assail	as sail
assault	as sault
astound	as tound
astray	a stray
attain	at tain
Atwood	At wood
balloon	bal loon
bassoon	bas soon
Belgium	Bel gium
bellow	bel low
billboard	*bill board*
Billie	Bil lie
blackboard	*black board*
blackmail	*black mail*
blackout	*black out*
Bradley	Brad ley
caffeine	caf feine
callous	cal lous
Calney	Cal ney
canteen	can teen
captain	cap tain
cashew	cash ew
cashier	cash ier
Cassie	Cas sie
Cathleen	Cath leen
centaur	cen taur
chalkboard	*chalk board*
chaplain	chap lain
chatroom	*chat room*
Chelsey	Chel sey
chickpea	*chick pea*

chimney	chim ney
Christie	Chris tie
classroom	*class room*
cockroach	cock roach
coffee	cof fee
collie	col lie
complain	com plain
complaint	com plaint
conceal	con ceal
Conroy	Con roy
contain	con tain
contour	con tour
convey	con vey
convoy	con voy
Conway	Con way
crossbow	*cross bow*
crossroads	*cross roads*
cupboard	*cup board*
Daniel	Dan iel
Delroy	Del roy
dogwood	*dog wood*
fallout	*fall out*
falsehood	false hood
fellow	fel low
fishhook	*fish hook*
Flossie	Flos sie
follow	fol low
foxhound	*fox hound*
frontier	fron tier
galley	gal ley
genius	gen ius
genteel	gen teel
Gilroy	Gil roy
glamour	glam our
Guthrie	Guth rie
Haggai	Hag gai
handout	*hand out*
handrail	*hand rail*
hangnail	*hang nail*
hollow	hol low
homey	hom ey
honey	hon ey
igloo	ig loo
impair	im pair
impeach	im peach
increase	in crease
indeed	in deed
indoor	in door
infield	in field
instead	in stead
issue	is sue
Jeffrey	Jef frey
jigsaw	jig saw
jockey	jock ey
Kelsey	Kel sey
kidney	kid ney
Kingsley	Kings ley
Leslie	Les lie
levee	lev ee
Lindsay	Lind say
liquid	liq uid
	*li quid
Ludlow	Lud low
luncheon	lunch eon
magpie	mag pie
maltreat	mal treat
manhood	man hood
Mansfield	Mans field
Matthew	Mat thew
medley	med ley

memoir	mem oir	*restroom*	*rest room*
Mickey	Mick ey	Rodney	Rod ney
midday	mid day	Roscoe	Ros coe
mildew	mil dew	*rundown*	*run down*
milkweed	*milk weed*	*runway*	*run way*
minnow	min now	sallow	sal low
miscount	mis count	*scrapbook*	*scrap book*
mislaid	mis laid	selfie	self ie
mislead	mis lead	senior	sen ior
mistook	mis took	shadow	shad ow
mistreat	mis treat	shallow	shal low
money	Mon ey	shampoo	sham poo
monkey	mon key	*shutdown*	*shut down*
monsoon	mon soon	sinew	sin ew
monstrous	mon strous	sixteen	six teen
Moscow	Mos cow	sixteenth	six teenth
movie	mov ie	soldier	sol dier
Mumbai	Mum bai	Spaniard	Span iard
mushroom	mush room	spaniel	span iel
nephew	neph ew	*springboard*	*spring board*
offshoot	*off shoot*	*Springfield*	*Spring field*
osprey	os prey	*standpoint*	*stand point*
pageant	pag eant	Stanley	Stan ley
Pasteur	Pas teur	statue	stat ue
penguin	pen guin	subway	sub way
pigtail	pig tail	succeed	suc ceed
pillow	pil low	*sunbeam*	*sun beam*
pinkie	pink ie	sundae	sun dae
pinpoint	*pin point*	Sunday	Sun day
pinwheel	*pin wheel*	*sunscreen*	*sun screen*
pompous	pomp ous	sustain	sus tain
Presley	Pres ley	swallow	swal low
pulley	pul ley	*swimsuit*	*swim suit*
raccoon	rac coon	tallow	tal low
redwood	*red wood*	tattoo	tat too

textbook	*text book*	valley	val ley
tiptoe	*tip toe*	value	val ue
tissue	tis sue	venue	ven ue
Tolkien	Tol kien	villain	vil lain
Tolstoy	Tol stoy	*walkway*	*walk way*
topsoil	*top soil*	wallow	wal low
Trixie	Trix ie	Whitney	Whit ney
trolley	trol ley	widow	wid ow
Tuesday	Tues day	Willie	Wil lie
tugboat	*tug boat*	willow	wil low
unearth	un earth	Willow	Wil low
unfair	un fair	window	win dow
unknown	un known	*windshield*	*wind shield*
unload	un load	Winslow	Wins low
unsound	un sound	*withdraw*	*with draw*
untie	un tie	*withdrawn*	*with drawn*
upkeep	up keep	*withdrew*	*with drew*
upload	up load	*without*	*with out*
uproar	up roar	*withstood*	*with stood*
uproot	up root	yellow	yel low
upstream	up stream	zombie	zom bie

CE

closed - VCE

- Some words may have syllables that appear to be **VCE**, but they have short vowel sounds. For example, the word **fragile** is pronounced **/fraj-il/,** not with a long **/i/** sound. Those words are not included in this list. See the **VCE** imposters lists for those words.
- Words marked with *italics* are compound words.

accuse	ac cuse
acquire	ac quire
adhere	ad here
admire	ad mire
advice	ad vice
advise	ad vise
alpine	al pine
aspire	as pire
assume	as sume
assure	as sure
astride	a stride
athlete	ath lete
attire	at tire
azure	az ure
backbone	*back bone*
backfire	*back fire*
backstroke	*back stroke*
bagpipe	*bag pipe*
baptize	bap tize
bathrobe	*bath robe*
capsize	cap size
capture	cap ture
cascade	cas cade
cashmere	cash mere
cellphone	*cell phone*
clambake	*clam bake*
classmate	*class mate*
clothesline	*clothes line*
collide	col lide
combine	com bine
commute	com mute
compare	com pare
compete	com pete
compile	com pile
complete	com plete
comprise	com prise
compute	com pute
concave	con cave
concede	con cede
concise	con cise
conclude	con clude
concrete	con crete
confide	con fide
confuse	con fuse
console	con sole
conspire	con spire
consume	con sume

contrite	con trite
convene	con vene
costume	cos tume
culture	cul ture
cupcake	*cup cake*
decade	dec ade
deluge	del uge
dictate	dic tate
drugstore	*drug store*
empire	em pire
engrave	en grave
exclude	ex clude
figure	fig ure
flagpole	*flag pole*
folklore	folk lore
folktale	*folk tale*
fracture	frac ture
Francene	Fran cene
franchise	fran chise
frostbite	*frost bite*
fructose	fruc tose
frustrate	frus trate
Gentile	Gen tile
gesture	ges ture
Glendale	Glen dale
graphite	graph ite
grindstone	*grind stone*
halfpipe	*half pipe*
handmade	*hand made*
handshake	*hand shake*
hillside	*hill side*
hitchhike	*hitch hike*
ignite	ig nite
immune	im mune
impede	im pede
implore	im plore
impose	im pose
impure	im pure
incite	in cite
incline	in cline
include	in clude
induce	in duce
inflame	in flame
inflate	in flate
inhale	in hale
injure	in jure
inquire	in quire
insane	in sane
inscribe	in scribe
inside	in side
inspire	in spire
insure	in sure
intake	in take
intrude	in trude
invade	in vade
invite	in vite
jackknife	*jack knife*
lactose	lac tose
landscape	*land scape*
landslide	*land slide*
lecture	lec ture
legume	leg ume
lengthwise	length wise
Maldives	Mal dives
manhole	*man hole*
manmade	*man made*
membrane	mem brane
methane	meth ane
milkshake	*milk shake*
misplace	mis place

mistake	mis take
misuse	mis use
mixture	mix ture
module	mod ule
mundane	mun dane
neckline	*neck line*
Neptune	Nep tune
nickname	nick name
obtuse	*ob tuse*
oboffshore	*off shore*
offside	*off side*
online	*on line*
onshore	*on shore*
oppose	op pose
oxide	*ox ide*
pancake	*pan cake*
penknife	*pen knife*
picture	pic ture
pollute	pol lute
postpone	post pone
posture	pos ture
pothole	*pot hole*
pressure	pres sure
Primrose	Prim rose
primrose	prim rose
pristine	pris tine
puncture	punc ture
quagmire	quag mire
rapture	rap ture
reptile	rep tile
rupture	rup ture
sandstone	*sand stone*
sapphire	sap phire
satire	sat ire
schedule	sched ule
scripture	scrip ture
sculpture	sculp ture
shipshape	*ship shape*
stampede	stam pede
stockade	stock ade
stockpile	*stock pile*
subdue	sub due
subscribe	sub scribe
subside	sub side
sunshine	*sun shine*
suppose	sup pose
syndrome	syn drome
textile	tex tile
texture	tex ture
tombstone	*tomb stone*
translate	trans late
tribute	trib ute
Truesdale	Trus dale
umpire	um pire
unlike	un like
update	*up date*
upgrade	*up grade*
vaccine	vac cine
venture	ven ture
volume	vol ume
welfare	wel fare
wildlife	*wild life*
windpipe	*wind pipe*
wishbone	*wish bone*

CR

closed-R controlled

- Students should be familiar with **R**-controlled combinations before attempting these words.
- Words in *italics* are compound words.

Abner	Ab ner
absorb	ab sorb
absurd	ab surd
accord	ac cord
actor	ac tor
ad verse	ad verse
adder	ad der
adverb	ad verb
affirm	af firm
afford	af ford
after	af ter
Albert	Al bert
altar	al tar
alter	al ter
amber	am ber
anchor	an chor
answer	an swer
anther	an ther
antler	ant ler
Astor	As tor
backyard	*back yard*
banner	ban ner
banter	ban ter
batter	bat ter
Baxter	Bax ter
beggar	beg gar
blackbird	*black bird*
Blackburn	*Black burn*
Bosworth	Bos woth
Bradburn	Brad burn
Bradford	Brad ford
Buster	Bus ter
camper	camp er
cancer	can cer
canter	can ter
Caspar	Cas par
catbird	*cat bird*
cavern	cav ern
cellar	cel lar
censor	cen sor
center	cen ter
Chandler	Chan dler
chapter	chap ter
chatter	chat ter
checkers	check ers
Chester	Ches ter
cinder	cin der
clamber	clam ber
clamor	clam or
clapper	clap per
clatter	clat ter
clever	clev er

Clifford	Clif ford
clipper	clip per
clockwork	*clock work*
cluster	clus ter
clutter	clut ter
cobbler	cob bler
collar	col lar
collards	col lards
color	col or
Colter	Col ter
concern	con cern
concert	con cert
concord	con cord
Concord	Con cord
concur	con cur
confer	con fer
conform	con form
Connor	Con nor
conquer	con quer
convert	con vert
copper	cop per
culvert	cul vert
custard	cus tard
dagger	dag ger
debtor	debt or
Denmark	Den mark
Denver	Den ver
dessert	des sert
Dexter	Dex ter
differ	dif fer
dinner	din ner
disarm	dis arm
filter	fil ter
flatter	flat ter
flipper	flip per

fluster	flus ter
flutter	flut ter
fodder	fod der
foghorn	*fog horn*
folder	fold er
foster	fos ter
fritter	frit ter
gander	gan der
gender	gen der
Gilbert	Gil bert
ginger	gin ger
gizzard	giz zard
glimmer	glim mer
glitter	glit ter
govern	gov ern
grammar	gram mar
gunner	gun ner
gutter	gut ter
halter	hal ter
hammer	ham mer
hamper	ham per
hamster	ham ster
hazard	haz ard
Hector	Hec tor
Hester	Hes ter
hinder	hin der
honor	hon or
hopper	hop per
hunger	hun ger
hunter	hunt er
import	im port
inborn	in born
inchworm	*inch worm*
infer	in fer
inform	in form

inner	in ner
insert	in sert
intern	in tern
invert	in vert
inward	in ward
jabber	jab ber
jester	jest er
juggler	jug gler
jumper	jump er
knickers	knick ers
lacquer	lac quer
ladder	lad der
landlord	*land lord*
landmark	*land mark*
lantern	lan tern
latter	lat ter
Lester	Les ter
letter	let ter
Lindberg	Lind berg
Lindhurst	Lind hurst
litter	lit ter
lizard	liz ard
lobster	lob ster
longhorn	*long horn*
lumber	lum ber
luster	lus ter
mallard	mal lard
manner	man ner
manners	man ners
manor	man or
master	mas ter
matter	mat ter
member	mem ber
Milburn	Mil burn
Mister	mis ter
modern	mod ern
monarch	mon arch
monster	mon ster
muffler	muf fler
muster	mus ter
mutter	mut ter
nectar	nec tar
network	*net work*
Oscar	Os car
otter	ot ter
Oxnard	Ox nard
pamper	pam per
panther	pan ther
passport	*pass port*
password	*pass word*
pastor	pas tor
pasture	pas ture
patchwork	*patch work*
patter	pat ter
pattern	pat tern
pepper	pep per
pester	pes ter
pilfer	pil fer
pillar	pil lar
pitchfork	*pitch fork*
Pittsburgh	Pitts burgh
plaster	plas ter
platform	plat form
platter	plat ter
plunder	plun der
ponder	pon der
poplar	pop lar
potter	pot ter
printer	print er
Proctor	Proc tor

pronghorn	prong horn	sil ver	sil ver
prosper	pros per	*silkworm*	*silk worm*
Radburn	Rad burn	simmer	sim mer
rampart	ram part	sister	sis ter
rapport	rap port	Skinner	Skin ner
record	rec ord	skipper	skip per
Redford	Red ford	slander	slan der
Richard	Rich ard	slender	slen der
Robert	Rob ert	slipper	slip per
rocker	rock er	slumber	slum ber
Rockford	Rock ford	smolder	smol der
roster	ros ter		*smold er
rubber	rub ber	soccer	soc cer
rudder	rud der	somber	som ber
runner	run ner	spatter	spat ter
sandbar	*sand bar*	Spencer	Spen cer
Sanford	San ford	splendor	splen dor
Saturn	Sat urn	splinter	splin ter
scabbard	scab bard		*splint er
scanner	scan ner	sponsor	spon sor
scatter	scat ter	sputter	sput ter
scepter	scep ter	squander	squan der
scholar	schol ar	Stafford	Staf ford
scissors	scis sors	stagger	stag ger
sculptor	sculp tor	Stamford	Stam ford
sensor	sen sor	stammer	stam mer
setter	set ter	standard	stan dard
settler	set tler	Stanford	Stan ford
shatter	shat ter	stirrup	stir rup
shelter	shel ter	*stockyard*	*stock yard*
shepherd	shep herd	Stoddard	Stod dard
shimmer	shim mer	stopper	stop per
shipyard	*ship yard*	structure	struc ture
shudder	shud der	stubborn	stub born
shutter	shut ter	stutter	stut ter

submerge	sub merge	upper	up per
suburb	sub urb	upward	up ward
suffer	suf fer	utter	ut ter
sugar	sug ar	valor	val or
sulfur	sul fur	vendor	ven dor
summer	sum mer	Victor	Vic tor
sunburn	*sun burn*	victor	vic tor
support	sup port	vulgar	vul gar
swagger	swag ger	Wadsworth	Wads worth
tamper	tam per	Waldorf	Wal dorf
tatter	tat ter	wander	wan der
temper	tem per	Webster	Web ster
tender	ten der	whenever	when ever
tenor	ten or	whisper	whis per
thinner	thin ner	Wilbur	Wil bur
thunder	thun der	Wilmer	Wil mer
timber	tim ber	Windsor	Wind sor
toddler	tod dler	*windstorm*	*wind storm*
totter	tot ter	*windsurf*	*wind surf*
tractor	trac tor	winner	win ner
transfer	trans fer	winter	win ter
transform	trans form	wizard	wiz ard
transport	trans port	wrapper	wrap per
trapper	trap per	Xander	Xan der
tremor	trem or	yonder	yon der
Trevor	Tre vor	Yonkers	Yon kers
trigger	trig ger	Zander	Zan der
tumbler	tum bler	Zephyr	Zeph yr
twitter	twit ter	zipper	zip per
udder	ud der		
under	un der		
unfurl	un furl		

OC

open-closed

- Many syllables that are open will have the schwa sound, so they will not make the long vowel sound. Beginning students who are learning open/closed should only be given words that make the long vowel sounds and not the schwa.
- Words in *italics* are compound words.

adopt	a dopt	canal	ca* nal
adrift	a drift	Cecil	Ce cil
adult	a dult	Cedric	Ce dric
atop	a top	Cephas	Ce phas
bagel	ba gel	chorus	cho rus
Barack	Ba rack	chosen	cho sen
basic	ba sic	client	cli ent
basin	ba sin	climax	cli max
basis	ba sis	Clovis	Clo vis
baton	ba ton	coed	co ed
began	be gan	crisis	cri sis
begin	be gin	Cuban	Cu ban
begun	be gun	cubic	cu bic
behalf	be half	cypress	cy press
beheld	be held	Cyprus	Cy prus
beset	be set	Cyrus	Cy rus
Bhutan	Bhu tan	decent	de cent
Boaz	Bo az	deduct	de duct
Brazil	Bra* zil	defect	de fect
Bryson	Bry son	defend	de fend
bypass	by pass	deflect	de flect
Cabul	Ca* bul	demand	de mand
cadet	ca* det	depend	de pend
Canaan	Ca naan	depict	de pict

depress	de press
descend	de scend
descent	de scent
detach	de tach
detect	de tect
detest	de test
detract	de tract
DeWitt	De Witt
digest	di gest
direct	di* rect
final	fi nal
floral	flo ral
florist	flo rist
fluent	flu ent
fluid	flu id
focal	fo cal
focus	fo cus
fragrant	fra grant
Fremont	Fre mont
frequent	fre quent
frozen	fro zen
frugal	fru gal
Gabon	Ga bon
genus	ge nus
giant	gi ant
gluten	glu ten
Goshen	Go shen
Grayson	Gray son
Haran	Ha ran
haven	ha ven
hazel	ha zel
hijack	hi jack
human	hu man
humid	hu mid
hybrid	hy brid
hydrant	hy drant
hyphen	hy phen
icon	i con
idol	i dol
Iran	I ran
Iraq	I raq
Irish	I rish
iron	i ron
item	i tem
Jacob	Ja cob
Japan	Ja pan
Jesus	Je sus
Jonah	Jo nah
Joseph	Jo seph
Judah	Ju dah
Judith	Ju dith
kebab	ke bab
Koran	Ko ran
label	la bel
Lagos	La gos
latex	la tex
legal	le gal
Leland	Le land
lichen	li chen
lilac	li lac
local	lo cal
Loren	Lo ren
lotus	lo tus
Macon	Ma con
mason	ma son
matron	ma tron
Micah	Mi cah
migrant	mi grant
minus	mi nus
Moab	Mo ab

modem	mo dem
moment	mo ment
morass	mo rass
Moses	Mo ses
motel	mo tel
mucus	mu cus
mural	mu ral
music	mu sic
myself	my self
Nahum	Na hum
naked	na ked
nasal	na sal
naval	na val
neglect	ne glect
neon	ne on
Nepal	Ne pal
Noah	No ah
nomad	no mad
open	o pen
oral	o ral
oval	o val
patrol	pa trol
patron	pa tron
pilot	pi lot
poem	po em
poet	po et
Poland	Po land
Polish	Po lish
predict	pre dict
pretend	pre tend
pretext	pre text
prevent	pre vent
profess	pro fess
program	pro gram
propel	pro pel
protect	pro tect
protest	pro test
proton	pro ton
protract	pro tract
prudent	pru dent
Purim	Pu rim
python	py thon
raven	ra ven
react	re act
rebuff	re buff
recent	re cent
recess	re cess
refill	re fill
reflect	re flect
reflex	re flex
refresh	re fresh
refund	re fund
regal	re gal
regret	re gret
reject	re ject
respect	re spect
respond	re spond
restrict	re strict
result	re sult
riot	ri ot
rival	ri val
robot	ro bot
robust	ro bust
rodent	ro dent
Roman	Ro man
Romans	Ro mans
Rudolf	Ru dolf
ruin	ru in
rural	ru ral
sacred	sa cred

Salem	Sa lem
scenic	sce nic
secret	se cret
sepal	se pal
sequel	se quel
sequin	se quin
serum	se rum
Shalom	Sha lom
silent	si lent
sinus	si nus
siphon	si phon
siren	si ren
slogan	slo gan
spinal	spi nal
spiral	spi ral
spoken	spo ken
stamen	sta men
Stephen	Ste phen
Steven	Ste ven
stolen	sto len
stupid	stu pid
stylus	sty lus
Sudan	Su dan
sumac	su mac
Sweden	Swe den
theist	the ist
thorax	tho rax
Tibet	Ti bet
Titus	Ti tus
topaz	to paz
total	to tal
totem	to tem
Travon	Tra von
trial	tri al
tripod	tri pod
triumph	tri umph
truant	tru ant
tumult	tu mult
tunic	tu nic
tyrant	ty rant
unit	u nit
Uruk	U ruk
vacant	va cant
vegan	ve gan
Venus	Ve nus
Viking	Vi king
vinyl	vi nyl
viral	vi ral
virus	vi rus
vital	vi tal
woven	wo ven
yodel	yo del
Yupik	Yu pik
zenith	ze nith
Zion	Zi on

OL

open-CLE

- The **OL** syllable pattern is rare.
- All open vowel syllables in this list have long vowel sounds and not schwa.

Bible	Bi ble	sable	sa ble
cable	ca ble	scruple	scru ple
cycle	cy cle	staple	sta ple
idle	i dle	stifle	sti fle
ladle	la dle	table	ta ble
maple	ma ple	title	ti tle
noble	no ble	trifle	tri fle

open-open

simple

no schwa

- Most of the words in this list end in the **-Y** suffix, but there are some that have other open syllables.
- There are no schwa sounds in this list. For the Open-Open pattern with schwa, see the list on the following page.

baby	ba by	Macy	Ma cy
Cleo	Cle o	navy	na vy
cozy	co zy	Navy	Na vy
crazy	cra zy	phony	pho ny
defy	de fy	photo	pho to
deny	de ny	Plato	Pla to
Grady	Gra dy	Pluto	Plu to
guru	gu ru	Provo	Pro vo
halo	ha lo	Ruby	Ru by
hazy	ha zy	ruby	ru by
hobo	ho bo	silo	si lo
holy	ho ly	solo	so lo
icy	i cy	Stacy	Sta cy
Ivy	I vy	Toby	To by
ivy	i vy	Tracy	Tra cy
Jody	Jo dy	trophy	tro phy
judo	ju do	Tutu	Tu tu
Lacy	La cy	veto	ve to
lady	la dy	Waco	Wa co
lazy	la zy	zany	za ny
Lehi	Le hi	zebu	ze bu
logo	lo go		

open-open

advanced & schwa

- Open syllables will usually have either the long vowel sound or the schwa sound.
- Beginning students who are learning open/closed should only be given words that make the long vowel sounds and not the schwa. See the previous Open-Open list for words that do not have schwa.

Cana	Ca na	peso	pe so
Chico	Chi co	pita	pi ta
china	chi na	Plano	Pla no
China	Chi na	plaza	pla za
cobra	co bra	pupa	pu pa
Cuba	Cu ba	quota	quo ta
Fiji	Fi ji	Roma	Ro ma
flora	flo ra	Rosa	Ro sa
gala	ga la	saga	sa ga
Ghana	Gha na	Sasha	Sa sha
llama	lla ma	soda	so da
Mali	Ma li	sofa	so fa
mesa	me sa	sushi	su shi
mocha	mo cha	tuna	tu na
		yoga	yo ga

OV

open-vowel team

- Many syllables that are open will have the schwa sound, so they will not make the long vowel sound. Beginning students who are learning open/closed should only be given words that make the long vowel sounds and not the schwa.

around	a round
askew	a skew
avoid	a void
await	a wait
away	a way
befriend	be friend
behead	be head
belie	be lie
belief	be lief
below	be low
beneath	be neath
beseech	be seech
besiege	be siege
besought	be sought
bestow	be stow
betray	be tray
Brunei	Bru nei
canoe	ca noe
career	ca reer
cocoa	co coa
cocoon	co coon
decay	de cay
deceit	de ceit
deceive	de ceive
decoy	de coy
decree	de cree
defeat	de feat
degree	de gree
delay	de lay
despair	de spair
destroy	de stroy
detail	de tail
detain	de tain
detour	de tour
Detroit	De troit
devout	de vout
Friday	Fri day
genie	ge nie
Hebrew	He brew
hygiene	hy giene
Jamie	Ja mie
Julie	Ju lie
kazoo	ka zoo
Kuwait	Ku wait
lagoon	la goon
LeRoy	Le Roy
luau	lu au
Marie	Ma rie
maroon	ma roon
melee	me lee
mellow	mel low

meow	me ow
pious	pi ous
platoon	pla toon
plywood	ply wood
porous	por ous
preschool	pre school
prevail	pre vail
preview	pre view
proceed	pro ceed
proclaim	pro claim
profound	pro found
pronoun	pro noun
protein	pro tein
rebound	re bound
rebuild	re build
receipt	re ceipt
reclaim	re claim
recoil	re coil
recount	re count
recruit	re cruit
redeem	re deem
refrain	re frain
regain	re gain
restrain	re strain
retail	re tail
retain	re tain
retreat	re treat
reveal	re veal
review	re view
Riley	Ri ley
series	se ries
thyroid	thy roid
today	to day
tryout	try out
tycoon	ty coon
typhoon	ty phoon

OE

open-VCE

- Syllables that are open will usually either have the open vowel sound or the schwa sound.
- Beginning students who are learning open/closed should only be given words that make the long vowel sounds and not the schwa.
- Some syllables may appear to be **VCE**, but they have short vowel sounds. For example, the word **fragile** is pronounced **/fraj-il/**, not with a long **/i/** sound. See the **VCE** imposters section for those words.

adore	a dore	decode	de code
ashore	a shore	deduce	de duce
aside	a side	deface	de face
atone	a tone	define	de fine
awake	a wake	delete	de lete
awoke	a woke	demote	de mote
became	be came	denote	de note
before	be fore	deplete	de plete
behave	be have	deprive	de prive
berate	be rate	derive	de rive
beside	be side	describe	de scribe
besides	be sides	desire	de sire
canine	ca nine	despise	de spise
Chinese	Chi nese	despite	de spite
chlorine	chlo rine	device	de vice
climate	cli mate	devise	de vise
crusade	cru sade	dilute	di lute
cyclone	cy clone	feline	fe line
debate	de bate	female	fe male
decide	de cide	finite	fi nite
declare	de clare	future	fu ture
decline	de cline	galore	ga lore

genome	ge nome
glucose	glu cose
gyrate	gy rate
humane	hu mane
irate	i rate
locate	lo cate
mature	ma ture
microbe	mi crobe
migrate	mi grate
Mobile	Mo bile
mobile	mo bile
mutate	mu tate
nature	na ture
parade	pa rade
polite	po lite
precede	pre cede
precise	pre cise
prescribe	pre scribe
preside	pre side
presume	pre sume
primate	pri mate
procure	pro cure
produce	pro duce
profile	pro file
profuse	pro fuse
promote	pro mote
protrude	pro trude
provide	pro vide
provoke	pro voke
rebate	re bate
recede	re cede
recline	re cline
recluse	re cluse
reduce	re duce
refine	re fine
refuse	re fuse
restore	re store
retire	re tire
revise	re vise
revive	re vive
revoke	re voke
rotate	ro tate
salute	sa lute
secrete	se crete
serene	se rene
skyline	*sky line*
supreme	su preme
vacate	va cate

OR

open-R controlled

- Syllables that are open will usually either have the long vowel sound, or the schwa sound.
- Beginning students who are learning open/closed should only be given words that make the long vowel sounds and not the schwa.
- Some syllables ending in **E** in this list may appear to be **VCE** syllables, but they are in fact **R**-controlled. The **E** has been added for a different reason than to make the vowel long. For example, in the word **preserve**, the **E** has been added because English spelling rules state that words should not end in the letter **V**. Words that end in the **V** sound have an **E** added to the end of them. Other examples of this would be the words **have, give,** and **deserve.** Words that end in -**SE** have the **E** to show that the word is not plural.

adorn	a dorn
crater	cra ter
defer	de fer
deform	de form
depart	de part
deport	de port
deserve	de serve
deter	de ter
fever	fe ver
fiber	fi ber
flavor	fla vor
flyer	fly er
gopher	go pher
Grover	Gro ver
homer	ho mer
humor	hu mor
Jafar	Ja far
Jamar	Ja mar
juror	ju ror
kosher	ko sher
labor	la bor
lemur	le mur
liter	li ter
lunar	lu nar
Luther	Lu ther
major	ma jor
meter	me ter
minor	mi nor
miser	mi ser
molar	mo lar
motor	mo tor
paper	pa per
pliers	pli ers
polar	po lar
prefer	pre fer
preserve	pre serve
prior	pri or
Pryor	Pry or
quasar	qua sar
quaver	qua ver

radar ra dar
razor ra zor
recur re cur
refer re fer
reform re form
regard re gard
return re turn
reverse re verse
rhubarb rhu barb
rotor ro tor
rumor ru mor
saber sa ber
savor sa vor
skier ski er
Skyler Sky ler
sober so ber
solar so lar
sonar so nar
spider spi der
Stuart Stu art
Sumer Su mer
super su per
taper ta per
tapir ta pir
tumor tu mor
tutor tu tor
Tyler Ty ler
vapor va por
viper vi per
visor vi sor
wafer wa fer
wager wa ger
yogurt yo gert

VC

vowel team-closed

- Syllables that are closed will usually make the short vowel sound, or the schwa sound.
- Beginning students who are learning open/closed should only be given words that make the short vowel sounds and not the schwa.
- Words in *italics* are compound words.

ailment	ail ment
airbag	*air bag*
aircraft	*air craft*
airship	*air ship*
augment	aug ment
August	Au gust
Austin	Aus tin
autumn	au tumn
awful	aw ful
Beacon	Bea con
beaten	beat en
Beaumont	Beau mont
beeswax	*bees wax*
bluegrass	*blue grass*
blueprint	*blue print*
bookbag	*book bag*
bookend	*book end*
booklet	book let
brainwash	*brain wash*
breakfast	*break fast*
breathless	breath less
broadband	*broad band*
broadcast	*broad cast*
cauldron	caul dron
chairman	*chair man*
cheerful	cheer ful
coastal	coast al
council	coun cil
counsel	coun sel
countess	coun tess
countless	*count less*
couplet	cou plet
coupon	cou pon
courtship	*court ship*
cousin	cous in
Cowan	Cow an
crawfish	*craw fish*
crayon	cray on
crooked	crook ed
crouton	crou ton
Dayton	Day ton
deacon	dea con
deaden	dead en
deafen	deaf en
deepen	deep en
diesel	die sel
doorbell	*door bell*
doorknob	*door knob*

doorstep	*door step*	Houston	Hous ton
doubtless	*doubt less*	*jaywalk*	*jay walk*
doughnut	*dough nut*	Jewel	Jew el
downcast	*down cast*	journal	jour nal
downfall	*down fall*	joystick	joy stick
downhill	*down hill*	kayak	kay ak
eardrum	*ear drum*	Keaton	Kea ton
earmuffs	*ear muffs*	*keypad*	*key pad*
feedback	*feed back*	*kneecap*	*knee cap*
flourish	flour ish	Laurel	Lau rel
foolish	fool ish	lawful	law ful
foothill	*foot hill*	leaden	lead en
footprint	*foot print*	leaflet	leaf let
footstep	*foot step*	*leapfrog*	*leap frog*
freedom	free dom	leaven	leav en
fruitful	fruit ful	loosen	loos en
gleeful	glee ful	Louis	Lou is
Goodman	*Good man*	Lowell	Low ell
goodwill	*good will*	loyal	loy al
gourmet	gour met	maiden	maid en
groundhog	*ground hog*	*mailbox*	*mail box*
grownup	*grown up*	*mailman*	*mail man*
hairpin	*hair pin*	*mainland*	*main land*
hayloft	*hay loft*	moisten	mois ten
haystack	*hay stack*	*moonlit*	*moon lit*
Heaven	Heav en	mournful	mourn ful
headband	*head band*	mouthful	mouth ful
headdress	*head dress*	neutral	neu tral
headland	*head land*	neutron	neu tron
headrest	*head rest*	*Newman*	*New man*
healthful	health ful	*newscast*	*news cast*
heighten	height en	*newsstand*	*news stand*
heiress	heir ess	*Oakland*	*Oak land*
housefly	*house fly*	*oilskin*	*oil skin*
houseplant	*house plant*	*outdid*	*out did*

outlet	*out let*
outwit	*out wit*
Owen	Ow en
painless	*pain less*
paintbrush	*paint brush*
peaceful	peace ful
peacock	pea cock
peanut	*pea nut*
playful	play ful
playoff	*play off*
poison	poi son
Powell	Pow ell
raindrop	*rain drop*
rainfall	*rain fall*
raisin	rai sin
rayon	ray on
Reagan	Rea gan
reason	rea son
roundtrip	*round trip*
roundup	*round up*
royal	roy al
saucepan	*sauce pan*
sawdust	*saw dust*
sawmill	*saw mill*
scoundrel	scoun drel
seagull	*sea gull*
sealant	seal ant
seamstress	seam stress
seashell	*sea shell*
seasick	*sea sick*
season	sea son
showoff	*show off*
snowfall	*snow fall*
snowman	*snow man*
soundtrack	*sound track*
southwest	*south west*
steamship	*steam ship*
straighten	straight en
teapot	*tea pot*
teardrop	*tear drop*
Thailand	Thai land
toilet	toi let
toothbrush	*tooth brush*
toothpick	*tooth pick*
toucan	tou can
towel	tow el
Townsend	*Town send*
township	*town ship*
treadmill	*tread mill*
treason	trea son
trowel	trow el
vowel	vow el
waitress	wait ress
weaken	weak en
weapon	weap on
weasel	wea sel
weekend	*week end*
weevil	wee vil
weightless	weight less
Wheaton	Wheat on
woodchuck	*wood chuck*
wooden	wood en
woodland	*wood land*
Woodstock	*Wood stock*
woodwind	*wood wind*
woolen	wool en

VL

vowel team-CLE

- Words with the **VL** pattern are rare.

beagle	bea-gle
beetle	bee-tle
dawdle	daw dle
needle	nee dle
steeple	stee ple
trouble	trou ble
wheedle	whee dle

VO

vowel team-open

- Most of the words that have the **VO** pattern end in **-y** or **-ly**, however there are a few that end in a regular open vowel (for example, **auto, Haiti, maybe**)

auto	au to	Haiti	Hai ti
beauty	beau-ty	haughty	haugh ty
Boise	Boi se	heavy	heav y
Cairo	Cai ro	juicy	juic y
cheery	cheer y	laundry	laun dry
chewy	chew y	leafy	leaf y
chiefly	chief ly	lousy	lous y
cloudy	cloud y	mainly	main ly
country	coun try	maybe	may be
county	coun ty	mealy	meal y
creamy	cream y	moody	mood y
creepy	creep y	naughty	naugh ty
daily	dai ly	nearby	near by
dainty	dain ty	nearly	near ly
dairy	dair y	needy	need y
daisy	dai sy	newly	new ly
deadly	dead ly	noisy	nois y
dearly	dear ly	outcry	out cry
friendly	friend ly	poultry	poul try
gaudy	gaud y	Pueblo	Pueb lo
gawky	gawk y	rainy	rain y
gloomy	gloom y	ready	read y
goody	good y	roomy	room y
greasy	greas y	rowdy	row dy
greedy	greed y	saintly	saint ly
grouchy	grouch y	scrawny	scrawn y
guilty	guilt y	Sheila	Shei la
hairy	hair y	showy	show y

sleepy sleep y
sneaky sneak y
snowy snow y
soapy soap y
speedy speed y
squeaky squeak y
steady stead y
stealthy stealth y
treaty trea ty

weakly weak ly
wealthy wealth y
weary wea ry
weedy weed y
weekly week ly
weighty weight y
woody wood y
wooly wool y

VV

vowel team-vowel team

- Words in *italics* are compound words.
- The majority of **VV** words are compound words However, there are some words that are not compounds (for example, **goalie, hooray, jealous**).

bloodstream	*blood stream*	*freeway*	*free way*
boomtown	*boom town*	goalie	goal ie
boyfriend	*boy friend*	goatee	goat ee
boyhood	*boy hood*	Greeley	Gree ley
breakdown	*break down*	*greenhouse*	*green house*
breakthrough	*break through*	*greyhound*	*grey hound*
chainsaw	*chain saw*	*headway*	*head way*
Chauncey	Chaun cey	*hearsay*	*hear say*
chieftain	chief tain	*heartbeat*	*heart beat*
cookbook	*cook book*	heirloom	heir loom
cookie	cook ie	hoodie	hood ie
cookout	*cook out*	hooray	hoo ray
countdown	*count down*	*houseboat*	*house boat*
courthouse	*court house*	jealous	jeal ous
courtroom	*court room*	journey	jour ney
daybreak	*day break*	joyous	joy ous
daydream	*day dream*	*keyboard*	*key board*
doorway	*door way*	*lawsuit*	*law suit*
download	*down load*	*lighthouse*	*light house*
downpour	*down pour*	*lookout*	*look out*
downstairs	*down stairs*	*mainstream*	*main stream*
downstream	*down stream*	maintain	main tain
downtown	*down town*	meadow	mead ow
fairway	*fair way*	*meatloaf*	*meat loaf*
foolproof	*fool proof*	*moonbeam*	*moon beam*
footstool	*foot stool*	mountain	moun tain

mouthpiece	mouth piece	seacoast	sea coast
nightgown	night gown	seafood	sea food
nighthawk	night hawk	seaweed	sea weed
outbound	out bound	seesaw	see saw
outbreak	out break	Shawnee	Shaw nee
outdoor	out door	snowboard	snow board
outfield	out field	snowplow	snow plow
outgrew	out grew	soundproof	sound proof
outgrow	out grow	southeast	south east
outgrown	out grown	soybean	soy bean
outlaw	out law	stairway	stair way
outlook	out look	steamboat	steam boat
outweigh	out weigh	streetlight	street light
playground	play ground	sweetheart	sweet heart
powwow	pow wow	teaspoon	tea spoon
prairie	prai rie	teepee	tee pee
proofread	proof read	throughout	through out
railroad	rail road	toadstool	toad stool
railway	rail way	toenail	toe nail
rainbow	rain bow	touchdown	touch down
raincoat	rain coat	toupee	tou pee
raucous	rau cous	townhouse	town house
reindeer	rein deer	viewpoint	view point
rookie	rook ie	voicemail	voice mail
rowboat	row boat	weekday	week day
sailboat	sail boat	wheelchair	wheel chair
schoolhouse	school house	Woodrow	Wood row
screenplay	screen play	zealous	zeal ous

VE

vowel team-CLE

- The majority of **VE** words are compound words However, there are some words that are not compounds (for example, **measure, leisure, treasure**).
- Words in *italics* are compound words.

airfare — *air fare*
airline — *air line*
airplane — *air plane*
austere — aus tere
beehive — *bee hive*
beeline — *bee line*
bookcase — *book case*
briefcase — *brief case*
coastline — *coast line*
creature — crea ture
daycare — *day care*
daytime — *day time*
deadline — *dead line*
earlobe — *ear lobe*
earphone — *ear phone*
earthquake — *earth quake*
footnote — *foot note*
foursquare — *four square*
hayride — *hay ride*
haywire — *hay wire*
headline — *head line*
headphones — *head phones*
keepsake — *keep sake*
keyhole — *key hole*
keystone — *key stone*
leisure — lei sure
meantime — *mean time*
meanwhile — *mean while*
measure — meas ure
moisture — mois ture
outcome — *out come*
outdone — *out done*
outline — *out line*
outside — *out side*
pleasure — pleas ure
rawhide — *raw hide*
roommate — *room mate*
seashore — *sea shore*
seizure — sei zure
showcase — *show case*
snowflake — *snow flake*
streamlined — *stream lined*
teammate — *team mate*
threadbare — *thread bare*
toothpaste — *tooth paste*
treasure — treas ure
wayside — *way side*

VR

vowel team-R-controlled

- Words in *italics* are compound words.
- Students should be familiar with **R**-controlled words before attempting these words.
- **W**-controlled vowel teams (**WAR, WOR**) are also included in this list, since they are considered by some teachers to be **R**-controlled.

airport	*air port*	*earthworm*	*earth worm*
auburn	au burn	*eastward*	*east ward*
author	au thor	flounder	floun der
awkward	awk ward	flower	flow er
Baylor	Bay lor	*foolhardy*	*fool hardy*
beaker	beak er	footer	foot er
blowtorch	*blow torch*	Fowler	Fowl er
blueberry	*blue berry*	freezer	freez er
bluebird	*blue bird*	freighter	freight er
bookmark	*book mark*	geyser	gey ser
Boulder	Boul der	*glowworm*	*glow worm*
brainstorm	*brain storm*	guitar	gui tar
Brewster	Brew ster	Hawthorn	Haw thorn
chowder	chow der	Hayward	Hay ward
cleaner	clean er	header	head er
cleanser	cleans er	*headfirst*	*head first*
cleav er	cleav er	heater	heat er
Cooper	Coop er	Heather	Heath er
cougar	cou gar	heather	heath er
counter	coun ter	heifer	heif er
courtyard	*court yard*	*housework*	*house work*
coward	cow ard	Howard	How ard
cower	cow er	keeper	keep er
crowbar	*crow bar*	*keyword*	*key word*
downward	*down ward*	laughter	laugh ter

launder	laun der	*schoolwork*	*school work*
lawyer	law yer	*schoolyard*	*school yard*
layer	lay er	schooner	schoon er
leader	lead er	scooter	scoot er
leather	leath er	*seahorse*	*sea horse*
leopard	leop ard	sewer	sew er
loiter	loi ter	shower	show er
lower	low er	skewer	skew er
meager	mea ger	smother	smooth er
neither	nei ther	sneaker	sneak er
Newark	New ark	*snowstorm*	*snow storm*
newborn	*new born*	speaker	speak er
outburst	*out burst*	steward	stew ard
outer	out er	Stewart	Stew art
outskirts	*out skirts*	suitor	suit or
oyster	oys ter	*sweatshirt*	*sweat shirt*
painter	paint er	tailor	tai lor
pauper	pau per	Taylor	Tay lor
pewter	pew ter	teacher	teach er
player	play er	*teamwork*	*team work*
pointer	point er	toaster	toast er
powder	pow der	tower	tow er
prayer	pray er	trawler	trawl er
reader	read er	trooper	troop er
reaper	reap er	trousers	trou sers
rooster	roost er	voucher	vouch er
router	rout er	waiter	wait er
sailor	sail or	weather	weath er
saucer	sau cer	Weaver	Weav er
saunter	saun ter	Wheeler	wheel er
schnauzer	schnau zer	youngster	young ster

EC

VCE-closed

- **VCE** is a pattern that is found at the end of a base word or the end of a syllable, not in the beginning or middle. Suffixes can be added on to **VCE**, making it appear to be in the middle of a word, but it will not be in the beginning or middle of the base word.
- Because **VCE** is an end pattern, most of the words that follow the **EC** pattern are compound words. That is because compound words are simply the joining together of two fully-formed bases/words.
- The only words in this list that are not compounds are words that end in the suffix **-ful. (graceful, hopeful, etc.)** The suffix **-ful** means "full of."
- Words in *italics* are compound words.

baseball *base ball*
basement *base ment*
careful care ful
careless *care less*
Cleveland Cleve land
farewell *fare well*
fireman *fire man*
forecast *fore cast*
foreman *fore man*
foremost *fore most*
foretell *fore tell*
graceful grace ful
grateful grate ful
hateful hate ful
homeland *home land*
homeless *home less*
homesick *home sick*
homespun *home spun*
homestretch *home stretch*
hopeful hope ful
hopeless *hope less*
icecap *ice cap*
Iceland *Ice land*
lifeless *life less*
lifelong *life long*
lifespan *life span*
likeness like ness
livestock *live stock*
makeshift *make shift*
makeup *make up*
movement move ment
pavement pave ment
priceless *price less*
purebred *pure bred*
racetrack *race track*
rosebush *rose bush*
sagebrush *sage brush*
salesman *sales man*
shameful shame ful
shameless *shame less*

sidestep	side step
sidetrack	side track
sidewalk	side walk
smokestack	smoke stock
spacecraft	space craft
spaceship	space ship
spineless	spine less
statement	state ment
timeless	time less
tireless	tire less
useful	use ful
wasteful	waste ful
wasteland	waste land
whitecap	white cap
whitewash	white wash
wireless	wire less

EL

VCE-CLE

(EL none)

- In my research I found no two-syllable words that followed the **EL** pattern. However, I left this blank page, so that if you find any words that follow the **EL** pattern, you can list them here.

EO

VCE-open

- **VCE** is a pattern that is found at the end of a base word, not in the beginning or middle. Suffixes can be added on to **VCE**, but it will not be in the beginning or middle of the base part of the word.
- The only words that follow the **EO** pattern are the ones that end in the **-LY** suffix.
- Words in *italics* are compound words.

barely	bare ly	merely	mere ly
firefly	*fire fly*	namely	name ly
homely	home ly	rarely	rare ly
likely	like ly	safety	safe ty
lonely	lone ly	stately	state ly

EV

VCE-vowel team

- **VCE** is a pattern that is found at the end of a base word, not in the beginning or middle. Suffixes can be added on to **VCE**, but it will not be in the beginning or middle of the base part of the word.
- The words that follow the **EV** pattern are all compound words.

carefree	*care free*	*lifeguard*	*life guard*
coleslaw	*cole slaw*	*nineteen*	*nine teen*
driveway	*drive way*	*nosebleed*	*nose bleed*
firehouse	*fire house*	*notebook*	*note book*
fireproof	*fire proof*	*safeguard*	*safe guard*
firewood	*fire wood*	*scapegoat*	*scape goat*
foreground	*fore ground*	*scarecrow*	*scare crow*
forehead	*fore head*	*scoreboard*	*score board*
gateway	*gate way*	*sideways*	*side ways*
grapefruit	*grape fruit*	*skateboard*	*skate board*
homegrown	*home grown*	*stagecoach*	*stage coach*
homeroom	*home room*	*strikeout*	*strike out*
homeschool	*home school*	*timepiece*	*time piece*
homestead	*home stead*	*warehouse*	*ware house*
hometown	*home town*	*whiteboard*	*white board*
Lakewood	*Lake wood*	*widespread*	*wide spread*
lifeboat	*life boat*		

EE

vowel team-vowel team

- **VCE** is a pattern that is found at the end of a base word, not in the beginning or middle. Suffixes can be added on to **VCE**, but it will not be in the beginning or middle of the base part of the word.
- In my research, I was only able to find one **EE** word. I have provided this page, so you can add more words if you find them.

Yuletide *Yule tide*

ER

VCE-R-controlled

- The words that follow the **ER** pattern are all compound words.
- Students should be familiar with the **R**-controlled phonograms before attempting these words.

fireworks	*fire works*
framework	*frame work*
graveyard	*grave yard*
homeward	*home ward*
homework	*home work*
iceberg	*ice berg*
rosemary	*rose mary*
Shreveport	*Shreve port*
sideburns	*side burns*
tapeworm	*tape worm*
trademark	*trade mark*

RC

R controlled-closed

- Some of the closed syllables may have the schwa sound.
- Words in *italics* are compound words.
- Students should be familiar with the **R**-controlled phonograms before attempting these words.

Aaron	Aar on	Charlton	Charl ton
aftermath	*after math*	cherish	cher ish
aftershock	*after shock*	Churchill	Church ill
Arab	Ar ab	coral	cor al
ardent	ar dent	Corbin	Cor bin
arid	ar id	Cordell	Cor dell
Armand	Ar mand	Corinth	Cor inth
armpit	*arm pit*	Cornell	Cor nell
arrest	ar rest	cornet	cor net
artist	ar tist	*cornstarch*	*corn starch*
barracks	bar racks	corral	cor ral
barrel	bar rel	correct	cor rect
barren	bar ren	corrupt	cor rupt
Bergman	Berg man	current	cur rent
Bertrand	Ber trand	darken	dark en
Boris	Bor is	Darnell	Dar nell
Burnett	Bur nett	Derrick	Der rick
carbon	car bon	ferment	fer ment
carob	car ob	ferret	fer ret
carol	car ol	for ceps	for ceps
carpet	car pet	*forbid*	*for bid*
carrot	car rot	forceful	force ful
carton	car ton	forest	for est

forgive	*for give*	hurtful	hurt ful
forgot	*for got*	jargon	jar gon
forklift	*fork lift*	Jordan	Jor dan
formal	for mal	kernel	ker nel
format	for mat	Kirkland	Kirk land
fortress	for tress	Kurdish	Kurd ish
furnish	fur nish	margin	mar gin
furthest	fur thest	market	mar ket
garden	gar den	marshal	mar shal
Gareth	Gar eth	Martin	Mar tin
garish	gar ish	martyr	mar tyr
garland	gar land	marvel	mar vel
garlic	gar lic	merit	mer it
garment	gar ment	Merlin	Mer lin
garnet	gar net	moral	mor al
garnish	gar nish	Morgan	Mor gan
garret	gar ret	Morris	Mor ris
Gerald	Ger ald	morsel	mor sel
gerbil	ger bil	mortal	mor tal
German	Ger man	Morton	Mor ton
girlish	girl ish	Norman	Nor man
harden	hard en	Norris	Nor ris
hardship	*hard ship*	*northwest*	*north west*
harmful	harm ful	Norton	Nor ton
harmless	*harm less*	Norwalk	Nor walk
harness	har ness	orbit	or bit
harvest	har vest	orchid	or chid
herald	her ald	Ordell	Or dell
hermit	her mit	organ	or gan
heron	her on	orphan	or phan
herself	*her self*	Orson	Or son
hornet	hor net	Orwell	Or well
horrid	hor rid	parcel	par cel
horseback	*horse back*	pardon	par don
hurrah	hur rah	parent	par ent

Paris	Par is
parish	par ish
parrot	par rot
parsnip	pars nip
parson	par son
percent	per cent
perfect	per fect
perhaps	per haps
permit	per mit
perplex	per plex
persist	per sist
person	per son
portal	por tal
Portland	*Port land*
quarrel	quar rel
sarcasm	sar casm
Sardis	Sar dis
scarlet	scar let
Scarlett	Scar lett
scornful	scorn ful
sermon	ser mon
serpent	ser pent
servant	serv ant
Sharon	Shar on
sharpen	sharp en
sherbet	sher bet
sheriff	sher iff
Sherlock	Sher lock
Sherwin	Sher win
shortcut	*short cut*
shorten	short en
shortness	short ness
shortstop	*short stop*
skirmish	skir mish
snorkel	snor kel
spirit	spir it
squirrel	squir rel
starfish	*star fish*
stirrup	stir rup
surpass	sur pass
surplus	sur plus
target	tar get
tariff	tar iff
tarnish	tar nish
tartan	tar tan
Terrell	Ter rel
thermal	ther mal
thermos	ther mos
Thornton	Thorn ton
Thurman	Thur man
torrent	tor rent
turban	tur ban
Turkish	Turk ish
turnip	tur nip
turret	tur ret
urgent	ur gent
varnish	var nish
verbal	ver bal
verdict	ver dict
vermin	ver min
Vermont	Ver mont
Vernon	Ver non
versus	ver sus
virgin	vir gin
whirlwind	*whirl wind*
yardstick	*yard stick*

RL

R controlled-CLE

- The **RL** combination is rare.
- Students should be familiar with the **R**-controlled phonograms before attempting these words.

chortle	chor tle
circle	cir cle
curdle	cur dle
gargle	gar gle
gurgle	gur gle
hurdle	hur dle
hurtle	hur tle
purple	pur ple
sparkle	spar kle
startle	star tle
turtle	tur tle

RO

R controlled-open

- Most of the words that follow the **RO** pattern end in the suffixes **-Y** or **-LY**. However, there are a few that do not **(cargo, larva**, etc).
- Many syllables that are open will have the schwa sound, so they will not make the long vowel sound. Beginning students who are learning open/closed should only be given words that make the long vowel sounds and not the schwa.
- Students should be familiar with the **R**-controlled phonograms before attempting these words.
- Words in *italics* are compound words.

army	ar my	forty	for ty
Barry	Bar ry	furry	fur ry
berry	ber ry	Gary	Gar y
Bertha	Ber tha	Gerry	Ger ry
cargo	car go	hardly	hard ly
Carly	Car ly	hardy	har dy
carry	car ry	Harry	Har ry
Cary	Car y	jerky	jerk y
cherry	cher ry	Jerry	Jer ry
circa	cir ca	Kerry	Ker ry
Clara	Clar a	largely	large ly
clergy	cler gy	larva	lar va
Cory	Cor y	marry	mar ry
curly	curl y	Marsha	Mar sha
curry	cur ry	Martha	Mar tha
curtsy	curt sy	Mary	Mar y
Darby	Dar by	Mercy	Mer cy
Darcy	Dar cy	mercy	mer cy
derby	der by	merry	mer ry
dirty	dirt y	parka	par ka
ferry	fer ry	partly	part ly
flurry	flur ry	party	par tyy

Percy	Per cy	sturdy	stur dy
perky	perk y	tardy	tar dy
Perry	Per ry	Terry	Ter ry
Peru	Pe ru	thorny	thorn y
quarry	quar ry	torso	tor so
scurry	scur ry	Urdu	Ur du
shortly	short ly	vary	var y
sorry	sor ry	Verna	Ver na
stormy	storm y	very	ver y

RV

R controlled-vowel team

- Students should be familiar with the **R**-controlled phonograms before attempting these words.
- Words in *italics* are compound words.

afternoon	*after noon*
argue	ar gue
armchair	*arm chair*
array	ar ray
arrow	ar row
Barney	Bar ney
birthday	*birth day*
cardboard	*card board*
Carlee	Car lee
Carlow	Car low
cartoon	car toon
certain	cer tain
charcoal	*char coal*
Charlie	Char lie
circuit	cir cuit
Corey	Cor ey
corkscrew	*cork screw*
curfew	cur few
curtail	cur tail
curtain	cur tain
Darcie	Dar cie
Darrow	Dar row
foreign	for eign
furlough	fur lough
furrow	fur row
Har ry	Har ry
hardwood	*hard wood*
Harley	Har ley
Harlow	Har low
harpoon	har poon
harrow	har row
horsehair	*horse hair*
horseplay	*horse play*
horseshoe	*horse shoe*
hurray	hur ray
hurried	hur ried
jersey	jer sey
kerchief	ker chief
larvae	lar vae
marrow	mar row
mermaid	mer maid
Murphey	Mur phey
Murray	Mur ray
narrow	nar row
nervous	ner vous
northeast	*north east*
Norway	Nor way
ordain	or dain
ordeal	or deal
parkway	*park way*
parsley	pars ley
perceive	per ceive

pertain	per tain
porpoise	por poise
portrait	por trait
portray	por tray
pursue	pur sue
pursuit	pur suit
sergeant	ser geant
Sherwood	Sher wood
Shirley	Shir ley
sorrow	sor row
sparrow	spar row
surround	sur round
survey	sur vey
terrain	ter rain
thirteen	thir teen
thirteenth	thir teenth
thorough	thor ough
Thurgood	Thur good
Thursday	Thurs day
Turkey	Tur key
turkey	tur key
turmoil	tur moil
turnout	*turn out*
virtue	vir tue
workbook	*work book*
workout	*work out*

RE

R controlled-VCE

- Words in *italics* are compound words.
- Students should be familiar with the **R**-controlled phonograms before attempting these words.

afterlife	*after life*	perfume	per fume
arcade	ar cade	perspire	per spire
arrive	ar rive	pervade	per vade
barcode	*bar code*	*porthole*	*port hole*
birthplace	*birth place*	sardine	sar dine
corrode	cor rode	surprise	sur prise
forbade	for bade	survive	sur vive
fortune	for tune	termite	ter mite
hardware	*hard ware*	turbine	tur bine
hormone	hor mone	*turnpike*	*turn pike*
narrate	nar rate	*turnstile*	*turn stile*

RR

R controlled-R controlled

- Words in *italics* are compound words.
- Students should be familiar with the **R**-controlled phonograms before attempting these words.

arbor	ar bor	mortar	mor tar
archer	ar cher	murder	mur der
armor	ar mor	murmur	mur mur
Arthur	Ar thur	northern	north ern
barber	bar ber	orchard	or chard
barter	bar ter	order	or der
charger	char ger	Parker	Park er
charter	char ter	parlor	par lor
corner	cor ner	partner	part ner
forlorn	for lorn	perform	per form
further	fur ther	perturb	per turb
Gardner	Gard ner	Porter	Por ter
garter	gar ter	porter	por ter
girder	gird er	quarter	quar ter
harbor	har bor	server	serv er
Harford	Har ford	tartar	tar tar
Herbert	Her bert	terror	ter ror
horror	hor ror	torture	tor ture
marker	mark er	Turner	Tur ner
mirror	mir ror		

Schwa

The word lists in this section are all two-syllable words. For more words with schwa, see the words lists for 3-7 syllables.

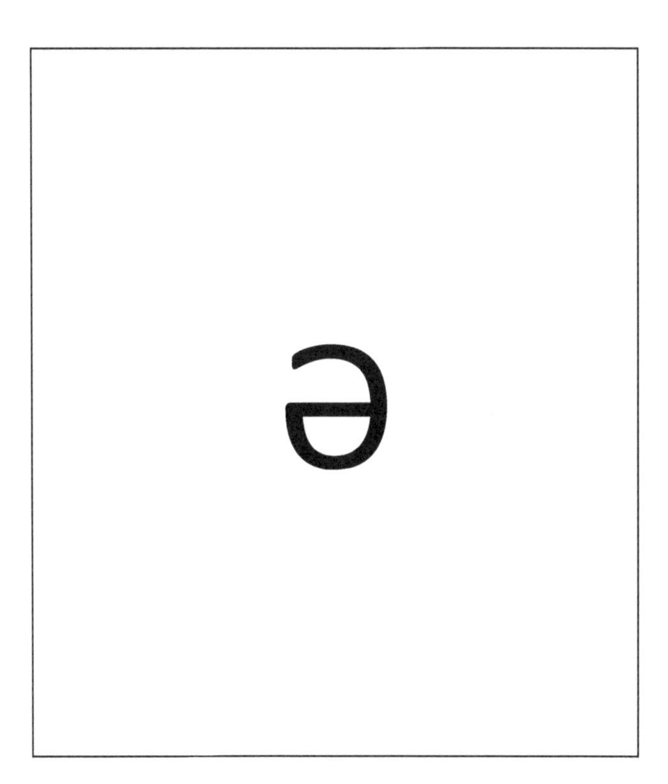

Schwa

Beginning A-

- In this word list, the **bold** print indicates the accented/stressed syllable in the word and the underlined print indicates the schwa syllable.
- Occasionally, words beginning with **A** will not be schwa, such as in the word **able**. However, most of the time when a word begins with the letter **A**, the **A-** is a is schwa sound.
- Beginning **A-** and ending **-A** words are good sets of words to introduce the schwa concept, because they are very predictable.
- In beginning **A-** words, the accent/stress is always on the second syllable.

a vert	a **vert**	accord	ac **cord**
abate	a **bate**	account	ac **count**
abduct	ab **duct**	accuse	ac **cuse**
abide	a **bide**	acquire	ac **quire**
ablaze	a **blaze**	acquit	ac **quit**
aboard	a **board**	across	a **cross**
abode	a **bode**	acute	a **cute**
abound	a **bound**	ad verse	ad **verse**
about	a **bout**	adapt	a **dapt**
abreast	a **breast**	afar	a **far**
abridge	a **bridge**	afflict	af **flict**
abroad	a **broad**	afford	af **ford**
abrupt	a **brupt**	affront	af **front**
absorb	ab **sorb**	afield	a **field**
abstain	ab **stain**	afire	a **fire**
absurd	ab **surd**	afloat	a **float**
abuse	a **buse**	afraid	a **fraid**
abyss	a **byss**	afresh	a **fresh**
acclaim	ac **claim**	again	a **gain**
accord	ac **cord**	against	a **gainst**

aghast	a **ghast**
ago	a **go**
agree	a **gree**
aground	a **ground**
ahead	a **head**
ajar	a **jar**
akin	a **kin**
alarm	a **larm**
alas	a **las**
alight	a **light**
align	a **lign**
alike	a **like**
alive	a **live**
allege	al **lege**
allow	al **low**
allude	al **lude**
allure	al **lure**
alone	a **lone**
along	a **long**
aloof	a **loof**
aloud	a **loud**
amass	a **mass**
amaze	a **maze**
amend	a **mend**
amid	a **mid**
amiss	a **miss**
among	a **mong**
amount	a **mount**
amuse	a **muse**
annoy	an **noy**
anoint	a **noint**
apart	a **part**
apiece	a **piece**
appall	ap **pall**
appeal	ap **peal**
appear	ap **pear**
appease	ap **pease**
applaud	ap **plaud**
applause	ap **plause**
apply	ap **ply**
appoint	ap **point**
appraise	ap **praise**
approve	ap **prove**
approach	ap **proach**
arise	a **rise**
around	a **round**
array	ar **ray**
arrive	ar **rived**
ascend	as **cend**
ascent	as **cent**
ashore	a **shore**
aside	a **side**
askew	a **skew**
asleep	a **sleep**
aspire	as **pire**
assail	as **sail**
assault	as **sault**
assent	as **sent**
assert	as **sert**
assess	as **sess**
assign	as **sign**
assist	as **sist**
assume	as **sume**
assure	as **sure**
astound	as **tound**
astray	as **tray**
astride	a **stride**
atone	a **tone**
atop	a **top**
attach	at **tach**

attack at **tack**
attain at **tain**
attempt at **tempt**
attend at **tend**
attest at **test**
attire at **tire**
attract at **tract**
avoid a **void**
await a **wait**
awake a **wake**
award a **ward**
aware a **ware**
away a **way**
awoke a **woke**
awry a **wry**
baton ba **ton**
Brazil Bra **zil**
cadet ca **det**
canal ca **nal**
career ca **reer**
galore ga **lore**
garage ga **rage**
gazelle ga **zelle**
Haran Ha **ran**
harass ha **rass**
Jafar Ja **far**
Jamar Ja **mar**
Japan Ja **pan**
kazoo ka **zoo**
lacrosse la **crosse**
lagoon la **goon**
Lahore La **hore**
lapel la **pel**
machine ma **chine**
malign ma **lign**
manure ma **nure**
Marie Ma **rie**
marine ma **rine**
maroon ma **roon**
mature ma **ture**
parade pa **rade**
parole pa **role**
ravine ra **vine**
sarong sa **rong**

Schwa

Ending -A

- In this word list, the **bold** print indicates the accented/stressed syllable in the word and the underlined print indicates the schwa syllable.
- Beginning **A-** and ending **-A** words are good sets of words to introduce the schwa concept, because they are very predictable. Beginning **A-** words are much more common.
- In ending **-A** words, the accent/stress is always on the first syllable.

balsa	**bal** sa	mocha	**mo** cha
China	**Chi** na	panda	**pan** da
circa	**cir** ca	parka	**par** ka
Clara	**Clar** a	pasta	**pas** ta
cobra	**co** bra	Perga	**Per** ga
comma	**com** ma	Petra	**Pet** ra
Cuba	**Cu** ba	pita	**pi** ta
Dhaka	**Dhak** a	pizza	**piz** za
feta	**fet** a	plasma	**plas** ma
flora	**flor** a	plaza	**pla** za
gala	**ga** la	pupa	**pu** pa
Ghana	**Gha** na	quota	**quo** ta
Glenda	**Glen** da	Roma	**Ro** ma
guava	**gua** va	Rosa	**Ro** sa
Kaska	**Kas** ka	saga	**sa** ga
Keisha	**Kei** sha	salsa	**sal** sa
Kenya	**Ken** ya	Sasha	**Sa** sha
larva	**lar** va	Shasta	**Shas** ta
Linda	**Lin** da	Shawna	**Shawn** a
Malta	**Mal** ta	Sheba	**She** ba
mesa	**me** sa	Sheena	**Sheen** a

Sheila **Shei** la

soda **so** da

sofa **so** fa

stanza **stan** za

Tampa **Tam** pa

Tasha **Ta** sha

Thea **The** a

Tonga **Ton** ga

trauma **trau** ma

tuba **tu** ba

Tulsa **Tul** sa

tuna **tu** na

tundra **tun** dra

Twyla **Twy** la

Umma **Um** ma

Verna **Ver** na

via **vi** a

Wanda **Wan** da

yoga **yo** ga

yucca **yuc** ca

zebra **ze** bra

Schwa

1st syllable

Closed

- In this word list, the **bold** print indicates the accented/stressed syllable in the word and the underlined print indicates the schwa syllable.
- In this set of words, the accent/stress is always on the second syllable and the first syllable is closed.
- Instead of the closed syllable making a short vowel sound, it makes the schwa vowel sound. This is because the closed syllable is located in the unstressed syllable of the word.

abduct ab **duct**
absorb ab **sorb**
abstain ab **stain**
absurd ab **surd**
acclaim ac **claim**
accord ac **cord**
account ac **count**
accuse ac **cuse**
acquire ac **quire**
acquit ac **quit**
afflict af **flict**
afford af **ford**
affront af **front**
allege al **lege**
allot al **lot**
allow al **low**
allude al **lude**
allure al **lure**
annoy an **noy**
appall ap **pall**

appeal ap **peal**
appear ap **pear**
appease ap **pease**
applaud ap **plaud**
applause ap **plause**
apply ap **ply**
appoint ap **point**
appraise ap **praise**
approach ap **proach**
approve ap **prove**
ascend as **cend**
ascent as **cent**
aspire as **pire**
assent as **sent**
assert as **sert**
assess as **sess**
assign as **sign**
assist as **sist**
assume as **sume**
assure as **sure**

astound	as **tound**
attach	at **tach**
attack	at **tack**
attain	at **tain**
attempt	at **tempt**
attend	at **tend**
attest	at **test**
attire	at **tire**
attract	at **tract**
balloon	bal **loon**
bassoon	bas **soon**
collage	col **lage**
collapse	col **lapse**
collect	col **lect**
collide	col **lide**
commit	com **mit**
compel	com **pel**
compete	com **pete**
compile	com **pile**
complain	com **plain**
complaint	com **plaint**
complete	com **plete**
con nect	con **nect**
concern	con **cern**
concise	con **cise**
conclude	con **clude**
concoct	con **coct**
concur	con **cur**
condemn	con **demn**
condense	con **dense**
confer	con **fer**
confess	con **fess**

confide	con **fide**
confirm	con **firm**
conform	con **form**
confront	con **front**
confuse	con **fuse**
connect	con **nect**
conquer	con **quer**
consent	con **sent**
consist	con **sist**
console	con **sole**
conspire	con **spire**
constrict	con **strict**
consult	con **sult**
consume	con **sume**
contain	con **tain**
contempt	con **tempt**
contend	con **tend**
contrite	con **trite**
contrive	con **trive**
control	con **trol**
converse	con **verse**
convex	con **vex**
convey	con **vey**
convict	con **vict**
convince	con **vince**
frontier	fron **tier**
Hassan	Has **san**
massage	mas **sage**
pollute	pol **lute**
possess	pos **sess**

Schwa

2nd syllable

Closed

- In this word list, the **bold** print indicates the accented/stressed syllable in the word and the underlined print indicates the schwa syllable.
- In this set of words, the accent/stress is always on the first syllable. The second closed syllable says the schwa sound, instead of the short vowel sound, because it is in the unstressed syllable of the word.

Aaron	**Aar** on
absent	**ab** sent
acrid	**ac** rid
Adam	**Ad** am
agent	**a** gent
ailment	**ail** ment
Akron	**Ak** ron
Allen	**Al** len
almond	**al** mond
Ammon	**Am** mon
Amos	**A** mos
angel	**an** gel
anthem	**an** them
anvil	**an** vil
April	**A** pril
apron	**a** pron
Arab	**Ar** ab
Aram	**A** ram
ardent	**ar** dent
arson	**ar** son
ashen	**ash** en
Ashton	**Ash** ton
aspen	**as** pen
Athens	**Ath** ens
atlas	**at** las
Austin	**Aus** tin
avid	**av** id
axis	**ax** is
Babel	**Ba** bel
bacon	**ba** con
Baden	**Ba** den
bagel	**ba** gel
Baldwin	**Bald** win
ballad	**bal** lad
ballast	**bal** last
ballot	**bal** lot
balsam	**bal** sam
bandit	**ban** dit
banquet	**ban** quet
baron	**ba** ron

barrel **bar** rel
barren **bar** ren
basil **bas** il
basin **ba** sin
basis **ba** sis
basket **bas** ket
Beacon **Bea** con
beaten **beat** en
beckon **beck** on
Bergman **Berg** man
Bertrand **Ber** trand
Bethel **Beth** el
bishop **bish** op
blossom **Blos** som
Boris **Bor** is
Boston **Bos** ton
Brandon **Bran** don
Branson **Bran** son
Bryson **Bry** son
Calvin **Cal** vin
camel **cam** el
Cana **Ca** na
cancel **can** cel
cannon **can** non
canvas **can** vas
caper **ca** per
carbon **car** bon
carcass **car** cass
carob **car** ob
carol **car** ol
Caroll **Car** oll
carpet **car** pet
carrot **car** rot
carton **car** ton
casket **cas** ket

cauldron **caul** dron
central **cen** tral
Cephas **Ce** phas
challenge **chal** lenge
channel **chan** nel
chapel **chap** el
Chapman **Chap** man
Charlton **Charl** ton
chicken **chick** en
chisel **chis** el
chosen **cho** sen
christen **chris** ten
Christmas **Christ** mas
civil **civ** il
Claxton **Clax** ton
Clement **Clem** ent
Cleveland **Cleve** land
client **cli** ent
Clifton **Clif** ton
Clinton **Clin** ton
closet **clos** et
coastal **coast** al
coffin **cof** fin
colon **co** lon
Colton **Col** ton
comet **com** et
common **com** mon
compass **com** pass
constant **con** stant
Corinth **Cor** inth
cotton **cot** ton
council **coun** cil
counsel **coun** sel
cousin **cous** in
covet **cov** et

Cowan **Cow** an
Cranston **Cran** ston
crayon **cray** on
crescent **cres** cent
cricket **crick** et
crimson **crim** son
crisis **cri** sis
Crockett **Crock** ett
crystal **crys** tal
Crystal **Crys** tal
Cuban **Cu** ban
cumin **cu** min
current **cur** rent
custom **cus** tom
customs **cus** toms
cymbal **cym** bal
cypress **cy** press
Cyprus **Cy** prus
Dallas **Dal** las
Dalton **Dal** ton
dampen **damp** en
darken **dark** en
Dayton **Day** ton
deacon **dea** con
deaden **dead** en
deafen **deaf** en
devil **dev** il
diesel **die** sel
Felton **Fel** ton
fidget **fidg** et
final **fi** nal
Finland **Fin** land
flannel **flan** nel
flatten **flat** ten
flaxen **flax** en
floral **flo** ral
fluent **flu** ent
fluid **flu** id
focal **fo** cal
fossil **fos** sil
fragment **frag** ment
fragrant **fra** grant
Frances **Fran** ces
Francis **Fran** cis
Franklin **Frank** lin
freedom **free** dom
frequent **fre** quent
freshen **fresh** en
frighten **fright** en
frigid **frig** id
fritter **frit** ter
frozen **fro** zen
frugal **fru** gal
Fulton **Ful** ton
funnel **fun** nel
gadget **gadg** et
gallant **gal** lant
gallon **gal** lon
gallop **gal** lop
gander **gan** der
garden **gar** den
garland **gar** land
garment **gar** ment
garnet **gar** net
garret **gar** ret
gavel **gav** el
Gerald **Ger** ald
gerbil **ger** bil
German **Ger** man
giant **gi** ant

gibbon **gib** bon
giblets **gib** lets
gingham **ging** ham
given **giv** en
gladden **glad** den
glimmer **glim** mer
glisten **glis** ten
global **glob** al
gluten **glu** ten
glutton **glut** ton
goblet **gob** let
goblin **gob** lin
golden **gold** en
Goshen **Go** shen
Gospel **Gos** pel
Grayson **Gray** son
Gresham **Gresh** am
Gretchen **Gret** chen
Gretel **Gret** el
griffin **grif** fin
grovel **grov** el
gymnast **gym** nast
habit **hab** it
haddock **had** dock
hamlet **ham** let
Hampton **Hamp** ton
Hannah **Han** nah
happen **hap** pen
harden **hard** en
harness **har** ness
Haskel **Has** kel
hasten **has** ten
hatchet **hatch** et
haven **ha** ven
havoc **hav** oc
hazel **ha** zel
Heaven **Heav** en
Hebron **He** bron
heighten **height** en
helmet **hel** met
herald **her** ald
hermit **her** mit
heron **her** on
hidden **hid** den
Hilton **Hil** ton
honest **hon** est
hornet **hor** net
horrid **hor** rid
hostel **hos** tel
hostess **host** ess
human **hu** man
humid **hu** mid
hundred **hun** dred
husband **hus** band
hybrid **hy** brid
hydrant **hy** drant
hyphen **hy** phen
Iceland **Ice** land
idol **i** dol
illness **ill** ness
infant **in** fant
ingot **in** got
inland **in** land
inlet **in** let
instant **in** stant
island **is** land
item **i** tem
jackal **jack** al
jacket **jack** et
Jackson **Jack** son

Jacob	**Ja** cob
jargon	**jar** gon
Jewel	**Jew** el
Jonah	**Jo** nah
Jordan	**Jor** dan
Joseph	**Jo** seph
journal	**jour** nal
Judah	**Ju** dah
judgment	**judg** ment
Judith	**Ju** dith
Justin	**Jus** tin
Kansas	**Kan** sas
Keaton	**Kea** ton
Kendall	**Ken** dall
Kenneth	**Ken** neth
kernel	**ker** nel
kindness	**kind** ness
kingdom	**king** dom
Kingston	**Kings** ton
Kirkland	**Kirk** land
kitchen	**kitch** en
kitten	**kit** ten
label	**la** bel
Landon	**Lan** don
Latin	**Lat** in
Laurel	**Lau** rel
lea ven	**leav** en
leaden	**lead** en
leaflet	**leaf** let
legal	**le** gal
legend	**leg** end
Leland	**Le** land
lemon	**lem** on
lengthen	**length** en
lentil	**len** til
lessen	**less** en
lesson	**les** son
level	**lev** el
Lewis	**Lew** is
lichen	**li** chen
lighten	**light** en
liken	**lik** en
likeness	**like** ness
limit	**lim** it
limpid	**lim** pid
Lincoln	**Lin** coln
Lubbock	**Lub** bock
Lyndon	**Lyn** don
maggot	**mag** got
magnet	**mag** net
maiden	**maid** en
Malcolm	**Mal** colm
mallet	**mal** let
mammal	**mam** mal
mammoth	**mam** moth
mantel	**man** tel
margin	**mar** gin
market	**mar** ket
marshal	**mar** shal
Martin	**Mar** tin
martyr	**mar** tyr
marvel	**mar** vel
mason	**ma** son
mattress	**mat** tress
measles	**mea** sles
medal	**med** al
melon	**mel** on
Memphis	**Mem** phis
mental	**men** tal
merchant	**mer** chant

Merlin	**Mer** lin
Merrill	**Mer** rill
metal	**met** al
method	**meth** od
Micah	**Mi** cah
midland	**mid** land
migrant	**mi** grant
millet	**mil** let
Milton	**Mil** ton
minstrel	**min** strel
Mitchell	**Mitch** ell
mitten	**mit** ten
model	**mod** el
modem	**mo** dem
modest	**mod** est
molten	**mol** ten
moment	**mo** ment
mongrel	**mon** grel
moral	**mor** al
Morgan	**Mor** gan
morsel	**mor** sel
mortal	**mor** tal
Morton	**Mor** ton
Moses	**Mo** ses
movement	**move** ment
muffin	**muf** fin
mural	**mu** ral
musket	**mus** ket
Muslim	**Mus** lim
muslin	**mus** lin
mussel	**mus** sel
mutant	**mu** tant
mutton	**mut** ton
napkin	**nap** kin
nasal	**na** sal
naval	**na** val
Nelson	**Nel** son
neutral	**neu** tral
Newman	**New** man
nickel	**nick** el
Nissan	**Nis** san
novel	**nov** el
Noah	**No** ah
Norman	**Nor** man
Norton	**Nor** ton
oven	**ov** en
open	**o** pen
organ	**or** gan
orphan	**or** phan
Orson	**Or** son
oval	**o** val
Owen	**Ow** en
oxen	**ox** en
packet	**pack** et
paddock	**pad** dock
pagan	**pa** gan
pallid	**pal** lid
pamphlet	**pam** phlet
panel	**pan** el
parcel	**par** cel
pardon	**par** don
parent	**par** ent
parrot	**par** rot
parson	**par** son
patent	**pat** ent
patron	**pa** tron
pavement	**pave** ment
peasant	**peas** ant
pedal	**ped** al
pellet	**pel** let

pendant	**pend** ant
pennant	**pen** nant
peril	**per** il
person	**per** son
petal	**pet** al
phantom	**phan** tom
pheasant	**pheas** ant
picket	**pick** et
pigment	**pig** ment
pilgrim	**pil** grim
pilot	**pi** lot
piston	**pis** ton
pita	**pi** ta
Pithom	**Pith** om
pivot	**piv** ot
pixel	**pix** el
placid	**plac** id
plaintiff	**plain** tiff
planet	**plan** et
plankton	**plank** ton
plastic	**plas** tic
pleasant	**pleas** ant
plummet	**plum** met
pocket	**pock** et
poem	**po** em
poet	**po** et
poison	**poi** son
Poland	**Po** land
pollen	**pol** len
portal	**por** tal
possum	**pos** sum
postal	**post** al
Powell	**Pow** ell
pregnant	**preg** nant
Preston	**Pres** ton
pretzel	**pret** zel
prison	**pris** on
problem	**prob** lem
profit	**prof** it
prophet	**proph** et
proven	**prov** en
prudent	**pru** dent
puffin	**puf** fin
pummel	**pum** mel
pumpkin	**pump** kin
quarrel	**quar** rel
quicken	**quick** en
rabbit	**rab** bit
racket	**rack** et
raisin	**rai** sin
random	**ran** dom
ransom	**ran** som
rapid	**rap** id
rascal	**ras** cal
raven	**ra** ven
Reagan	**Rea** gan
reason	**rea** son
rebel	**reb** el
recent	**re** cent
reckless	**reck** less
reckon	**reck** on
rectum	**rec** tum
regal	**re** gal
restless	**rest** less
ribbon	**rib** bon
riches	**rich** es
Richmond	**Rich** mond
ridden	**rid** den
rigid	**rig** id
riot	**ri** ot

ripen	**rip** en
risen	**ris** en
rival	**ri** val
rivet	**riv** et
robin	**rob** in
rocket	**rock** et
rodent	**ro** dent
Roman	**Ro** man
Romans	**Ro** mans
rotten	**rot** ten
royal	**roy** al
rugged	**rug** ged
rural	**ru** ral
Russell	**Rus** sell
ruthless	**ruth** less
Sabbath	**Sab** bath
sacred	**sa** cred
sadden	**sad** den
Saffron	**Saf** fron
salad	**sal** ad
Salem	**Sa** lem
salmon	**salm** on
sandal	**san** dal
satin	**sat** in
scallop	**scal** lop
scandal	**scan** dal
scarlet	**scar** let
Scarlett	**Scar** lett
scoundrel	**scoun** drel
sealant	**seal** ant
seamstress	**seam** stress
season	**sea** son
second	**sec** ond
secret	**se** cret
segment	**seg** ment
seldom	**sel** dom
sepal	**se** pal
sequel	**se** quel
sermon	**ser** mon
serpent	**ser** pent
servant	**serv** ant
seven	**sev** en
seventh	**sev** enth
shaken	**shak** en
Shannon	**Shan** non
Sharon	**Shar** on
sharpen	**sharp** en
shaven	**shav** en
sherbet	**sher** bet
sheriff	**sher** iff
Sherwin	**Sher** win
shorten	**short** en
shortness	**short** ness
shovel	**shov** el
shrivel	**shriv** el
shrunken	**shrunk** en
sicken	**sick** en
sickness	**sick** ness
Sidon	**Si** don
signal	**sig** nal
silent	**si** lent
silken	**silk** en
siphon	**si** phon
siren	**si** ren
skillet	**skil** let
slacken	**slack** en
slogan	**slo** gan
snippet	**snip** pet
snorkel	**snor** kel
Snowden	**Snow** den

socket	**sock** et
soften	**soft** en
solid	**sol** id
sonnet	**son** net
spinal	**spi** nal
spiral	**spi** ral
spirit	**spir** it
squadron	**squad** ron
squirrel	**squir** rel
stagnant	**stag** nant
stamen	**sta** men
Stanton	**Stan** ton
statement	**state** ment
stencil	**sten** cil
Stephen	**Ste** phen
Stetson	**Stet** son
stiffen	**stif** fen
Stillman	**Still** man
Stockton	**Stock** ton
stolen	**sto** len
stomach	**stom** ach
straighten	**straight** en
strengthen	**strength** en
stricken	**strick** en
Strickland	**Strick** land
striven	**striv** en
stupid	**stu** pid
sudden	**sud** den
sullen	**sul** len
sultan	**sul** tan
summit	**sum** mit
summon	**sum** mon
sunken	**sunk** en
Sweden	**Swe** den
sweeten	**sweet** en
swivel	**swiv** el
swollen	**swol** len
symbol	**sym** bol
symptom	**symp** tom
system	**sys** tem
tablet	**tab** let
taken	**tak** en
talent	**tal** ent
talon	**tal** on
target	**tar** get
tartan	**tar** tan
tassel	**tas** sel
tempest	**tem** pest
tenant	**ten** ant
tendon	**ten** don
tendril	**ten** dril
tennis	**ten** nis
tepid	**tep** id
Texas	**Tex** as
Thailand	**Thai** land
thermal	**ther** mal
thermos	**ther** mos
thicken	**thick** en
thicket	**thick** et
Thomas	**Thom** as
Thornton	**Thorn** ton
threaten	**threat** en
Thurman	**Thur** man
ticket	**tick** et
tidal	**ti** dal
tighten	**tight** en
timid	**tim** id
tinsel	**tin** sel
toilet	**toi** let
token	**to** ken

Torah **To** rah
torrent **tor** rent
total **to** tal
totem **to** tem
towel **tow** el
transit **tran** sit
travel **trav** el
treason **trea** son
Trenton **Tren** ton
trial **tri** al
tribal **trib** al
trinket **trin** ket
***trink** et
triplet **trip** let
Tristan **Tris** tan
trodden **trod** den
trowel **trow** el
truant **tru** ant
Truman **Tru** man
trumpet **trum** pet
tunnel **tun** nel
turban **tur** ban
turnip **tur** nip
turret **tur** ret
tyrant **ty** rant
urban **ur** ban
urgent **ur** gent
valid **val** id
vandal **van** dal
vassal **vas** sal
vegan **ve** gan
venom **ven** om
verbal **ver** bal
vermin **ver** min
Vernon **Ver** non

vessel **ves** sel
victim **vic** tim
vinyl **vi** nyl
viral **vi** ral
visit **vis** it
vital **vi** tal
vivid **viv** id
vocal **vo** cal
vomit **vom** it
vowel **vow** el
wagon **wag** on
waken **wak** en
Walden **Wal** den
wallet **wal** let
wallop **wal** lop
Waltham **Wal** tham
Walton **Wal** ton
wanton **wan** ton
warden **war** den
warrant **war** rant
Warren **War** ren
weaken **weak** en
weapon **weap** on
weasel **wea** sel
weevil **wee** vil
Wendell **Wen** dell
Wharton **Whar** ton
Wheaton **Wheat** on
whiten **whit** en
wicket **wick** et
widen **wid** en
Wilson **Wil** son
Wilton **Wil** ton
Winston **Win** ston
wisdom **wis** dom

witness **wit** ness

woman **wom** an

women **wom** en

wooden **wood** en

woolen **wool** en

worsen **wors** en

woven **wo** ven

written **writ** ten

Yemen **Yem** en

yodel **yo** del

Zaanan **Zaan** an

VCE Imposters

VCE imposters

-IVE

/ĭ v/

- There are several syllables that appear to be **VCE** syllables, but are not. For this list of **-IVE** words, the **E** at the end of the word is there because one of our English spelling conventions is that no English word will have the letter **V** at the end of the word.

active	**ac** tive
captive	**cap** tive
cursive	**cur** sive
festive	**fes** tive
furtive	**fur** tive
massive	**mas** sive
motive	**mo** tive
native	**na** tive
olive	**ol** ive
passive	**pas** sive
pensive	**pen** sive
restive	**res** tive

VCE imposters

-ILE

/əl/

/ī l/

- There are several syllables that appear to be **VCE** syllables, but are not. **-ILE** is one of those suffixes.
- In different dialects, **-ILE** may be pronounced with a long **/ī/**, with a schwa sound, or with another sound, such as the **u** sound in **pull**.

agile	**ag** ile
docile	**doc** ile
fertile	**fer** tile
fragile	**frag** ile
futile	**fu** tile
hostile	**hos** tile
missile	**mis** sile
mobile	**mo** bile
sterile	**ster** ile

VCE imposters
-ACE/-ICE/-UCE
/ ĭ s/

- There are several syllalbes that appear to be **VCE** syllables, but are not. For this list of **-ACE, -ICE, -UCE** words, the **E** does not make the vowel sound long. Instead, the **E** at the end of the word is there because it tells the reader to use the soft **C** sound (**/s/** in **celery**), instead of the hard **C** sound (**/k/** in **cat**).

-ACE

furnace	**fur** nace
grimace	**grim** ace
Horace	**Hor** ace
menace	**men** ace
necklace	**neck** lace
palace	**pal** ace
preface	**pref** ace
solace	**sol** ace
surface	**sur** face
terrace	**ter** race

-UCE

lettuce	**let** tuce

-ICE

chalice	**chal** ice
cornice	**cor** nice
crevice	**crev** ice
jaundice	**jaun** dice
justice	**jus** tice
lattice	**lat** tice
malice	**mal** ice
notice	**no** tice
novice	**nov** ice
office	**of** fice
practice	**prac** tice
Prentice	**Pren** tice
service	**ser** vice
solstice	**sol** stice

VCE imposters

-AGE

/ĭ j/

- There are several syllables that appear to be **VCE** syllables, but are not. For this list of **-AGE** words, the **E** does not make the vowel sound long. Instead, the **E** at the end of the word is there because it tells the reader to use the soft **G** sound (**/j/** in giraffe), instead of the hard **G** sound (**/g/** in **goat**).

Suffix -AGE

adage	**ad** age	hostage	**hos** tage
assuage	as **suage**	image	**im** age
baggage	**bag** gage	language	**lan** guage
bandage	**band** age	leakage	**leak** age
barrage	bar **rage**	luggage	**lug** gage
blockage	**block** age	manage	**man** age
breakage	**break** age	massage	mas **sage**
cabbage	**cab** bage	message	**mes** sage
carriage	**car** riage	mileage	**mile** age
collage	col **lage**	mirage	mi **rage**
cottage	**cot** tage	mortgage	**mort** gage
courage	**cour** age	outage	**out** age
cribbage	**crib** bage	package	**pack** age
damage	**dam** age	passage	**pas** sage
dosage	**dos** age	pillage	**pil** lage
drainage	**drain** age	plumage	**plum** age
footage	**foot** age	portage	**por** tage
forage	**for** age	postage	**post** age
garage	ga **rage**	ravage	**rav** age
garbage	**gar** bage	rummage	**rum** mage
homage	**hom** age	salvage	**sal** vage

sausage **sau** sage

savage **sav** age

scrimmage **scrim** mage

seepage **seep** age

sewage **sew** age

shortage **short** age

storage **sort** age

suffrage **suf** frage

vantage **van** tage

village **vil** lage

vintage **vin** tage

voltage **volt** age

voyage **voy** age

wattage **watt** age

wreckage **wreck** age

yardage **yard** age

VCE imposters

-ISE/-ASE

/ĭs/

- There are several suffixes that appear to be **VCE** syllables, but are not.
- The words in this list have **-SE** at the end of them. The **E** at the end does not make the vowel sound long. Instead, it follows the **S** to show that the word is not a plural. Other words that are not **VCE** imposters also use an **E** after an **S** to indicate that the word is not plural. Examples are **house, mouse, cause,** and **dense.**

mortise	**mor** tise
premise	**prem** ise
promise	**prom** ise
purchase	**pur** chase
treatise	**trea** tise

Longer Words by Number of Syllables

3 Syllables

- In this list, the stressed syllable is indicated by **bold** print, and the schwa syllable is indicated by <u>underlined</u> print. These may vary based on dialect.
- In multi-syllable words, you will often find that one or more syllables in the word have a vowel schwa sound. This can be confusing for students who have learned that open syllables make a long vowel sound and closed syllables make a short vowel sound. Teaching students about the schwa sound is a valuable tool in teaching them to decode multi-syllable words.
- As student read longer words, they need to learn more how to "flex" the vowels. This means to try out different vowel sounds to see which one sounds like it fits in the word. The most common flex would be to try out the schwa sound for the different vowels in a multi-syllable word. Here are some examples of open vowel syllables that make the schwa sound instead of the long vowel sound:

  al m<u>a</u> nac   ar b<u>i</u> trate   an t<u>e</u> lope

- For the majority of 3 syllable words, the accent/stress will be on the first or second syllable. Only a few words stress the final syllable. This is because the accent/stress is usually focused on the base word, and final syllables in longer words are usually suffixes.

abacus	**ab** <u>a</u> cus
abandon	a **ban** <u>don</u>
abdicate	**ab** di cate
	***ab** dic ate
abdomen	**ab** do <u>men</u>
Abilene	**Ab** <u>i</u> lene
abnormal	ab **nor** <u>mal</u>
abolish	<u>a</u> **bol** ish
Abraham	**A** <u>bra</u> ham
absolute	**ab** <u>so</u> lute
absorbent	<u>ab</u> **sorb** <u>ent</u>
absorbing	<u>ab</u> **sorb** ing
absorption	<u>ab</u> **sorp** <u>tion</u>
abundance	<u>a</u> **bun** <u>dance</u>
abundant	<u>a</u> **bun** <u>dant</u>
acceptance	ac **cept** <u>ance</u>
accident	**ac** <u>ci</u> dent
accountant	<u>ac</u> **count** <u>ant</u>
accounting	<u>ac</u> **count** ing
accurate	**ac** <u>cu</u> <u>rate</u>
	ac <u>cur</u> <u>ate</u>
accustom	<u>ac</u> **cus** <u>tom</u>
achievement	<u>a</u> **chieve** <u>ment</u>
acoustic	<u>a</u> **cous** tic
acreage	**a** cre age
acrobat	**ac** ro bat
acronym	**ac** ro nym

acrylic	a **cryl** ic
activist	**ac** tiv ist
actual	**ac** tu al
addicted	ad **dict** ed
addiction	ad **dic** tion
addition	ad **di** tion
additive	**ad** di tive
adequate	**ad** e quate
adherence	ad **her** ence
adhesion	ad **he** sion
adhesive	ad **he** sive
adjacent	ad **ja** cent
adjective	**ad** jec tive
adjustment	ad **just** ment
admiral	**ad** mi ral
	***ad** mir al
admission	ad **mis** sion
admittance	ad **mit** tance
admonish	ad **mon** ish
Adonai	Ad o **nai**
adoption	a **dop** tion
adornment	a **dorn** ment
adulthood	a **dult** hood
advancement	ad **vance** ment
advantage	ad **van** tage
adventure	ad **ven** ture
advertise	**ad** ver tise
advisor	ad **vi** sor
advocate	**ad** vo cate
aerial	**aer** i al
aerobic	aer **o** bic
aerospace	**aer** o space
affection	af **fec** tion
affliction	af **flic** tion
affluent	**af** flu ent
African	**Af** ri can
Agatha	**Ag** a tha
agency	**a** gen cy
agenda	a **gen** da
aggravate	**ag** gra vate
aggression	ag **gres** sion
aggressive	ag **gres** sive
agility	a **gil** i ty
agitate	**ag** i tate
agnostic	ag **nos** tic
agreement	a **gree** ment
Aisha	A **i** sha
Alaska	A **las** ka
Alastair	**Al** a stair
albatross	**al** ba tross
albino	al **bi** no
alchemy	**al** che my
algebra	**al** ge bra
alias	**a** li as
alibi	**al** i bi
alien	**a** li en
allegiance	al **le** giance
allergic	al **ler** gic
allergy	**al** ler gy
alliance	al **li** ance
allocate	**al** lo cate
allowance	al **low** ance
almanac	**al** ma nac
almighty	al **might** y
aloha	a **lo** ha
alpaca	al **pac** a
alphabet	**al** pha bet
already	al **read** y
alternate	**al** ter nate
altitude	**al** ti tude

Alyssa	Al **ys** sa
amateur	**am** a teur
amazement	a **maze** ment
amazing	a **maz** ing
ambition	am **bi** tion
ambitious	am **bi** tious
amethyst	**am** e thyst
ammonia	am **mo** nia
amnesia	am **ne** sia
amnesty	**am** nes ty
amplify	**am** pli fy
amputate	**am** pu tate
amusement	a **muse** ment
amusing	a **mus** ing
Anaheim	**An** a heim
Analee	**An** a lee
analog	**an** a log
analyze	**an** a lyze
ancestor	**an** ces tor
ancestral	an **ces** tral
ancestry	**an** ces try
Anchorage	**An** chor age
anchovy	**an** cho vy
Andorra	An **dor** ra
Andrea	**An** dre a
anecdote	**an** ec dote
Angola	An **go** la
	*Ang **o** la
Anguilla	An **guil** la
animal	**an** i mal
announcer	an **nounc** er
	*an **noun** cer
annoyance	an **noy** ance
annual	**an** nu al
Antarctic	ant **arc** tic

anteater	**ant** eat er
antelope	**an** te lope
antenna	an **ten** na
Anthony	**An** tho ny
antidote	**an** ti dote
antifreeze	**an** ti freeze
Antioch	**An** ti och
antonym	**an** to nym
aorta	a **or** ta
apartment	a **part** ment
apathy	**ap** a thy
apostle	a **pos** tle
apparel	ap **par** el
apparent	ap **par** ent
appealing	ap **peal** ing
appearance	ap **pear** ance
appendix	ap **pen** dix
appetite	**ap** pe tite
appliance	ap **pli** ance
applicant	**ap** pli cant
apprehend	ap pre **hend**
apprentice	ap **pren** tice
approval	ap **prov** al
apricot	**ap** ri cot
aptitude	**ap** ti tude
aquatic	a **qua** tic
aqueduct	**a** que duct
aquifer	**a** qui fer
Aquila	A **quil** a
Arabic	**Ar** a bic
arachnid	a **rach** nid
arbitrate	**ar** bi trate
archery	**ar** cher_y
architect	**ar** chi tect
arena	a **re** na

argument	**ar** gu ment
arisen	a **ris** en
Arlington	**Ar** ling ton
armada	ar **ma** da
armistice	**ar** mi stice
armory	**ar** mor y
aroma	a **ro** ma
arrangement	ar **range** ment
arrival	ar **ri** val
arrogant	**ar** ro gant
arroyo	ar **roy** o
arsenal	**ar** se nal
arsenic	**ar** se nic
artery	**ar** ter y
arthritis	ar **thri** tis
arthropod	**ar** thro pod
artichoke	**ar** ti choke
article	**ar** ti cle
artifact	**ar** ti fact
artisan	**ar** ti san
artistic	ar **tis** tic
artistry	**art** ist ry
Aruba	A **ru** ba
Arvada	Ar **va** da
asbestos	as **bes** tos
ascension	as **cen** sion
Ashanti	A **shan** ti
Ashkelon	**Ash** ke lon
asocial	a **so** cial
aspirin	**as** pi rin
	*as pir in
Asriel	**As** ri el
assassin	as **sas** sin
assemble	as **sem** ble
assembly	as **sem** bly
assessment	as **sess** ment
assignment	as **sign** ment
assistance	as **sis** tance
assistant	as **sis** tant
assorted	as **sort** ed
assortment	as **sort** ment
assumption	as **sump** tion
assurance	as **sur** ance
asterisk	**as** ter isk
asteroid	**as** ter oid
astonish	as **ton** ish
astronaut	**as** tro naut
asylum	a **sy** lum
atheist	**a** the ist
Athena	A **the** na
athletic	ath **let** ic
Atlanta	At **lan** ta
atomic	a **tom** ic
atonement	a **tone** ment
atrocious	a **tro** cious
attachment	at **tach** ment
Attalia	At ta **li** a
attendance	at **tend** ance
attendant	at **ten** dant
attention	at **ten** tion
attentive	at **ten** tive
attitude	**at** ti tude
attorney	at **tor** ney
attraction	at **trac** tion
attractive	at **trac** tive
attribute	at **trib** ute
	at trib ute
auctioneer	auc tion **eer**
audacious	au **da** cious
audible	**au** di ble

audience	**au** di ence
audio	**au** di o
audition	au **di** tion
Augusta	Au **gus** ta
Augustus	Au **gus** tus
Aurora	Au **ro** ra
Australia	Aus **tral** ia
Australian	Aus **tral** ian
Austria	**Aus** tri a
authentic	au **then** tic
authorize	**au** thor ize
autistic	au **tis** tic
autograph	**au** to graph
automate	**au** to mate
autopsy	au **top** sy
avalanche	**av** a lanche
avatar	**av** a tar
a nue	**av** e nue
a rage	**av** er age
awaken	a **wak** en
axiom	**ax** i om
azalea	a **zal** ea
babushka	ba **bush** ka
Babyon	**Bab** y lon
backgammon	**back** gam mon
badminton	**bad** min ton
Bahamas	Ba **ha** mas
Bakersfield	**Ba** kers field
balcony	**bal** co ny
baloney	ba **lo** ney
Baltimore	**Bal** ti more
banana	ba **nan** a
bandanna	ban **dan** na
Bangalore	**Ban** ga lore
Bangladesh	**Ban** gla desh
banister	**ban** is ter
Barbados	Bar **ba** dos
barbaric	bar **bar** ic
barbecue	**bar** be cue
barnacle	**bar** na cle
baroness	**bar** on ess
barricade	**bar** ri cade
barrier	**bar** ri er
barrio	**bar** ri o
battery	**bat** ter y
Battista	Bat **ti** sta
beautiful	**beau** ti ful
beautify	**beau** ti fy
becoming	be **com** ing
bedraggled	be **drag** gled
beginner	be **gin** ner
beginning	be **gin** ning
behavior	be **hav** ior
Belarus	Be la **rus**
belated	be **lat** ed
Belinda	Be **lin** da
belongings	be **long** ings
Benedict	**Ben** e dict
benefit	**ben** e fit
Bengali	Ben **ga** li
Benjamin	**Ben** ja min
Bermuda	Ber **mu** da
Bethany	**Beth** a ny
Bethlehem	**Beth** le hem
Bethsaida	Beth **sai** da
Beverly	**Bev** er ly
bewilder	be **wil** der
biblical	**bib** li cal
bicycle	**bi** cy cle
bikini	bi **ki** ni

bilingual	bi **lin** gual
billionaire	**bil** lion aire
bionic	bi **on** ic
Birmingham	**Bir** ming ham
blasphemy	**blas** phe my
bodily	**bod** i ly
Bogota	**Bo** go ta
boisterous	**bois** ter ous
Bolivar	Bol **i** var
bologna	bo **lo** gna
boomerang	**boo** mer ang
botany	**bot** a ny
Brittany	**Brit** ta ny
broccoli	**broc** co li
bronchitis	bron **chi** tis
buffalo	**buf** fa lo
Bulgaria	Bul **gar** i a
bulletin	**bul** le tin
burgundy	**bur** gun dy
burglary	**bur** gla ry
burial	**bur** i al
burrito	bur **ri** to
Burundi	Bu **run** di
calcium	**cal** ci um
calculate	**cal** cu late
Calcutta	Cal **cut** ta
calendar	**cal** en dar
calico	**cal** i co
calorie	**cal** or ie
camcorder	**cam** cord er
Cameron	**Cam** er on
Cameroon	Cam e **roon**
camouflage	**cam** ou flage
Canada	**Can** a da
canary	ca **nar** y
candidate	**can** di date
cannibal	**can** ni bal
cannoli	can **no** li
canopy	**can** o py
cantaloupe	**can** ta loupe
Cantonese	Can ton **ese**
capable	**ca** pa ble
capacity	ca **pac** i ty
capital	**cap** i tal
capitol	**cap** i tol
caramel	**car** a mel
caravan	**car** a van
cardiac	**car** di ac
caribou	**car** i bou
carnation	car **na** tion
carnival	**car** ni val
carnivore	**car** ni vore
carpenter	**car** pen ter
carpentry	**car** pen try
carrier	**car** ri er
Carrollton	Car roll ton
cartilage	**car** ti lage
Cassandra	Cas **san** dra
casserole	**cas** se role
Cassidy	**Cas** sid y
castanets	cas ta **nets**
casual	**cas** u al
Catalan	**Cat** a lan
catalog	**cat** a log
catalyst	**cat** a lyst
catamount	**cat** a mount
catapult	**cat** a pult
cataract	**cat** a ract
category	**cat** e gor y
cathedral	ca **the** dral

cavalry	**cav** al ry
cavity	**cav** i ty
Cecelia	Ce **ce** lia
celebrate	**cel** e brate
Celena	Ce **le** na
celery	**cel** er y
cellulose	**cel** lu lose
Celsius	**cel** si us
centigrade	**cen** ti grade
centipede	**cen** ti pede
ceramic	ce **ram** ic
cereal	**ce** re al
certainly	**cer** tain ly
certainty	**cer** tain ty
certify	**cer** ti fy
champion	**cham** pi on
chandelier	**chan** de lier
chaotic	cha **ot** ic
chaparral	chap ar ral
chaperone	**chap** er one
character	**char** ac ter
chariot	**char** i ot
charisma	cha **ris** ma
charity	**char** i ty
chemical	**chem** i cal
chemistry	**chem** is try
Chesapeake	**Ches** a peake
Chicago	Chi **ca** go
chickadee	**chick** a dee
chimpanzee	chim pan **zee**
chinchilla	chin **chil** la
chivalry	**chiv** al ry
chlorophyll	**chlo** ro phyll
christening	**chris** ten ing
Christopher	**Chris** to pher
chromosome	**chro** mo some
chronicle	**chron** i cle
Chronicles	**Chron** i cles
chrysalis	**chrys** a lis
cicada	ci **ca** da
Cierra	Ci **er** ra
cilium	**cil** i um
cinema	**cin** e ma
cinnamon	**cin** na mon
circular	**cir** cu lar
circulate	**cir** cu late
circumstance	**cir** cum stance
citizen	**cit** i zen
civilian	ci **vil** ian
civilized	**civ** i lized
clarify	**clar** i fy
clarinet	clar i **net**
Clarissa	Cla **ris** sa *Clar **is** sa
clarity	**clar** i ty
classical	**clas** si cal
classify	**clas** si fy
Claudia	**Clau** di a
Clementine	**Clem** en tine
clerical	**cler** i cal
Clorinda	Clor **in** da
cockatoo	**cock** a too
coincide	co in **cide**
colander	**col** an der
collection	col **lec** tion
collector	col **lec** tor
collision	col **li** sion
colonist	**col** o nist
colonize	**col** o nize
colony	**col** o ny

colorful	**col** or ful
coloring	**col** or ing
colorless	**col** or less
colossal	co **los** sal
Colossians	Co **los** sians
Columbus	Co **lum** bus
combustion	com **bus** tion
comedy	**com** e dy
comical	**com** i cal
commander	com **mand** er
commandment	com **mand** ment
commandments	com **mand** ments
commencement	com **mence** ment
commercial	com **mer** cial
commission	com **mis** sion
commitment	com **mit** ment
committee	com **mit** tee
commotion	com **mo** tion
communion	com **mu** nion
communism	**com** mu nism
communist	**com** mu nist
commuter	com **mut** er
Comoros	Com o ros
companion	com **pan** ion
company	**com** pa ny
compartment	com **part** ment
compassion	com **pas** sion
compensate	**com** pen sate
competence	**com** pe tence
competent	**com** pe tent
complacent	com **pla** cent
complement	**com** ple ment
completely	com **plete** ly
completion	com **ple** tion
complexion	com **plex** ion
compliant	com **pli** ant
complicate	**com** pli cate
compliment	**com** pli ment
component	com **po** nent
composer	com **pos** er
composite	com **pos** ite
comprehend	com pre **hend**
compromise	**com** pro mise
compulsion	com **pul** sion
computer	com **put** er
concentrate	**con** cen trate
concentric	con **cen** tric
conception	con **cep** tion
concerning	con **cern** ing
concerto	con **cer** to
concession	con **ces** sion
conclusion	con **clu** sion
conclusive	con **clu** sive
concussion	con **cus** sion
condiment	**con** di ment
condition	con **di** tion
conductor	con **duc** tor
conference	**con** fer ence
confession	con **fes** sion
confetti	con **fet** ti
confidence	**con** fi dence
confident	**con** fi dent
confiscate	**con** fis cate
conformity	con **form** i ty
confusion	con **fu** sion
congested	con **gest** ed
congregate	**con** gre gate
congruent	con **gru** ent
conifer	**co** ni fer
conjunction	con **junc** tion

connection	con **nec** tion
consciousness	**con** scious ness
consensus	con **sen** sus
consequence	**con** se quence
consider	con **sid** er
consistent	con **sist** ent
consonant	**con** so nant
constitute	**con** sti tute
construction	con **struc** tion
constructive	con **struc** tive
consumer	con **sum** er
consumption	con **sump** tion
contagious	con **ta** gious
container	con **tain** er
contemplate	**con** tem plate
contented	con **tent** ed
contention	con **ten** tion
contentment	con **tent** ment
contestant	con **test** ant
continent	**con** ti nent
continue	con **tin** ue
contortion	con **tor** tion
contraband	**con** tra band
contraction	con **trac** tion
contradict	con tra **dict**
contraption	con **trap** tion
contrary	**con** trar y
contribute	con **trib** ute
concoction	con **coc** tion
convenient	con **ven** ient
conversion	con **ver** sion
conviction	con **vic** tion
corduroy	**cor** du roy
cornea	**cor** ne a
corona	co **ro** na
coroner	**cor** o ner
corporal	**cor** por al
corpuscle	cor pus cle
correction	cor **rec** tion
correspond	cor re **spond**
corridor	**cor** ri dor
corrosion	cor **ro** sion
cosmetic	cos **met** ic
counselor	**coun** sel or
countenance	**coun** te nance
counteract	coun ter **act**
counterfeit	**coun** ter feit
courageous	cou **ra** geous
courteous	**cour** te ous
courtesy	**cour** te sy
covenant	**cov** e nant
covering	**cov** er ing
coyote	coy **o** te
cranberry	**cran** ber ry
cranium	**cra** ni um
creation	cre **a** tion
creative	cre **a** tive
creator	cre **a** tor
credentials	cre **den** tials
credible	**cred** i ble
creditor	**cred** i tor
crescendo	cre **scen** do
Cressida	**Cres** si da
criminal	**crim** i nal
critical	**crit** i cal
criticism	**crit** i cism
criticize	**crit** i cize
Croatia	Cro **a** tia
crocodile	**croc** o dile
cruelty	**cru** el ty

crusader	cru **sad** er
crustacean	crus **ta** cean
crystallize	**crys** tal lize
cubicle	**cu** bi cle
cucumber	**cu** cum ber
culminate	**cul** mi nate
cultivate	**cul** ti vate
cumbersome	**cum** ber some
Cunningham	**Cun** ning ham
curable	**cur** a ble
curious	**cu** ri ous
	***cur** i ous
currency	**cur** ren cy
currently	**cur** rent ly
custody	**cus** to dy
customer	**cus** tom er
cuticle	**cu** ti cle
cylinder	**cyl** in der
Cynthia	**Cyn** thi a
daffodil	**daf** fo dil
Dalmatian	Dal **ma** tian
Damascus	Da **mas** cus
dangerous	**dan** ger ous
deceitful	de **ceit** ful
December	De **cem** ber
deception	de **cep** tion
deceptive	de **cep** tive
decided	de **cid** ed
decimal	**dec** i mal
decipher	de **ci** pher
decision	de **ci** sion
decisive	de **ci** sive
declaration	dec la **ra** tion
decompose	de com **pose**
decorate	**dec** o rate
dedicate	**ded** i cate
	ded i cate
deduction	de **duc** tion
defective	de **fec** tive
defendant	de **fend** ant
defensive	de **fen** sive
defiance	de **fi** ance
defiant	de **fi** ant
deficient	de **fi** cient
definite	**def** i nite
degrading	de **grad** ing
	de **grad** ing
dehydrate	de **hy** drate
dejected	de **ject** ed
	de **ject** ed
Delaney	De **la** ney
	De **la** ney
Delaware	**Del** a ware
	Del a ware
delegate	**del** e gate
	del e gate
delicate	**del** i cate
delicious	de **li** cious
delighted	de **light** ed
delightful	de **light** ful
deliver	de **liv** er
delusion	de **lu** sion
demeanor	de **mean** or
demerit	de **mer** it
Democrat	**Dem** o crat
demolish	de **mol** ish
	de **mol** ish
demonstrate	**dem** on strate
denial	de **ni** al
density	**den** si ty

department	de **part** ment
departure	de **par** ture
dependence	de **pend** ence
dependent	de **pend** ent
deposit	de **pos** it
depression	de **pres** sion
deputy	**dep** u ty
derelict	**der** e lict
descendant	de **scend** ant
	de **scend** ant
description	de **scrip** tion
	de **scrip** tion
descriptive	de **scrip** tive
	de scrip tive
deserted	de **sert** ed
designate	**des** ig nate
	des ig nate
desolate	**des** o late
desperate	**des** per ate
Destiny	**Des** ti ny
destitute	**des** ti tute
	des ti tute
destroyer	de **stroy** er
destruction	de **struc** tion
destructive	de **struc** tive
detective	de **tec** tive
detector	de **tec** tor
detention	de **ten** tion
detergent	de **ter** gent
determine	de **ter** mine
determined	de **ter** mined
devastate	**dev** as tate
develop	de **vel** op
devious	**de** vi ous
devoted	de **vot** ed
devotion	de **vo** tion
diagnose	di ag **nose**
	di ag **nose**
diagram	**di** a gram
dialect	**di** a lect
dialogue	**di** a logue
diaphragm	**di** a phragm
dictator	**dic** ta tor
difficult	**dif** fi cult
digestion	di **ges** tion
	di **ges** tion
dignified	**dig** ni fied
dignity	**dig** ni ty
dilemma	di **lem** ma
	di **lem** ma
diligent	**dil** i gent
dimension	di **men** sion
	di **men** sion
diminish	di **min** ish
dinosaur	**di** no saur
diploma	di **plo** ma
diplomat	**dip** lo mat
	dip lo mat
direction	di **rec** tion
	di **rec** tion
directly	di **rect** ly
	di **rect** ly
director	di **rect** tor
disabled	dis **a** bled
disagree	dis a **gree**
disappear	dis ap **pear**
disappoint	dis ap **point**
disapprove	dis ap **prove**
disaster	dis **as** ter
	dis **as** ter

disbelief	dis be **lief**
disciple	dis **ci** ple
discipline	**dis** ci pline
discolor	dis **col** or
discomfort	dis **com** fort
disconnect	dis con **nect**
discourage	dis **cour** age
discover	dis **cov** er
discredit	dis **cred** it
disembark	dis em **bark**
disfigure	dis **fig** ure
disgraceful	dis **grace** ful
disgruntled	dis **grun** tled
dishearten	dis **heart** en
dishonest	dis **hon** est
dishonor	dis **hon** or
disinfect	dis in **fect**
dislocate	dis **lo** cate
disloyal	dis **loy** al
dismissal	dis **miss** al
disorder	dis **or** der
dispenser	dis **pens** er
displeasure	dis **pleas** ure
disregard	dis re **gard**
disrespect	dis re **spect**
dissipate	**dis** si pate
distasteful	dis **taste** ful
distinction	dis **tinc** tion
distinctive	dis **tinc** tive
distinguish	dis **tin** guish
distribute	dis **trib** ute
	dis **trib** ute
disturbance	dis **turb** ance
diversion	di **ver** sion
	di **ver** sion
dividend	**div** i dend
	div i dend
division	di **vi** sion
divisor	di **vi** sor
document	**doc** u ment
domestic	do **mes** tic
dominant	**dom** i nant
dominate	**dom** i nate
Dominique	**Dom** i nique
domino	**dom** i no
donation	do **na** tion
Dorothy	**Dor** o thy
dramatic	dra **mat** ic
dramatist	dram **a** tist
dramatize	**dram** a tize
drapery	**drap** er y
drudgery	**drudg** er y
dubious	**du** bi ous
duplicate	**du** pli cate
durable	**du** ra ble
duration	du **ra** tion
dutiful	**du** ti ful
dynamic	dy **nam** ic
dynamite	**dy** na mite
dynasty	**dy** nas ty
eccentric	ec **cen** tric
ecstatic	ec **stat** ic
Ecuador	**Ec** ua dor
edible	**ed** i ble
edition	e **di** tion
editor	**ed** i tor
educate	**ed** u cate
effortless	**ef** fort less
Egyptian	E **gyp** tian
eightieth	**eight** i eth

elastic	e **las** tic
elderly	**eld** er ly
election	e **lec** tion
elective	e **lec** tive
Electra	E **lec** tra
electron	e **lec** tron
elegance	**el** e gance
elegant	**el** e gant
element	**el** e ment
elephant	**el** e phant
elevate	**el** e vate
eleven	e **lev** en
eleventh	e **lev** enth
Elinor	**El** i nor
Elisha	E **li** sha
Ellington	**El** ling ton
Elliot	**El** li ot
eloquent	**el** o quent
elusive	e **lu** sive
embankment	em **bank** ment
embargo	em **bar** go
embarrass	em **bar** rass
embassy	**em** bas sy
embezzle	em **bez** zle
embody	em **bod** y
embroider	em **broi** der
embryo	**em** bry o
emerald	**em** er ald
Emery	**Em** er y
emigrant	**em** i grant
emigrate	**em** i grate
eminent	**em** i nent
emission	e **mis** sion
emotion	e **mo** tion
emperor	**em** per or

emphasis	**em** pha sis
emphasize	**em** pha size
employee	em **ploy** ee
employer	em **ploy** er
employment	em **ploy** ment
enable	en **a** ble
enamel	e **nam** el
encircle	en **cir** cle
enclosure	en **clo** sure
encompass	en **com** pass
encounter	en **coun** ter
encourage	en **cour** age
endanger	en **dan** ger
endeavor	en **deav** or
endocrine	**en** do crine
endurance	en **dur** ance
enemy	**en** e my
energize	**en** er gize
energy	**en** er gy
engagement	en **gage** ment
engineer	en gi **neer**
engraving	en **grav** ing
enigma	e **nig** ma
enjoyment	en **joy** ment
enlargement	en **large** ment
enlighten	en **light** en
enliven	en **liv** en
enormous	e **nor** mous
enrollment	en **roll** ment
entangle	en **tan** gle
enterprise	**en** ter prise
entertain	en ter **tain**
entirely	en **tire** ly
entitle	en **ti** tle
entreaty	en **treat** y

envelop	en **vel** op
envelope	**en** ve lope
envious	**en** vi ous
envision	en **vi** sion
Ephesians	E **phe** sians
Ephesus	**Eph** e sus
Ephraim	**Eph** ra im
episode	**ep** i sode
epistle	e **pis** tle
equation	e **qua** tion
equator	e **qua** tor
equinox	**e** qui nox
eraser	e **ras** er
erosion	e **ro** sion
erratic	er **rat** ic
eruption	e **rup** tion
essential	es **sen** tial
establish	es **tab** lish
estimate	**es** ti mate
eternal	e **ter** nal
ethical	**eth** i cal
etiquette	**et** i quette
Eucharist	**Eu** cha rist
Evansville	**Ev** ans ville
Everest	**Ev** er est
evidence	**ev** i dence
evident	**ev** i dent
exactly	ex **act** ly
examine	ex **am** ine
example	ex **am** ple
excavate	**ex** ca vate
excellence	**ex** cel lence
excellent	**ex** cel lent
exception	ex **cep** tion
excessive	ex **ces** sive
excitement	ex **cite** ment
exciting	ex **cit** ing
exclusive	ex **clu** sive
excursion	ex **cur** sion
exercise	**ex** er cise
exertion	ex **er** tion
exhaustion	ex **haus** tion
exhibit	ex **hib** it
existence	ex **ist** ence
Exodus	**Ex** o dus
exotic	ex **ot** ic
expansion	ex **pan** sion
expensive	ex **pen** sive
explicit	ex **plic** it
explorer	ex **plor** er
explosion	ex **plo** sion
explosive	ex **plo** sive
exponent	ex **po** nent
exposure	ex **po** sure
expression	ex **pres** sion
expressive	ex **pres** sive
expressly	ex **press** ly
expressway	ex **press** way
expulsion	ex **pul** sion
exquisite	ex **quis** ite
extension	ex **ten** sion
extensive	ex **ten** sive
exterior	ex **te** ri or
external	ex **ter** nal
extinction	ex **tinc** tion
extinguish	ex **tin** guish
fabulous	**fab** u lous
factory	**fac** to ry
factual	**fac** tu al
faculty	**fac** ul ty

Fahrenheit	**Fahr** en heit
falafel	fa la fel
familiar	fa **mil** iar
family	**fam** i ly
fanatic	fa **nat** ic
fantastic	fan **tas** tic
fantasy	**fan** ta sy
farsighted	***far*** *sight ed*
fascinate	**fas** ci nate
fastener	**fas** ten er
favorite	**fa** vor ite
Fayetteville	**Fay** ette ville
feasible	**fea** si ble
federal	**fed** er al
fellowship	**fel** low ship
	fel low ship
feminine	**fem** i nine
Ferdinand	**Fer** di nand
ferocious	fe **ro** cious
fertilize	**fer** ti lize
festival	**fes** ti val
feudalism	**feu** dal ism
fiancé	fi **an** ce
fiftieth	**fif** ti eth
filament	**fil** a ment
finalist	**fi** nal ist
finally	**fi** nal ly
financial	fi **nan** cial
	fi **nan** cial
fishery	**fish** er y
flamingo	fla **min** go
flammable	**flam** ma ble
flattery	**flat** ter y
flavoring	**fla** vor ing
flexible	**flex** i ble
Florida	**Flor** i da
fluctuate	**fluc** tu ate
fluorescent	fluo **res** cent
follower	**fol** low er
following	**fol** low ing
Fontana	Fon ta na
forbidden	for **bid** den
forgiveness	for **give** ness
forgotten	for **got** ten
formation	for **ma** tion
formula	**for** mu la
forsaken	for **sak** en
fortieth	**for** ti eth
fortify	**for** ti fy
fortunate	**for** tu nate
foundation	foun **da** tion
Francisco	Fran **cis** co
fraternal	fra **ter** nal
frivolous	**friv** o lous
fugitive	**fu** gi tive
Fullerton	**Ful** ler ton
furious	fu ri ous
furnishings	**fur** nish ings
furniture	**fur** ni ture
futility	fu **til** i ty
Gabriel	**Ga** bri el
Gabrielle	Ga bri **elle**
galactic	ga **lac** tic
Galatians	Ga **la** tians
galaxy	**gal** ax y
Galilee	**Gal** i lee
gallery	**gal** ler y
galoshes	ga **losh** es
Gambia	Gam bi a
gardener	**gar** den er

gardenia	gar **de** nia
gasoline	gas o line
gathering	**gath** er ing
gazebo	ga **ze** bo
gelatin	**gel** a tin
general	**gen** er al
generate	**gen** er ate
generic	ge **ner** ic
generous	**gen** er ous
Genesis	**Gen** e sis
genetic	ge **net** ic
genial	**gen** i al
gentleman	**gen** tle man
genuine	**gen** u ine
Germany	**Ger** ma ny
germinate	**ger** mi nate
gibberish	**gib** ber ish
Gibraltar	Gi **bral** tar
gigabyte	**gig** a byte
gigantic	gi **gan** tic
	gi **gan** tic
gingerly	**gin** ger ly
Gloria	**Glor** i a
glorify	**glor** i fy
glossary	**glos** sa ry
Golgotha	Gol **go** tha
Goliath	Go **li** ath
Gomorrah	Go **mor** rah
gondola	**gon** do la
gondolier	gon do **lier**
gorilla	gor **il** la
government	**gov** ern ment
governor	**gov** er nor
gradual	**grad** u al
graduate	**grad** u ate
	grad u ate
graffiti	graf **fi** ti
granola	gra **no** la
gratify	**grat** i fy
gratitude	**grat** i tude
Greensboro	**Greens** bo ro
Grenada	Gre **na** da
guarantee	guar an **tee**
guardian	**guard** i an
gullible	**gul** li ble
Guyana	Guy a na
gymnastic	gym **nas** tic
Habakkuk	Hab **ak** kuk
	Hab ak kuk
habitat	**hab** i tat
halibut	**hal** i but
Halloween	Hal low **een**
Hamilton	**Ham** il ton
handicap	**hand** i cap
handicraft	**hand** i craft
Hanukkah	**Ha** nuk kah
haphazard	hap **haz** ard
happily	**hap** pi ly
happiness	**hap** pi ness
harmonize	**har** mo nize
harmony	**har** mo ny
harpsichord	**harp** si chord
harrowing	**har** row ing
harvester	**har** ves ter
Hawaii	Ha **wai** i
heartily	**heart** i ly
heavenly	**heav** en ly
heavily	**heav** i ly
helium	**he** li um
Hemingway	**Hem** ing way

hemisphere	**hem** i sphere
Henderson	**Hen** der son
herbicide	**herb** i cide
herbivore	**her** bi vore
Hercules	**Her** cu les
heritage	**her** i tage
heroine	**her** o ine
heroism	**her** o ism
hesitant	**hes** i tant
hesitate	**hes** i tate
hexagon	**hex** a gon
hibernate	**hi** ber nate
hickory	**hick** o ry
hideous	**hid** e ous
Hispanic	His **pan** ic
historic	his **tor** ic
history	**hist** or y
holiday	**hol** i day
Hollywood	**Hol** ly wood
homicide	**hom** i cide
hominy	**hom** i ny
Honduras	Hon **du** ras
honesty	**hon** es ty
horizon	hor **i** zon
horrible	**hor** ri ble
Hosea	Ho **se** a
hospital	**hos** pi tal
however	how **ev** er
humorous	**hu** mor ous
Hungary	**Hun** ga ry
hungrily	**hun** gri ly
Huntington	Hun **ting** ton
Hyacinth	**Hy** a cinth
	Hy a cinth
hydrogen	**hy** dro gen
hyena	hy **e** na
hyphenate	**hy** phen ate
hypnosis	hyp **no** sis
hypnotize	**hyp** no tize
hypocrite	**hyp** o crite
icicle	**i** ci cle
Idaho	**I** da ho
idiom	**id** i om
igneous	**ig** ne ous
ignition	ig **ni** tion
ignorance	**ig** nor ance
ignorant	**ig** nor ant
iguana	i **gua** na
illegal	il **le** gal
Illinois	Il li **nois**
illusion	il **lu** sion
illustrate	**il** lus trate
imitate	**im** i tate
immature	im ma **ture**
immigrant	**im** mi grant
immigrate	**im** mi grate
imminent	**im** mi nent
immobile	im **mo** bile
immoral	im **mor** al
immortal	im **mor** tal
immunize	**im** mu nize
impala	im **pal** a
impartial	im **par** tial
impatient	im **pa** tient
imperfect	im **per** fect
implement	**im** ple ment
implicit	im **plic** it
impolite	im po **lite**
importance	im **por** tance
important	im **por** tant

imposing	im **pos** ing
impostor	im **post** er
impression	im **pres** sion
imprison	im **pris** on
improper	im **prop** er
improvement	im **prove** ment
improvise	**im** pro vise
impudent	im **pu** dent
impulsive	im **pul** sive
inactive	in **ac** tive
incentive	in **cen** tive
incessant	in **ces** sant
incident	**in** ci dent
incision	in **ci** sion
incisor	in **ci** sor
inclusion	in **clu** sion
incomplete	in com **plete**
incorrect	in cor **rect**
indebted	in **debt** ed
India	**In** di a
Indian	**In** di an
indicate	**in** di cate
indignant	in **dig** nant
indigo	**in** di go
Indira	In **di** ra
industry	**in** dus try
inertia	in **er** tia
infancy	**in** fan cy
infantry	**in** fan try
infection	in **fec** tion
infectious	in **fec** tious
infielder	**in** field er
infinite	**in** fi nite
inflation	in **fla** tion
inflection	in **flec** tion
influence	**in** flu ence
informal	in **for** mal
infrequent	in **fre** quent
ingenious	in **gen** ious
inhaler	in **hal** er
inherit	in **her** it
inhumane	in hu **mane**
initial	in **i** tial
injection	in **jec** tion
injury	**in** ju ry
injustice	in **jus** tice
innocence	**in** no cence
innocent	**in** no cent
inquiry	**in** quir y
inscription	in **scrip** tion
insecure	**in** se cure
insincere	in sin **cere**
insistent	in **sist** ent
insolent	**in** so lent
inspection	in **spec** tion
inspector	in **spec** tor
installment	in **stall** ment
instantly	**in** stant ly
instinctive	in **stinc** tive
institute	**in** sti tute
instruction	in **struc** tion
instructor	in **struc** tor
instrument	**in** stru ment
insulate	**in** su late
insulin	**in** su lin
insurance	in **sur** ance
integer	**in** te ger
integrate	**in** te grate
intellect	**in** tel lect
intensive	in **ten** sive

intention	in **ten** tion
interact	in ter **act**
intercept	**in** ter cept
interest	**in** ter est
interface	**in** ter face
internal	in **ter** nal
internet	**in** ter net
interpret	in **ter** pret
interrupt	in ter **rupt**
interstate	**in** ter state
interval	**in** ter val
internet	in ter **net**
interview	**in** ter view
intestine	in **tes** tine
intimate	**in** ti mate
intrepid	in **trep** id
intricate	**in** tri cate
introduce	in tro **duce**
inundate	**in** un date
invalid	in **val** id
invasion	in **va** sion
intention	in **ten** tion
inventive	in **ven** tive
inventor	in **ven** tor
investment	in **vest** ment
investor	in **ves** tor
inwardly	**in** ward ly
iodine	**i** o dine
	i o dine
Iowa	**I** o wa
ironic	i **ron** ic
irony	**i** ron y
irrigate	**ir** ri gate
irritate	**ir** ri tate
Isaiah	I **sa** iah
Ishmael	Ish ma el
Islamic	Is **lam** ic
islander	**is** land er
isolate	**i** so late
Israel	**Is** ra el
Israeli	Is **rae** li
Istanbul	**Is** tan bul
Italian	I **tal** ian
italic	i **tal** ic
Italy	**It** a ly
itemize	**i** tem ize
Ivanhoe	**I** van hoe
ivory	**i** vo ry
Jacksonville	**Jack** son ville
Jacqueline	**Jac** que line
	Jac que line
Jakarta	Ja **kar** ta
Jamaica	Ja **mai** ca
janitor	**jan** i tor
Japanese	Jap a **nese**
jealousy	**jeal** ous y
Jefferson	**Jef** fer son
Jennifer	**Jen** ni fer
jeopardize	**jeop** ard ize
jeopardy	**jeop** ard y
Jeremy	**Jer** e my
Jessica	**Jes** si ca
Jezebel	**Jez** e bel
Joachim	Jo **a** chim
Jonathan	**Jon** a than
Josephine	**Jo** se phine
Joshua	**Josh** u a
journalism	**jour** nal ism
journalist	**jour** nal ist
jovial	**jo** vi al

jubilant	**ju** bi lant
jubilee	ju bi **lee**
Judaism	**Ju** da ism
	Ju da sim
judicial	ju **di** cial
judicious	ju **di** cious
jujitsu	ju **jit** su
juniper	**ju** ni per
Jupiter	**Ju** pi ter
justify	**jus** ti fy
juvenile	**ju** ve nile
Kabuki	Ka **bu** ki
kangaroo	kan ga **roo**
Karachi	Ka ra chi
karate	ka **ra** te
katydid	**ka** ty did
Kazakhstan	**Ka** zahk stan
Kenisha	Ke **ni** sha
Kennedy	**Ken** ne dy
Kentucky	Ken **tuck** y
kerosene	**ker** o sene
kilowatt	**kil** o watt
Kimberly	**Kim** ber ly
kimono	ki **mo** no
	ki **mo** no
Kinshasa	Kin sha sa
koala	ko **a** la
Korean	Kor **e** an
Kosovo	Ko so vo
Kyrgyzstan	**Kyr** gyz stan
	Kyr gyz **stan**
laborer	**la** bor er
Lafayette	La fa **yette**
Lakeisha	Lak ei sha
Lancaster	**Lan** cas ter
	Lan cas ster
larceny	**lar** ce ny
Laredo	La **re** do
Larissa	La ris sa
Latasha	La **ta** sha
Latina	La **ti** na
Latino	La **ti** no
Latisha	La ti sha
latitude	**lat** i tude
Latoya	La toy a
Latvia	**Lat** vi a
lavender	**lav** en der
Lebanon	**Leb** a non
	Leb a non
legacy	**leg** a cy
lemonade	**lem** on ade
lenient	**le** ni ent
leotard	**le** o tard
leprechaun	**lep** re chaun
Lesotho	Le so tho
lettering	**let** ter ing
Lexington	**Lex** ing ton
liable	**li** a ble
liberal	**lib** er al
liberate	**lib** er ate
Liberty	**Lib** er ty
liberty	**lib** er ty
library	**li** brar y
licorice	**lic** or ice
	lic or ice
Liechtenstein	**Liech** ten stein
lieutenant	lieu **ten** ant
ligament	**lig** a ment
likable	**lik** a ble
limerick	**lim** er ick

limousine	lim ou **sine**
linear	**lin** e ar
literal	**lit** er al
literate	**lit** er ate
Livingston	**Liv** ing ston
lobbyist	**lob** by ist
location	lo **ca** tion
logical	**log** i cal
lollipop	**lol** li pop
lopsided	**lop** sid ed
lottery	**lot** ter y
Louisville	**Lou** is ville
lovable	**lov** a ble
loyalty	**loy** al ty
lubricate	**lu** bri cate
Lucinda	Lu **cin** da
luckily	**luck** i ly
ludicrous	**lu** di crous
lullaby	**lul** la by
luminous	**lu** mi nous
Luxembourg	**Lux** em bourg
luxury	**lux** u ry
	***lux** ur y
Macau	Ma **cau**
MacDougal	Mac **Dou** gal
machete	ma **chet** e
machinist	ma **chin** ist
mackerel	**mack** er el
mackintosh	**mack** in tosh
maddening	**mad** den ing
Madison	**Mad** i son
magazine	**mag** a zine
Magdalene	**Mag** da lene
magical	**mag** i cal
magician	ma **gi** cian
magistrate	**mag** is trate
magnetic	mag **net** ic
magnetism	**mag** net ism
magnetize	**mag** net ize
magnify	**mag** ni fy
magnitude	**mag** ni tude
Mahatma	Ma **hat** ma
maintenance	**main** te nance
majestic	ma **jes** tic
majesty	**ma** jes ty
majorette	ma jor **ette**
Malachi	**Mal** a chi
malady	**mal** a dy
Malawi	Ma **la** wi
Malaysia	Ma **lay** sia
malicious	ma **li** cious
malignant	ma **lig** nant
Mallory	**Mal** lo ry
management	**man** age ment
manager	**man** ag er
manatee	**man** a tee
Manchester	**Man** ches ter
Mandarin	**Man** da rin
Mandela	**Man** de la
mandolin	man do **lin**
maneuver	ma **neu** ver
maniac	**ma** ni ac
manicure	**man** i cure
Manila	Ma **nil** a
mannequin	**man** ne quin
mannerism	**man** ner ism
manual	**man** u al
manuscript	**man** u script
maraca	ma **ra** ca
marathon	**mar** a thon

margarine	**mar** ga rine
Margery	**Mar** ger y
marginal	**mar** gin al
Mariah	Mar **i** ah
marigold	**mar** i gold
Marilyn	**Mar** i lyn
marina	ma **ri** na
marinate	**mar** i nate
mariner	**mar** i ner
Marissa	Ma **ris** sa
maritime	**mar** i time
marmalade	**mar** ma lade
marshmallow	**marsh** mal low
Martinique	Mar ti **nique**
marvelous	**mar** vel ous
Maryland	**Mar** y land
mascara	mas **car** a
masculine	**mas** cu line
masonry	**ma** son ry
masquerade	mas quer **ade**
massacre	**mas** sa cre
masterful	**mas** ter ful
masterpiece	**mas** ter piece
mastery	**mas** ter y
maternal	ma **ter** nal
matinee	mat i **nee**
matriarch	**ma** tri arch
maximum	**max** i mum
meander	me **an** der
measurement	**meas** ure ment
mechanic	me **chan** ic
mechanism	**mech** an ism
medallion	me **dal** lion
media	**me** di a
median	**me** di an
medical	**med** i cal
medicate	**med** i cate
medicine	**med** i cine
meditate	**med** i tate
medium	**me** di um
megabyte	**meg** a byte
Melinda	Me **lin** da
Melissa	Me **lis** sa
melody	**mel** o dy
membership	**mem** ber ship
memento	me **men** to
memorize	**mem** or ize
menial	**me** ni al
menorah	me **nor** ah
mentally	**men** tal ly
Mercedes	Mer **ce** des
merchandise	**mer** chan dise
merciful	**mer** ci ful
merciless	**mer** ci less
mercury	**mer** cu ry
Mercury	**Mer** cu ry
Meredith	**Mer** e dith
meridian	me **rid** i an
mesmerize	**mes** mer ize
messenger	**mes** sen ger
Messiah	Mes **si** ah
metallic	me **tal** lic
metaphor	**met** a phor
meteor	**me** te or
metronome	**met** ro nome
Mexican	**Mex** i can
Miami	Mi **am** i
	Mi **am** i
Michigan	**Mich** i gan
midfielder	**mid** fiel der

midsummer	mid **sum** mer
midwinter	mid **win** ter
migration	mi **gra** tion
militant	**mil** i tant
militia	mi **li** tia
milligram	**mil** li gram
millionaire	mil lion **aire**
millipede	**mil** li pede
Milwaukee	Mil **wau** kee
minaret	min a **ret**
mineral	**min** er al
minimum	**min** i mum
minuet	min u **et**
minuscule	**min** is cule
miracle	**mir** a cle
Miriam	**Mir** i am
misbehave	mis be **have**
mischievous	**mis** chie vous
misconduct	mis **con** duct
misfortune	mis **for** tune
misgiving	mis **giv** ing
mispronounce	mis pro **nounce**
Missouri	Mis **sour** i
mistaken	mis **tak** en
mistletoe	**mis** tle toe
mockery	**mock** er y
moderate	**mod** er ate
Modesto	Mo **des** to
modify	**mod** i fy
molasses	mo **las** ses
molecule	**mol** e cule
momentous	mo **men** tous
momentum	mo **men** tum
	mo **men** tum
Monaco	**Mon** a co
monarchy	**mon** ar chy
Mongolia	Mon **go** li a
Monisha	Mo **ni** sha
monitor	**mon** i tor
monogram	**mon** o gram
monotone	**mon** o tone
Montana	Mon **tan** a
Montserrat	Mont ser **rat**
monument	**mon** u ment
moodily	**mood** i ly
Morocco	Mor **oc** co
mosaic	mo **sa** ic
mosquito	mos **qui** to
motherly	**moth** er ly
motivate	**mo** ti vate
motorist	**mo** tor ist
mountaineer	moun tain **eer**
mountainous	**moun** tain ous
movable	**mov** a ble
Mozambique	Mo zam **bique**
Muhammad	Mu **ham** mad
mulberry	**mul** ber ry
	mul ber ry
multiple	**mul** ti ple
multiply	**mul** ti ply
multitude	**mul** ti tude
munitions	mu **ni** tion
muscular	**mus** cu lar
museum	mu **se** um
musical	**mu** si cal
musician	mu **si** cian
musketeer	mus ket **eer**
Mustafa	Mu **sta** fa
mutation	mu **ta** tion
mutinous	**mu** ti nous

mutiny	**mu** ti ny
mutual	**mu** tu al
Myanmar	**My** an mar
myriad	**myr** i ad
mystery	**mys** ter y
mystify	**mys** ti fy
mythical	**myth** i cal
Naperville	**Na** per ville
narcissus	nar **cis** sus
narcotic	nar **cot** ic
narrative	**nar** ra tive
narrator	**nar** ra tor
Natasha	Na **ta** sha
national	**na** tion al
natural	**nat** u ral
nautical	**nau** ti cal
nautilus	**nau** ti lus
navigate	**nav** i gate
Nebraska	Ne **bras** ka
nebula	**neb** u la
nebulous	**neb** u lous
nectarine	**nec** tar ine
negative	**neg** a tive
negligent	**neg** li gent
neighborly	**neigh** bor ly
Netherlands	**Neth** er lands
Nevada	Ne **vad** a
nicotine	**nic** o tine
nightingale	**night** in gale
ninetieth	**nine** ti eth
Nineveh	**Nin** e veh
nitrogen	**ni** tro gen
nobility	no **bil** i ty
nocturnal	noc **tur** nal
nomadic	no **mad** ic
nominate	**nom** i nate
nominee	nom i **nee**
nostalgia	nos **tal** gia
nostalgic	nos **tal** gic
notable	**no** ta ble
notation	no **ta** tion
notify	**no** ti fy
nourishment	**nour** ish ment
novelist	**nov** el ist
novelty	**nov** el ty
November	Nov **em** ber
numeral	**nu** mer al
numerous	**nu** mer ous
nutrient	**nu** tri ent
nutrition	nu **tri** tion
nutritious	nu **tri** tious
oasis	o **a** sis
Obama	O **ba** ma
obelisk	**ob** e lisk
objection	ob **jec** tion
objective	ob **jec** tive
obnoxious	ob **nox** ious
	ob **nox** ious
observant	ob **serv** ant
obsession	ob **ses** sion
	ob **se** sion
obsolete	ob so **lete**
obstacle	**ob** sta cle
obstinate	**ob** sti nate
obstruction	ob **struc** tion
	ob **struc** tion
obvious	**ob** vi ous
occasion	oc **ca** sion
occupant	**oc** cu pant
occupy	**oc** cu py

occurrence	oc **cur** rence
ocelot	**oc** e lot
octagon	**oc** ta gon
Octavia	Oc **ta** vi a
October	Oc **to** ber
octopus	**oc** to pus
oddity	**odd** i ty
Odessa	O **des** sa
odious	**o** di ous
offensive	of **fen** sive
officer	**of** fi cer
official	of **fi** cial
Ohio	O **hi** o
Omaha	**O** ma ha
ominous	**om** i nous
omission	o **mis** sion
	o **mis** sion
omnivore	**om** ni vore
oncoming	**on** com ing
opener	**o** pen er
opening	**o** pen ing
operate	**op** er ate
opinion	o **pin** ion
opossum	o **pos** sum
opponent	op **po** nent
optical	**op** ti cal
optician	op **ti** cian
optional	**op** tion al
orator	**or** a tor
orchestra	**or** ches tra
orderly	**or** der ly
ordinance	**or** di nance
Oregon	**Or** e gon
	Or e gon
organic	or **gan** ic
organism	**or** gan ism
organize	**or** gan ize
orient	**or** i ent
origin	**or** i gin
	or i gin
oriole	**or** i ole
	or i ole
Orlando	Or **lan** do
ornament	**or** na ment
	or na ment
Orpheus	**Or** phe us
	Or phe us
orthodox	or **tho** dox
Osaka	O **sa** ka
	O sa ka
outdated	out **dat** ed
outrageous	out **ra** geous
outrigger	**out** rig ger
ovary	**o** va ry
pacifist	**pac** i fist
pacify	**pac** i fy
pagoda	pa **go** da
pajamas	pa **ja** mas
Pakistan	**Pa** ki stan
	***Pak** i stan
Palestine	**Pal** es tine
palisade	pal i **sade**
palmetto	pal **met** to
Panama	**Pan** a ma
pancreas	**pan** cre as
pantomime	**pan** to mime
paprika	pap **ri** ka
	pap **ri** ka
papyrus	pa **py** rus
parable	**par** a ble

parachute	**par** a chute
paradise	**par** a dise
paradox	**par** a dox
paragraph	**par** a graph
Paraguay	**Par** a guay
parakeet	**par** a keet
parallel	**par** al lel
	par al lel
paralyze	**par** a lyze
paramount	**par** a mount
paraphrase	**par** a phrase
parasite	**par** a site
parasol	**par** a sol
parental	pa **ren** tal
parliament	**par** lia ment
parody	**par** o dy
particle	**par** ti cle
partition	par **ti** tion
partnership	**part** ner ship
passenger	**pas** sen ger
passionate	**pas** sion ate
pastoral	**pas** tor al
pastrami	pas **tra** mi
paternal	pa **ter** nal
Patterson	**Pat** ter son
pathetic	pa **thet** ic
patriarch	**pa** tri arch
patriot	**pa** tri ot
patronage	**pa** tron age
patronize	**pa** tron ize
pavilion	pa **vil** ion
peculiar	pe **cu** liar
pedestal	**ped** es tal
pedicure	**ped** i cure
pedigree	**ped** i gree

pelican	**pel** i can
penalize	**pe** nal ize
penalty	**pen** al ty
pendulum	**pen** du lum
pentagon	**pen** ta gon
Pentecost	**Pen** te cost
	Pen te cost
peony	**pe** o ny
percentage	per **cent** age
perception	per **cep** tion
perceptive	per **cep** tive
Perceval	**Per** ce val
percussion	per **cus** sion
perfection	per **fec** tion
perforate	**per** for ate
performance	per **for** mance
perilous	**per** il ous
period	**pe** ri od
periscope	**per** i scope
permanent	**per** ma nent
permeate	**per** me ate
permission	per **mis** sion
pernicious	per **ni** cious
persecute	**per** se cute
persevere	per se **vere**
persimmon	per **sim** mon
persistent	per **sis** tent
personal	**per** son al
personnel	per son **nel**
perspective	per **spec** tive
persuasion	per **sua** sion
pertinent	**per** ti nent
pesticide	**pes** ti cide
petition	pe **ti** tion
petrify	**pet** ri fy

petticoat	**pet** ti coat
petunia	pe **tu** nia
Pharisee	**Phar** i see
pharmacist	**phar** ma cist
pharmacy	**phar** ma cy
Philemon	Phi **le** mon
Philippa	**Phil** ip pa
phobia	**pho** bi a
phonetic	pho **net** ic
phosphorus	**phos** phor us
physical	**phys** i cal
physician	phy **si** cian
physicist	**phys** i cist
pianist	**pi** an ist
piccolo	**pic** co lo
pictograph	**pic** to graph
picturesque	pic tur **esque**
pimento	pi **men** to
pinnacle	**pin** na cle
pioneer	pi o **neer**
piracy	**pi** ra cy
piranha	pi **ra** nha
pirouette	pir ou **ette**
pitiful	**pit** i ful
Placido	Pla **ci** do
plantation	plan **ta** tion
platinum	**plat** i num
platypus	**plat** y pus
pliable	**pli** a ble
pneumatic	pneu **mat** ic
pneumonia	pneu **mo** nia
podium	**po** di um
poetry	**po** et ry
	po et ry
poisonous	**poi** son ous
policy	**pol** i cy
polio	**po** li o
politic	**pol** i tic
polliwog	**pol** li wog
pollutant	pol **lu** tant
pollution	pol **lu** tion
Pomona	Po **mo** na
populate	**pop** u late
porcupine	**por** cu pine
portable	**port** a ble
portico	**por** ti co
portrayal	por **tray** al
Portugal	**Por** tu gal
Portuguese	**Por** tu guese
position	po **si** tion
positive	**pos** i tive
possession	pos **ses** sion
possessive	pos **ses** sive
possible	**pos** si ble
	pos si ble
possibly	**pos** si bly
potato	po **ta** to
potential	po **ten** tial
pottery	**pot** ter y
poverty	**pov** er ty
powdery	**pow** der y
powerful	**pow** er ful
practical	**prac** ti cal
precaution	pre **cau** tion
precedent	**prec** e dent
precipice	**prec** i pice
precision	pre **ci** sion
precocious	pre **co** cious
predator	**pred** a tor
predicate	**pred** i cate

prediction	pre **dic** tion
preference	**pref** er ence
prejudice	**prej** u dice
premature	pre ma **ture**
prescription	pre **scrip** tion
presently	**pres** ent ly
president	**pres** i dent
prevalent	**prev** a lent
prevention	pre **ven** tion
preventive	pre **ven** tive
previous	**pre** vi ous
Pricilla	Pri **cil** la
primary	**pri** ma ry
	pri ma ry
	***pri** mar y
primeval	pri **me** val
primitive	**prim** i tive
principal	**prin** ci pal
	prin ci pal
principle	**prin** ci ple
privacy	**pri** va cy
probable	**prob** a ble
probably	**prob** a bly
probation	pro **ba** tion
procedure	pro **ce** dure
procession	pro **ces** sion
prodigy	**prod** i gy
producer	pro **duc** er
production	pro **duc** tion
productive	pro **duc** tive
profession	pro **fes** sion
professor	pro **fes** sor
proficient	pro **fi** cient
profusion	pro **fu** sion
progressive	pro **gres** sive

prohibit	pro **hib** it
	pro **hib** it
	pro **hib** it
projectile	pro **jec** tile
	pro **jec** tile
projection	pro **jec** tion
projector	pro **jec** tor
prolific	pro **lif** ic
promenade	prom e **nade**
prominent	**prom** i nent
promotion	pro **mo** tion
propeller	pro **pel** ler
properly	**prop** er ly
property	**prop** er ty
prophecy	**proph** e cy
proportion	pro **por** tion
proposal	pro **pos** al
propulsion	pro **pul** sion
prosecute	**pros** e cute
prospective	pro **spec** tive
prospector	**pros** pec tor
prosperous	**pros** per ous
protection	pro **tec** tion
protective	pro **tect** ive
protector	pro **tec** tor
Protestant	**Prot** es tant
protoplasm	**pro** to plasm
protractor	**pro** trac tor
provided	pro **vid** ed
Providence	**Prov** i dence
provincial	pro **vin** cial
provision	pro **vi** sion
pseudonym	**pseu** do nym
puberty	**pu** ber ty
publicly	**pub** lic ly

publisher	**pub** lish er
pulverize	**pul** ver ize
punctuate	**punc** tu ate
punishment	**pun** ish ment
purify	**pu** ri fy
	***pur** i fy
Puritan	**Pu** ri tan
	***Pur** i tan
purity	**pu** ri ty
	***pur** i ty
purposeful	**pur** pose ful
purposely	**pur** pose ly
pyramid	**pyr** a mid
quadrangle	**quad** ran gle
quadruped	**quad** ru ped
quadruple	quad **ru** ple
quadruplet	quad **ru** plet
qualify	**qual** i fy
quality	**qual** i ty
quantity	**quan** ti ty
quarantine	**quar** an tine
quarterly	**quar** ter ly
quintuplet	quin **tu** plet
quizzical	**quiz** zi cal
quotation	quo **ta** tion
radiant	**ra** di ant
radiate	**ra** di ate
radical	**rad** i cal
radio	**ra** di o
radium	**ra** di um
radius	**ra** di us
Ramadan	Ram a dan
rational	**ra** tion al
reaction	re **ac** tion
readily	**read** i ly

realize	**re** al ize
reappear	re ap **pear**
reasoning	**rea** son ing
reassure	re as **sure**
rebellion	re **bel** lion
rebellious	re **bel** lious
recapture	re **cap** ture
receiver	re **ceiv** er
reception	re **cep** tion
recession	re **ces** sion
recital	re **cit** al
recognize	**rec** og nize
recollect	rec ol **lect**
recommend	rec om **mend**
recorder	re **cord** er
recording	re **cord** ing
recover	re **cov** er
rectangle	**rec** tan gle
rectify	**rec** ti fy
recycle	re **cy** cle
reduction	re **duc** tion
redundant	re **dun** dant
reelect	re e **lect**
referee	ref er **ee**
reference	**ref** er ence
reflection	re **flec** tion
reflector	re **flec** tor
refraction	re **frac** tion
refreshments	re **fresh** ments
refugee	ref u **gee**
refusal	re **fus** al
regarding	re **gard** ing
regiment	**reg** i ment
register	**reg** is ter
regretful	re **gret** ful

regular	**reg** u lar
regulate	**reg** u late
rehearsal	re **hears** al
reimburse	re im **burse**
reinforce	re in **force**
related	re **lat** ed
relation	re **la** tion
relative	**rel** a tive
relevant	**rel** e vant
religion	re **li** gion
religious	re **li** gious
reluctant	re **luc** tant
remainder	re **main** der
remedy	**rem** e dy
remember	re **mem** ber
reminisce	rem i **nisce**
remodel	re **mod** el
removal	re **mov** al
rendezvous	**ren** dez vous
renovate	**ren** o vate
repentance	re **pent** ance
repertoire	**rep** er toire
replica	**rep** li ca
reporter	re **port** er
represent	rep re **sent**
reprimand	**rep** ri mand
reproduce	re pro **duce**
republic	re **pub** lic
repulsive	re **pul** sive
requirement	re **quire** ment
resemblance	re **sem** blance
resemble	re **sem** ble
resentful	re **sent** ful
reservoir	**res** er voir
residence	**res** i dence
resident	**res** i dent
	res i dent
residue	**res** i due
resistance	re **sist** ance
resonate	**res** o nate
respectful	re **spect** ful
restaurant	**res** tau rant
restriction	re **stric** tion
retina	**ret** i na
retriever	re **triev** er
reunion	re **un** ion
revenue	**rev** e nue
reverence	**rev** er ence
revolting	re **volt** ing
revolver	re **volv** er
Richardson	**Rich** ard son
ridicule	**rid** i cule
rigorous	**rig** or ous
robbery	**rob** ber y
Roberta	Ro **ber** ta
Rochester	**Roch** es ter
rodeo	**ro** de o
	ro **de** o
romantic	ro **man** tic
	ro **man** tic
rotary	**ro** ta ry
rotation	ro **ta** tion
Rowena	Ro **we** na
royalty	**roy** al ty
sabotage	**sab** o tage
sacrament	**sac** ra ment
sacrifice	**sac** ri fice
safari	sa **fa** ri
salami	sa **la** mi
salary	**sal** a ry

Salinas	Sa li nas
saliva	sa **li** va
Salvador	**Sal** va dor
Samantha	Sam **an** tha
	*Sa **man** tha
Samoa	Sa **mo** a
sarcastic	sar **cas** tic
satisfy	**sat** is fy
saturate	**sat** u rate
Saturday	**Sat** ur day
sauerkraut	**sau** er kraut
Savannah	Sa **van** nah
savannah	sa **van** nah
saxophone	**sax** o phone
scarcity	**scar** ci ty
scavenger	**scav** en ger
scenery	**scen** er y
scholarly	**schol** ar ly
scholastic	scho **las** tic
scientist	**sci** en tist
scorpion	**scor** pi on
scrupulous	**scru** pu lous
seasonal	**sea** son al
seasoning	**sea** son ing
Seattle	Se **at** tle
secular	**sec** u lar
sediment	**sed** i ment
seemingly	**seem** ing ly
segregate	**seg** re gate
seismograph	**seis** mo graph
selection	se **lec** tion
semester	se **mes** ter
Semitic	Se **mit** ic
senator	**sen** a tor
Senegal	**Sen** e gal
sensation	sen **sa** tion
	sen **sa** tion
sensible	**sen** si ble
sensitive	**sen** si tive
sensory	**sen** sor y
sentiment	**sen** ti ment
September	Sep **tem** ber
	Sep **tem** ber
sequoia	se **quoi** a
serenade	ser e **nade**
serial	**se** ri al
serious	**se** ri ous
sesame	**ses** a me
seventeen	**sev** en teen
seventeenth	**sev** en teenth
shadowy	**shad** ow y
Shakeela	Sha **kee** la
Shakira	Sha **ki** ra
Shania	Sha **ni** a
Sheridan	**Sher** i dan
Sherisa	Sher **i** sa
shortcoming	**short** com ing
shrubbery	**shrub** ber y
Sicily	**Sic** i ly
siesta	si **es** ta
signature	**sig** na ture
signify	**sig** ni fy
silhouette	sil hou **ette**
silicon	**sil** i con
silvery	**sil** ver y
similar	**sim** i lar
simile	**sim** i le
simplify	**sim** pli fy
simulate	**sim** u late
Singapore	**Sin** ga pore

	***Sing** a pore
singular	**sin** gu lar
	***sing** u lar
sixtieth	**six** ti eth
sizable	**siz** a ble
skeleton	**skel** e ton
skeptical	**skep** ti cal
slavery	**slav** er y
slippery	**slip** per y
slovenly	**slov** en ly
	slov en ly
socialism	**so** cial ism
socialize	**so** cial ize
sodium	**so** di um
soluble	**sol** u ble
solution	so **lu** tion
sombrero	som **bre** ro
Somerby	**Som** er by
somersault	**som** er sault
sonata	so **na** ta
Sophia	So **phi** a
soprano	so **pran** o
sorcerer	**sor** cer er
sorceress	**sor** cer ess
souvenir	**sou** ve nir
spaghetti	spa **ghet** ti
sparingly	**spar** ing ly
spatula	**spat** u la
specialist	**spe** cial ist
specialize	**spe** cial ize
specific	spe **cif** ic
specify	**spec** i fy
specimen	**spec** i men
spectacle	**spec** ta cle
speculate	**spec** u late

spirited	**spir** it ed
sportsmanship	**sports** man ship
staccato	stac **ca** to
stadium	**sta** di um
stalactite	sta **lac** tite
stalagmite	sta **lag** mite
statistic	sta **tis** tic
steadily	**stead** i ly
Stephanie	**Steph** a nie
Stephanus	**Ste** pha nus
	***Steph** a nus
stereo	**ster** e o
sterilize	**ster** i lize
stethoscope	**steth** o scope
stewardess	**stew** ard ess
stimulate	**stim** u late
stimuli	**stim** u li
stimulus	**stim** u lus
straightforward	straight **for** ward
stratosphere	**strat** o sphere
strenuous	**stren** u ous
studio	**stu** di o
studious	**stu** di ous
subdivide	**sub** di vide
subjective	sub **jec** tive
submission	sub **mis** sion
submissive	sub **mis** sive
subscription	sub **scrip** tion
subsequent	**sub** se quent
substantial	sub **stan** tial
substitute	**sub** sti tute
subtitle	**sub** ti tle
subtraction	sub **trac** tion
suburban	sub **ur** ban
successful	suc **cess** ful

succession	suc **ces** sion
successive	suc **ces** sive
successor	suc **ces** sor
sufficient	suf **fi** cient
suffocate	**suf** fo cate
suffragist	**suf** fra gist
suggestion	sug **ges** tion
suitable	**suit** a ble
summarize	**sum** ma rize
summary	**sum** ma ry
sumptuous	**sump** tu ous
superscript	**su** per script
supervise	**su** per vise
supplement	**sup** ple ment
surgery	**sur** ger y
surrender	sur **ren** der
surroundings	sur **round** ings
surveyor	sur **vey** or
survival	sur **viv** al
survivor	sur **vi** vor
suspender	sus **pend** er
suspension	sus **pen** sion
suspicion	sus **pi** cion
suspicious	sus **pi** cious
Swaziland	**Swa** zi land
sweetener	**sweet** en er
Switzerland	**Switz** er land
sycamore	**syc** a more
syllable	**syl** la ble
Sylvester	Syl **ves** ter
symbolic	sym **bol** ic
symbolize	**sym** bol ize
symmetry	**sym** me try
sympathize	**sym** pa thize
sympathy	**sym** pa thy
symphony	**sym** pho ny
synagogue	**syn** a gogue
synchronize	**syn** chro nize
synonym	**syn** o nym
synopsis	syn **op** sis
synoptic	syn **op** tic
synthetic	syn **thet** ic
Syracuse	**Syr** a cuse
Syria	**Syr** i a
Tabitha	**Tab** i tha
Tacoma	Ta **co** ma
talented	**tal** ent ed
Talitha	Ta **li** tha
talkative	**talk** a tive
tambourine	tam bou **rine**
tangerine	tan ger **rine**
Tanisha	Ta **ni** sha
tantalize	**tan** ta lize
tapestry	**tap** es try
tarpaulin	tar **pau** lin
taxation	tax **a** tion
technical	**tech** ni cal
technician	tech **ni** cian
tedious	**te** di ous
teenager	**teen** ag er
telegram	**tel** e gram
telegraph	**tel** e graph
telephone	**tel** e phone
telescope	**tel** e scope
televise	**tel** e vise
temperate	**tem** per ate
temptation	temp **ta** tion
tenacious	te **na** cious
tendency	**ten** den cy
tenement	**ten** e ment

Tennessee	Ten nes **see**
tentacle	**ten** ta cle
tentative	**ten** ta tive
Teresa	Te **re** sa
terminal	**ter** mi nal
terminate	**ter** mi nate
terrible	**ter** ri ble
terrier	**ter** ri er
terrific	ter **rif** ic
terrify	**ter** ri fy
terrorism	**ter** ror ism
terrorist	**ter** ror ist
terrorize	**ter** ror ize
testament	**tes** ta ment
testify	**tes** ti fy
thanksgiving	thanks **giv** ing
therapist	**ther** a pist
therapy	**ther** a py
Theresa	The **re** sa
	*Ther **e** sa
thermostat	**ther** mo stat
thesaurus	the **sau** rus
thirtieth	**thir** ti eth
tiara	ti **ar** a
Tiffany	**Tif** fa ny
Timothy	**Tim** o thy
Tobias	To **bi** as
toboggan	to **bog** gan
together	to **geth** er
Tokelau	To ke **lau**
Toledo	To **le** do
tolerance	**tol** er ance
tolerant	**tol** er ant
tolerate	tol er ate
tomahawk	**tom** a hawk
tomato	to **ma** to
tomorrow	to **mor** row
Topeka	To **pe** ka
topical	**top** i cal
tornado	tor **na** do
torpedo	tor **pe** do
tortilla	tor **til** la
tournament	**tour** na ment
tourniquet	**tour** ni quet
towering	**tow** er ing
trachea	**tra** che a
tradition	tra **di** tion
tragedy	**trag** e dy
trampoline	**tram** po line
transaction	trans **ac** tion
transformer	trans **form** er
transfusion	trans **fu** sion
transistor	tran **sis** tor
transition	tran **si** tion
translation	trans **la** tion
translator	trans **la** tor
translucent	trans **lu** cent
transmission	trans **mis** sion
transmitter	trans **mit** ter
	***trans** mit ter
transparent	trans **par** ent
trapezoid	**trap** e zoid
traumatic	trau **mat** ic
traveler	**trav** el er
treacherous	**treach** er ous
treachery	**treach** er y
treasurer	**treas** ur er
treasury	**treas** ur y
tremendous	tre **men** dous
triangle	**tri** an gle

triathlon	tri **ath** lon
tricycle	**tri** cy cle
trilogy	**tril** o gy
Trinity	**Trin** i ty
triumphant	tri **um** phant
tropical	**trop** i cal
tsunami	tsu **na** mi
tuition	tu **i** tion
Tunisia	Tu ni sia
turbulent	**tur** bu lent
turpentine	**tur** pen tine
Tuvalu	**Tu** va lu
tuxedo	tux **e** do
twentieth	**twen** ti eth
typical	**typ** i cal
tyranny	**tyr** an ny
Uganda	U **gan** da
ultrasound	**ul** tra sound
Ulysses	U **lys** ses
umbrella	um **brel** la
unaware	un a **ware**
uncertain	un **cer** tain
uncommon	un **com** mon
unconcerned	un con **cerned**
unconscious	un **con** scious
uncover	un **cov** er
underneath	un der **neath**
understand	un der **stand**
uneasy	un **eas** y
unemployed	un em **ployed**
unequal	un **e** qual
uneven	un **e** ven
unfeeling	un **feel** ing
unfriendly	un **friend** ly
ungrateful	un **grate** ful
unhappy	un **hap** py
unhealthy	un **health** y
unicorn	**u** ni corn
uniform	**u** ni form
unify	**u** ni fy
unison	**u** ni son
universe	**u** ni verse
unlikely	un **like** ly
unlucky	un **luck** y
unprepared	un pre **pared**
unravel	un **rav** el
unruly	un **ru** ly
unsettled	un **set** tled
unshaken	un **sha** ken
unsightly	un **sight** ly
unstable	un **sta** ble
unsteady	un **stead** y
unwilling	un **will** ing
upbringing	up **bring** ing
upheaval	up **heav** al
Uranus	**U** ra nus
Uruguay	**U** ru guay
usual	**u** su al
utensil	u **ten** sil
uterus	**u** ter us
utility	u **til** i ty
utilize	**u** ti lize
vacancy	**va** can cy
vacation	va **ca** tion
vaccinate	**vac** ci nate
vagabond	**vag** a bond
vagina	va **gi** na
valentine	**val** en tine
Valerie	**Val** er ie
Vancouver	Van **cou** ver

vandalize	**van** dal ize
vanilla	va **nil** la
vanity	**van** i ty
various	**var** i ous
varsity	**var** si ty
vehicle	**ve** hi cle
velocity	ve **loc** i ty
venomous	**ven** om ous
ventricle	**ven** tri cle
veranda	ve **ran** da
versatile	**ver** sa tile
version	**ver** sion
vertebra	**ver** te bra
	ver te bra
vertebrate	**ver** te brate
vertical	**ver** ti cal
vertices	**ver** ti ces
veteran	**vet** er an
vibration	vi **bra** tion
victory	**vic** to ry
	***vic** tor y
video	**vid** e o
Vietnam	Vi et **nam**
	Vi et **nam**
vigilant	**vig** i lant
vigorous	**vig** or ous
vinegar	**vin** e gar
viola	vi **o** la
violate	**vi** o late
violence	**vi** o lence
violin	vi o lin
Virginia	Vir **gin** ia
virtual	**vir** tu al
visible	**vis** i ble
visitor	**vis** i tor
visual	**vis** u al
vitamin	**vi** ta min
vocalize	**vo** cal ize
volcanic	vol **can** ic
volcano	vol **ca** no
volunteer	vol **un** teer
wallaby	**wal** la by
warranty	**war** ran ty
Washington	**Wash** ing ton
watery	**wa** ter y
wearisome	**wea** ri some
Westminster	**West** min ster
whimsical	**whim** si cal
Whittaker	**Whit** ta ker
Wichita	**Wich** i ta
widower	**wid** ow er
wilderness	**wil** der ness
Wilkinson	**Wil** kin son
Wilmington	**Wil** ming ton
Wisconsin	Wis **con** sin
worshipper	**wor** ship per
Wyoming	Wy **o** ming
xylophone	**xy** lo phone
yellowish	**yel** low ish
yesterday	**yes** ter day
Yoruba	Yo ru ba
Zachary	**Za** cha ry
	*Zach a ry
Zambia	**Zam** bi a
Zanzibar	**Zan** zi bar
Zebedee	**Zeb** e dee
Zimbabwe	Zim **bab** we
zinnia	**zin** ni a
zucchini	zuc **chi** ni

4 Syllables

- In this list, the stressed syllable is indicated by **bold** print, and the schwa syllable is indicated by underlined print. These may vary based on dialect.
- In multi-syllable words, you will often find that one or more syllables in the word have a vowel schwa sound. This can be confusing for students who have learned that open syllables make a long vowel sound and closed syllables make a short vowel sound. Teaching students about the schwa sound is a valuable tool in teaching them to decode multi-syllable words.
- Four-syllable words often have more than one schwa sound. As student read longer words, they need to learn more how to "flex" the vowels. This means to try out different vowel sounds to see which one sounds like it fits in the word. The most common flex would be to try out the schwa sound for the different vowels in a multi-syllable word. Here are some examples of open vowel syllables that make the schwa sound instead of the long vowel sound:

ac a **dem** ic   **ac** cu ra cy   a **lu** mi num

- The accent/stress in a 4 syllable word will vary, and will be especially influenced by the suffixes in the word.

aberration	ab er **ra** tion	accuracy	**ac** cu ra cy
abolition	ab o **li** tion		*ac cur a cy
academic	ac a **dem** ic	accusation	ac cu **sa** tion
academy	a **cad** e my	accustomed	ac **cus** tom-ed
accelerate	ac **cel** er ate	acidity	a **cid** i ty
accentuate	ac **cen** tu ate	acknowledgment	ac **knowl** edg ment
acceptable	ac **cept** a ble	acquisition	ac qui **si** tion
accessible	ac **ces** si ble	Acropolis	A **crop** o lis
accessory	ac **ces** so ry	actually	**ac** tu al ly
accidental	ac ci **den** tal	acupuncture	**ac** u punc ture
accommodate	ac **com** mo date	adaptable	a **dapt** a ble
accompany	ac **com** pa ny	adaptation	ad ap **ta** tion
accomplishment	ac **com** plish ment	additional	ad **di** tion al
accordingly	ac **cord** ing ly	administer	ad **min** is ter
accordion	ac **cor** di on	admirable	**ad** mi ra ble
accumulate	ac **cu** mu late		*ad mir a ble

admiration	ad mi **ra** tion
admonition	ad mo **ni** tion
adolescent	ad o **les** cent
adorable	a **dor** a ble
advantageous	ad van **ta** geous
adventurous	ad **ven** tur ous
adversary	**ad** ver sar y
adversity	ad **ver** si ty
advertisement	ad ver **tise** ment
advertising	**ad** ver tis ing
aeronautic	aer o **nau** tic
affectionate	af **fec** tion ate
affirmative	af **firm** a tive
Afghanistan	Af **ghan** i stan
agility	a **gil** i ty
agitation	ag i **ta** tion
agonizing	**ag** o niz ing
agreeable	a **gree** a ble
agriculture	**ag** ri cul ture
Alabama	Al a **bam** a
Albania	Al **ba** ni a
Albuquerque	**Al** bu quer que
Alessandra	Al es **san** dra
Alexander	Al ex **an** der
Alexandra	Al ex **an** dra
Algeria	Al **ge** ri a
	Al **ger** i a
alimony	**al** i mo ny
allegory	**al** le go ry
	*al le gor y
alligator	**al** li ga tor
alphabetize	**al** pha bet ize
alteration	al ter **a** tion
alternative	al **ter** na tive
altimeter	al **tim** e ter
altogether	al to **geth** er
aluminum	a **lu** mi num
Amarillo	Am a **ril** lo
ambassador	am **bas** sa dor
	am **bas** sa dor
ambidextrous	am bi **dex** trous
ambiguous	am **big** u ous
ambivalent	am **biv** a lent
American	A **mer** i can
amiable	**a** mi a ble
ammunition	am mu **ni** tion
amphibian	am **phib** i an
amphibious	am **phib** i ous
amplifier	**am** pli fi er
anachronism	a **nach** ro nism
anaconda	an a **con** da
anesthesia	an es **the** sia
anesthetic	an es **the** tic
animated	**an** i mat ed
animation	an i **ma** tion
annexation	an nex **a** tion
annihilate	an **ni** hi late
anonymous	a **non** y mous
antagonism	an **tag** o nism
antagonist	an **tag** o nist
Antarctica	Ant **arc** ti ca
anthology	an **thol** o gy
antibody	**an** ti bod y
anticipate	an **tic** i pate
antiseptic	an ti **sep** tic
anxiety	anx **i** e ty
apathetic	ap a **thet** ic
apologize	a **pol** o gize
apology	a **pol** o gy
apostrophe	a **pos** tro phe

apparatus	ap pa **rat** us
appetizer	**ap** pe tiz er
appetizing	**ap** pe tiz ing
applicable	ap **pli** ca ble
application	ap pli **ca** tion
appreciate	ap **pre** ci ate
appreciative	ap **pre** cia tive
apprehension	ap pre **hen** sion
apprehensive	ap pre **hen** sive
approachable	ap **proach** a ble
appropriate	ap **pro** pri ate
approximate	ap **prox** i mate
aquamarine	a qua ma **rine**
aquarium	a **quar** i um
Arabia	A **ra** bi a
Arabian	A **ra** bi an
Aramaic	Ar a **ma** ic
arbitrary	**ar** bi trar y
architecture	**ar** chi tec ture
Argentina	Ar gen **ti** na
aristocrat	a **ris** to crat
arithmetic	a **rith** me tic
armadillo	ar ma **dil** lo
Armenia	Ar **me** ni a
articulate	ar **tic** u late
	ar **tic** u late
artificial	ar ti **fi** cial
artillery	ar **til** ler y
asparagus	as **par** a gus
aspiration	as pi **ra** tion
assassinate	as **sas** si nate
associate	as **so** ci ate
	as **so** ci ate
astonishment	as **ton** ish ment
astronomer	as **tron** o mer
astronomy	as **tron** o my
atmospheric	at mos **pher** ic
atypical	a **typ** i cal
audacity	au **dac** i ty
authority	au **thor** i ty
automatic	au to **mat** ic
automation	au to **ma** tion
automobile	au to mo **bile**
auxiliary	aux **il** ia ry
available	a **vail** a ble
aviation	a vi **a** tion
aviator	**a** vi a tor
avocado	a vo **ca** do
Azerbaijan	Az er bai jan
bacteria	bac **te** ri a
	bac **ter** i a
ballerina	bal le **ri** na
barbarian	bar **bar** i an
barometer	ba **rom** e ter
barracuda	bar ra **cu** da
Bartholomew	Bar **thol** o mew
beatitudes	be **a** ti tudes
begonia	be **go** ni a
benediction	ben e **dic** tion
beneficial	ben e **fi** cial
benevolent	be **nev** o lent
binoculars	bin **oc** u lars
biography	bi **og** ra phy
botanical	bo **tan** i cal
brutality	bru **tal** i ty
Bulgaria	Bul **gar** i a
calamity	ca **lam** i ty
calculation	cal cu **la** tion
calculator	**cal** cu la tor
California	Cal i **for** nia

Cambodia	Cam **bo** di a
Canadian	Ca **na** di an
capacity	ca **pac** i ty
capitalism	**cap** i tal ism
capitalize	**cap** i tal ize
captivity	cap **tiv** i ty
carbohydrate	car bo **hy** drate
	car bo **hy** drate
carbonated	**car** bon at ed
caricature	**car** i ca ture
carnivorous	car **niv** or ous
casualty	**cas** u al ty
catamaran	**cat** a ma ran
catastrophe	ca **tas** tro phe
category	**cat** e go ry
	***cat** e gor y
Catholicism	Ca **thol** i cism
cauliflower	**cau** li flow er
celebrated	**cel** e brat ed
celebration	cel e **bra** tion
cemetery	**cem** e ter y
centennial	cen **ten** ni al
centimeter	**cen** ti me ter
ceremony	**cer** e mo ny
certificate	cer **tif** i cate
championship	**cham** pi on ship
characterize	**char** ac ter ize
charitable	**char** i ta ble
Chattanooga	Chat ta **noo** ga
cholesterol	cho **les** ter ol
choreograph	**cho** re o graph
chrysanthemum	chry **san** the mum
Cincinnati	Cin cin **nat** i
Cinderella	Cin der **el** la
Cipriano	Ci pri **a** no

circulation	cir cu **la** tion
circumference	cir **cum** fer ence
citizenship	**cit** i zen ship
Cleopatra	Cle o **pa** tra
coagulate	co **ag** u late
coalition	co a **li** tion
coincidence	co **in** ci dence
Columbia	Co **lum** bi a
combination	com bi **na** tion
combustible	com **bus** ti ble
comedian	co **me** di an
comfortable	**com** fort a ble
commemorate	com **mem** or ate
commissioner	com **mis** sion er
commodity	com **mod** i ty
communicate	com **mu** ni cate
community	com **mu** ni ty
companionship	com **pan** ion ship
comparable	com **pa** ra ble
comparative	com **par** a tive
comparison	com **par** i son
compassionate	com **pas** sion ate
compatible	com **pat** i ble
compensation	com pen **sa** tion
competition	com pe **ti** tion
competitive	com **pet** i tive
competitor	com **pet** i tor
complexity	com **plex** i ty
complicated	**com** pli cat ed
complication	com pli **ca** tion
composition	com po **si** tion
comprehension	com pre **hen** sion
comprehensive	com pre **hen** sive
compulsory	com **pul** so ry
	*com **pul** sor y

concentration	con cen **tra** tion
condensation	con den **sa** tion
condescending	con de **scend** ing
conditioner	con **di** tion er
condolences	con **dol** en ces
confederate	con **fed** er ate
confidential	con fi **den** tial
confirmation	con fir **ma** tion
conformity	con **form** i ty
congratulate	con **grat** u late
congregation	con gre **ga** tion
Connecticut	Con **nect** i cut
conquistador	con **quis** ta dor
conscientious	con sci **en** tious
consecration	con se **cra** tion
consecutive	con **sec** u tive
consequently	**con** se quent ly
	con se quent ly
conservation	con ser **va** tion
conservative	con **serv** a tive
considerate	con **sid** er ate
consistency	con **sist** en cy
consolidate	con **sol** i date
conspicuous	con **spic** u ous
conspiracy	con **spir** a cy
constellation	con stel **la** tion
constituent	con **stit** u ent
constitution	con sti **tu** tion
consultation	con sul **ta** tion
contaminate	con **tam** i nate
contemplation	con tem **pla** tion
contemptible	con **tempt** i ble
continental	con ti **nen** tal
continual	con **tin** u al
continuous	con **tin** u ous

contradiction	con tra **dic** tion
controversial	con tro **ver** sial
controversy	**con** tro ver sy
convalescent	con va **les** cent
conventional	con **ven** tion al
conversation	con ver **sa** tion
convertible	con **vert** i ble
cooperate	co **op** er ate
coordinate	co **or** di nate
	co or di nate
Corinthians	Cor **in** thi ans
coronary	**cor** o nar y
coronation	cor o **na** tion
corporation	cor por **a** tion
correspondence	cor re **spon** dence
correspondent	cor re **spon** dent
corrugated	**cor** ru gat ed
criterion	cri **te** ri on
	cri **te** ri on
crucifixion	cru ci **fix** ion
cultivation	cul ti **va** tion
curriculum	cur **ric** u lum
custodian	cus **to** di an
customary	**cus** tom ar y
declaration	dec la **ra** tion
decorative	**dec** or a tive
decorator	**dec** or a tor
dedication	ded i **ca** tion
deficiency	de **fi** cien cy
definition	def i **ni** tion
delegation	del e **ga** tion
deliberate	de **lib** er ate
delirious	de **lir** i ous
delivery	de **liv** er y
democracy	de **moc** ra cy

democratic	dem o **crat** ic
demonstration	dem on **stra** tion
demonstrator	**dem** on stra tor
deodorant	de **o** dor ant
dependable	de **pend** a ble
desirable	de **sir** a ble
desolation	des o **la** tion
desperation	des per **a** tion
destination	des ti **na** tion
detrimental	det ri **men** tal
devastation	dev as **ta** tion
development	de **vel** op ment
dexterity	dex **ter** i ty
diabetes	di a **be** tes
	di a **be** tes
diabetic	di a **bet** ic
diagnosis	di ag **no** sis
	di ag **no** sis
diagonal	di **ag** o nal
diameter	di **am** e ter
diarrhea	di ar **rhe** a
dictionary	**dic** tion ar y
difficulty	**dif** fi cul ty
diminutive	di **min** u tive
diorama	di o **ram** a
diplomatic	dip lo **mat** ic
directory	di **rec** to ry
disability	dis a **bil** i ty
disadvantage	dis ad **van** tage
disagreement	dis a **gree** ment
disappearance	dis ap **pear** ance
disappointment	dis ap **point** ment
disapproval	dis ap **prov** al
disconcerted	dis con **cert** ed
discontented	dis con **tent** ed
discontinue	dis con **tin** ue
discourteous	dis **cour** te ous
discovery	dis **cov** er y
discriminate	dis **crim** i nate
disinfectant	dis in **fect** ant
disintegrate	dis **in** te grate
disorderly	dis **or** der ly
disorganized	dis **or** gan ized
disposable	dis **pos** a ble
disposition	dis po **si** tion
disqualify	dis **qual** i fy
disrespectful	dis re **spect** ful
dissatisfy	dis **sat** is fy
distribution	dis tri **bu** tion
diversity	di **ver** si ty
	di **ver** si ty
divinity	di **vin** i ty
divisible	di **vis** i ble
domesticate	do **mes** ti cate
domination	dom i **na** tion
Dominica	Dom **i** ni ca
	Dom i **ni** ca
dormitory	**dor** mi to ry
dromedary	**drom** e dar y
duplication	du pli **ca** tion
dyslexia	dys **lex** i a
ecology	e **col** o gy
economic	ec o **nom** ic
economist	e **con** o mist
economy	e **con** o my
ecosystem	**ec** o sys tem
education	ed u **ca** tion
educator	**ed** u ca tor
efficiency	ef **fi** cien cy
elaborate	e **lab** or ate

electrical	e **lec** tric al
electrician	e lec **tri** cian
electronic	e lec **tron** ic
elevation	el e **va** tion
elevator	**el** e va tor
eligible	**el** i gi ble
eliminate	e **lim** i nate
Elizabeth	E **liz** a beth
emancipate	e **man** ci pate
embarrassment	em **bar** rass ment
embroidery	em **broi** der y
emergency	e **mer** gen cy
emissary	**em** is sar y
emotional	e **mo** tion al
enchilada	en chi **la** da
encouragement	en **cour** age ment
energetic	en er **get** ic
engineering	en gi **neer** ing
enjoyable	en **joy** a ble
entertainer	en ter **tain** er
entertainment	en ter **tain** ment
enthusiasm	en **thu** si asm
entrepreneur	en tre pre **neur**
enunciate	e **nun** ci ate
environment	en **vi** ron ment
epidemic	ep i **dem** ic
Epiphany	E **piph** a ny
equality	e **qual** i ty
equivalent	e **quiv** a lent
eradicate	e **rad** i cate
Eritrea	Er i **tre** a
escalator	**es** ca la tor
Escondido	Es con **di** do
esophagus	e **soph** a gus
especially	es **pe** cial ly
espionage	**es** pi o nage
establishment	es **tab** lish ment
estimation	es ti **ma** tion
Estonia	Es **to** ni a
estuary	**es** tu ar y
eternity	e **ter** ni ty
eucalyptus	eu ca **lyp** tus
European	Eu ro **pe** an
evacuate	e **vac** u ate
evacuee	e **vac** u ee
evaluate	e **val** u ate
evaporate	e **vap** or ate
eventual	e **ven** tu al
evolution	ev o **lu** tion
exaggerate	ex **ag** ger ate
exasperate	ex **as** per ate
excavation	ex ca **va** tion
exceedingly	ex **ceed** ing ly
exceptional	ex **cep** tion al
exclamation	ex cla **ma** tion
execution	ex e **cu** tion
executive	ex **ec** u tive
exhibition	ex hi **bi** tion
exhilarate	ex **hil** a rate
expectation	ex pec **ta** tion
expedition	ex pe **di** tion
expenditure	ex **pend** i ture
	ex **pend** i ture
experience	ex **pe** ri ence
experiment	ex **per** i ment
expiration	ex pi **ra** tion
explanation	ex pla **na** tion
exploration	ex plor **a** tion
exterior	ex **te** ri or
exterminate	ex **ter** mi nate

extinguisher	ex **tin** guish er
extravagance	ex **trav** a gance
extravagant	ex **trav** a gant
extremity	ex **trem** i ty
Ezekiel	E **ze** ki el
facilitate	fa **cil** i tate
facility	fa **cil** i ty
favorable	**fa** vor a ble
February	**Feb** ru ar y
federation	fed er **a** tion
fermentation	fer men **ta** tion
fertilizer	**fer** ti liz er
festivity	fes **tiv** i ty
	fes **tiv** i ty
Filipina	Fil i **pi** na
Filipino	Fil i **pi** no
formidable	for **mi** da ble
	for **mi** da ble
forsythia	for **syth** i a
	for **syth** i a
fundamental	fun da **men** tal
gargantuan	gar **gan** tu an
generation	gen er **a** tion
generator	**gen** er a tor
geographic	ge o **graph** ic
geography	ge **og** ra phy
geologic	ge o **log** ic
geologist	ge **ol** o gist
geology	ge **ol** o gy
geometric	ge o **met** ric
geometry	ge **om** e try
geothermal	ge o **ther** mal
geranium	ge **ra** ni um
	ger a ni um
Gethsemane	Geth **sem** a ne
gladiator	**glad** i a tor
graduation	grad u **a** tion
grammatical	gram **mat** i cal
Guatemala	Gua te **ma** la
gymnasium	gym **na** si um
habitual	ha **bit** u al
hacienda	ha ci **en** da
hallelujah	hal le **lu** jah
harmonica	har **mon** i ca
harmonious	har **mo** ni ous
hemoglobin	**he** mo glo bin
hepatitis	hep a **ti** tis
hesitation	hes i **ta** tion
Hezekiah	Hez e **ki** ah
hibernation	hi ber **na** tion
hilarious	hi **lar** i ous
historian	his **to** ri an
historical	his **tor** i cal
Honolulu	Hon o **lu** lu
honorable	**hon** or a ble
honorary	**hon** or ar y
hospitable	hos **pi** ta ble
hospitalize	**hos** pi tal ize
humanity	hu **man** i ty
humidity	hu **mid** i ty
humiliate	hu **mil** i ate
hypocrisy	hy **poc** ri sy
hypotenuse	hy **pot** e nuse
hypothesis	hy **poth** e sis
	hy poth e sis
hysterical	hys **ter** i cal
identical	i **den** ti cal
illegible	il **leg** i ble
illiterate	il **lit** er ate
illogical	il **log** i cal

illuminate	il **lu** mi nate
illustration	il lus **tra** tion
illustrator	**il** lus tra tor
imitation	im i **ta** tion
immaculate	im **mac** u late
immediate	im **me** di ate
immigration	im mi **gra** tion
immunity	im **mu** ni ty
impassable	im **pass** a ble
imperial	im **pe** ri al
impersonate	im **per** son ate
impertinent	im **per** ti nent
impetuous	im **pet** u ous
impossible	im **pos** si ble
impoverish	im **pov** er ish
impractical	im **prac** ti cal
impurity	im **pu** ri ty
inaccurate	in **ac** cu rate
inadequate	in **ad** e quate
inanimate	in **an** i mate
inattentive	in at **ten** tive
inaudible	in **au** di ble
inaugurate	in **au** gu rate
incarnation	in car **na** tion
inclination	in cli **na** tion
incompetent	in **com** pe tent
inconvenience	in con **ven** ience
inconvenient	in con **ven** ient
incorporate	in **cor** por ate
incredible	in **cred** i ble
incubator	**in** cu ba tor
incurable	in **cur** a ble
indecision	in de **ci** sion
Independence	in de **pend** ence
independent	in de **pend** ent
Indiana	In di **an** a
indication	in di **ca** tion
indifferent	in **dif** fer ent
indigestion	in di **ges** tion
indignation	in dig **na** tion
Indonesia	In do **ne** sia
industrial	in **dus** tri al
industrious	in **dus** tri ous
inedible	in **ed** i ble
inefficient	in ef **fi** cient
inexpensive	in ex **pen** sive
infallible	in **fal** li ble
inferior	in **fe** ri or
infinitive	in **fin** i tive
infinity	in **fin** i ty
inflammable	in **flam** ma ble
inflammation	in flam **ma** tion
inflatable	in **flat** a ble
inflexible	in **flex** i ble
influential	in flu **en** tial
influenza	in flu **en** za
information	in for **ma** tion
infuriate	in **fu** ri ate
ingenuity	in ge **nu** i ty
ingratitude	in **grat** i tude
ingredient	in **gre** di ent
inhabitant	in **hab** it ant
inheritance	in **her** it ance
innovation	in no **va** tion
inoculate	in **oc** u late
inquisitive	in **quis** i tive
insignia	in **sig** ni a
insinuate	in **sin** u ate
inspection	in **spec** tion
inspiration	in spi **ra** tion

institution	in sti **tu** tion
instrumental	in stru **men** tal
insufficient	in suf **fi** cient
insulation	in su **la** tion
integration	in te **gra** tion
integrity	in **teg** ri ty
intelligent	in **tel** li gent
intensity	in **ten** si ty
intentional	in **ten** tion al
interactive	in ter **ac** tive
interesting	**in** ter est ing
	in ter est ing
interference	in ter **fer** ence
interior	in **te** ri or
interjection	in ter **jec** tion
intermission	in ter **mis** sion
intermittent	in ter **mit** tent
interpreter	in **ter** pret er
interrogate	in **ter** ro gate
interruption	in ter **rup** tion
intersection	in ter **sec** tion
intimidate	in **tim** i date
intolerant	in **tol** er ant
introduction	in tro **duc** tion
intuition	in tu **i** tion
intuitive	in **tu** i tive
inventory	**in** ven to ry
invertebrate	in **ver** te brate
investigate	in **ves** ti gate
invigorate	in **vig** or ate
invincible	in **vin** ci ble
invisible	in **vis** i ble
invitation	in vi **ta** tion
irrational	ir **ra** tion al
irregular	ir **reg** u lar
irrelevant	ir **rel** e vant
irrigation	ir ri **ga** tion
irritable	**ir** ri ta ble
irritation	ir ri **ta** tion
isolation	i so **la** tion
January	**Jan** u ar y
Jebediah	Jeb e **di** ah
Jedediah	Jed e **di** ah
Jeremiah	Jer e **mi** ah
Jeroboam	Jer o **bo** am
Jerusalem	Je **ru** sa lem
karaoke	ka ra **o** ke
Lamentations	Lam en **ta** tions
lavatory	**lav** a to ry
legendary	**leg** end ar y
legislation	leg is **la** tion
legislative	**leg** is la tive
	leg is la tive
legislator	**leg** is la tor
legitimate	le **git** i mate
Leonardo	Le o **nar** do
Leviticus	Le **vit** i cus
Liberia	Li **be** ri a
librarian	li **brar** i an
linoleum	li **no** le um
literally	**lit** er al ly
literature	**lit** er a ture
locomotion	lo co **mo** tion
locomotive	lo co **mo** tive
luxuriant	lux **u** ri ant
luxurious	lux **u** ri ous
macaroni	mac a **ro** ni
machinery	ma **chin** er y
Madagascar	Mad a **gas** car
magnesium	mag **ne** si um

magnificence	mag **nif** i cence
magnificent	mag **nif** i cent
	mag **nif** i cent
mahogany	ma **hog** a ny
majority	ma **jor** i ty
malaria	ma **lar** i a
malleable	**mal** le a ble
malnutrition	mal nu **tri** tion
mandatory	**man** da to ry
manipulate	ma **nip** u late
manufacture	man u **fac** ture
marionette	mar i on **ette**
marsupial	mar **su** pi al
Massachusetts	Mas sa **chu** setts
material	ma **te** ri al
matrimony	**mat** ri mo ny
maturity	ma **tu** ri ty
mechanical	me **chan** i cal
medication	med i **ca** tion
mediocre	me di **o** cre
meditation	med i **ta** tion
melodious	me **lo** di ous
memorial	me **mo** **ri** al
menagerie	me **nag** er ie
mercenary	**mer** ce nar y
meridian	me **rid** i an
metabolism	me **tab** o lism
metamorphic	met a **mor** phic
meteorite	**me** te or ite
methodical	me **thod** i cal
meticulous	me **tic** u lous
metropolis	me **trop** o lis
microscopic	mi cro **scop** ic
military	**mil** i tar y
millennium	mil **len** ni um
milliliter	**mil** li li ter
millimeter	**mil** li me ter
miniature	**min** i a ture
Minnesota	Min ne **so** ta
minority	mi **nor** i ty
	mi **nor** i ty
miraculous	mi **rac** u lous
	*mir **ac** u lous
miserable	**mis** er a ble
missionary	**mis** sion ar y
Mississippi	Mis is **sip** pi
misunderstand	mis un der **stand**
misunderstood	mis un der **stood**
modifier	**mod** i fi er
momentary	**mo** men tar y
monastery	**mon** as ter y
Mongolia	Mon **go** li a
monopolize	mo **nop** o lize
monopoly	mo **nop** o ly
monotheism	**mon** o the ism
monotony	mo **no** to ny
Montenegro	Mon te **ne** gro
Montgomery	Mont **gom** er y
	Mont **gom** er y
monumental	mon u **men** tal
morality	mor **al** i ty
	mor **al** i ty
motorcycle	**mo** tor cy cle
municipal	mu **nic** i pal
	*mu **ni** ci pal
mutually	**mu** tu al ly
mysterious	mys **te** ri ous
mythology	my **thol** o gy
Namibia	Na mib i a
nationalism	**na** tion al ism

naturalist	**nat** u ral ist
naturalize	**nat** u ral ize
naturally	**nat** u ral ly
navigation	nav i **ga** tion
necessary	**nec** es sar y
necessity	ne **ces** si ty
negotiate	ne **go** ti ate
Nehemiah	Ne he **mi** ah
Nicaragua	Nic a **ra** gua
Nigeria	Ni **ge** ri a
nomination	nom i **na** tion
noticeable	**no** tice a ble
notorious	no **tor** i ous
	no **tor** i ous
insecticide	in **sec** ti cide
numerator	**nu** mer a tor
numerical	nu **mer** i cal
nutritional	nu **tri** tion al
Obadiah	O ba **di** ah
obedient	o **be** di ent
	o **be** di ent
obligation	ob li **ga** tion
obliterate	ob **lit** er ate
	ob **lit** er ate
observation	ob ser **va** tion
occasional	oc **ca** sion al
occupation	oc cu **pa** tion
Octavia	Oc **ta** vi a
Odysseus	O **dys** se us
Oklahoma	O kla **ho** ma
Olympia	O **lym** pi a
omnivorous	om **niv** or ous
Ontario	On **tar** i o
operation	op er **a** tion
operator	**op** er a tor
opposition	op po **si** tion
optimistic	op ti **mis** tic
optometrist	op **tom** e trist
orangutan	or **ang** u tan
ordinary	**or** di nar y
oregano	o **reg** a no
origami	or i **ga** mi
original	o **rig** i nal
	*or **i** gi nal
originate	o **rig** i nate
	*or **i** gi nate
ornamental	or na **men** tal
orthodontist	or tho **don** tist
overwhelming	o ver **whelm** ing
pacifier	**pac** i fi er
palomino	pal o **mi** no
paralysis	pa **ral** y sis
paramedic	par a **med** ic
parochial	pa **ro** chi al
participant	par **tic** i pant
	*par **ti** ci pant
participate	par **tic** i pate
	*par **ti** ci pate
participle	**par** ti ci ple
particular	par **tic** u lar
Pasadena	**Pas** a de na
patriotic	pa tri **ot** ic
pedestrian	pe **des** tri an
penicillin	pen i **cil** lin
peninsula	pen **in** su la
Pennsylvania	Penn syl **va** nia
Peoria	Pe **or** i a
pepperoni	pep per **o** ni
perceptible	per **cep** ti ble
perennial	per **en** ni al

perimeter	pe **rim** e ter
	per **im** e ter
periodic	pe ri **od** ic
perishable	**per** ish a ble
perpetual	per **pet** u al
perpetuate	per **pet** u ate
perplexity	per **plex** i ty
persecution	per se **cu** tion
perseverance	per se **ver** ance
personally	**per** son al ly
perspiration	per spi **ra** tion
	*per spir **a** tion
pessimistic	pes si **mis** tic
petroleum	pe **tro** le um
phenomena	phe **nom** e na
phenomenal	phe **nom** e nal
phenomenon	phe **nom** e non
	phe **nom** e non
philanthropist	phi **lan** thro pist
philanthropy	phi **lan** thro py
Philippians	Phi **lip** pi ans
Philistia	Phi **lis** ti a
philosopher	phi **los** o pher
philosophy	phi **los** o phy
photographer	pho **tog** ra pher
photographic	pho to **graph** ic
pistachio	pis **tach** i o
plutonium	plu **to** ni um
political	po **lit** i cal
politician	pol i **ti** cian
polyester	pol y **es** ter
polytheism	pol y **the** ism
pomegranate	**pom** eg ran ate
	***pom** e gran ate
population	pop u **la** tion
portfolio	port **fo** li o
possibility	pos si **bil** i ty
potassium	po **tas** si um
practically	**prac** ti cal ly
precarious	pre **car** i ous
predecessor	pred e **ces** sor
predicament	pre **dic** a ment
prehistoric	pre his **tor** ic
prehistory	pre **his** to ry
premonition	pre mo **ni** tion
preoccupied	pre **oc** cu pied
preparation	prep a **ra** tion
preposition	prep o **si** tion
preposterous	pre **pos** ter ous
presentation	pres en **ta** tion
	pres en **ta** tion
preservation	pres er **va** tion
preservative	pre **ser** va tive
presidency	**pres** i den cy
presidential	pres i **den** tial
primarily	pri **ma** ri ly
	*pri **mar** i ly
prioritize	pri **or** i tize
priority	pri **or** i ty
proclamation	proc la **ma** tion
procrastinate	pro **cras** ti nate
	pro **cras** ti nate
professional	pro **fes** sion al
profitable	**prof** it a ble
prohibition	pro hi **bi** tion
propaganda	prop a **gan** da
proposition	prop o **si** tion
proprietor	pro **pri** e tor
prosecution	pros e **cu** tion
prosecutor	**pros** e cu tor

prosperity	pros **per** i ty
protagonist	pro **tag** o nist
proverbial	pro **ver** bi al
provisional	pro **vi** sion al
provocation	pro vo **ca** tion
psychiatrist	psy **chi** a trist
	psy **chi** a trist
psychologist	psy **chol** o gist
psychology	psy **chol** o gy
publication	pub li **ca** tion
publicity	pub **lic** i ty
	*pub **li** ci ty
pulmonary	**pul** mo nar y
pumpernickel	**pum** per nick el
punctuation	punc tu **a** tion
quesadilla	que sa **dil** la
radiation	ra di **a** tion
radiator	**ra** di a tor
ravioli	ra vi **o** li
realistic	re al **is** tic
reality	re **al** i ty
reasonable	**rea** son a ble
receptacle	re **cep** ta cle
recognition	rec og **ni** tion
recollection	rec ol **lec** tion
reconsider	re con **sid** er
Reconstruction	re con **struc** tion
recovery	re **cov** er y
recreation	rec re **a** tion
rectangular	rec **tan** gu lar
recuperate	re **cu** per ate
Reformation	Ref or **ma** tion
refrigerate	re **frig** er ate
regulation	reg u **la** tion
regurgitate	re **gur** gi tate
reliable	re **li** a ble
remarkable	re **mark** a ble
repetition	rep e **ti** tion
reproduction	re pro **duc** tion
Republican	Re **pub** li can
reputation	rep u **ta** tion
reservation	res er **va** tion
residential	res i **den** tial
resignation	res ig **na** tion
resolution	res o **lu** tion
respectable	re **spect** a ble
respectively	re **spec** tive ly
respiration	res pi **ra** tion
	*res pir **a** tion
responsible	re **spon** si ble
Resurrection	Res ur **rec** tion
retaliate	re **tal** i ate
Revelation	Rev e **la** tion
revolution	rev o **lu** tion
rhinoceros	rhi **noc** er os
	*rhi **no** cer os
rhododendron	rho do **den** dron
ridiculous	ri **dic** u lous
Romania	Ro **ma** ni a
Sacramento	Sac ra **men** to
salamander	**sal** a man der
salutation	sal u **ta** tion
Samaritan	Sa **mar** i tan
sanctuary	**sanc** tu ar y
sanitary	**san** i tar y
sanitation	san i **ta** tion
satisfaction	sat is **fac** tion
satisfactory	sat is **fac** to ry
	*sat is **fact** or y
scientific	sci en **tif** ic

secretary	**sec** re tar y
security	se **cu** ri ty
	*se **cur** i ty
segregation	seg re **ga** tion
semifinal	sem i **fi** nal
seminary	**sem** i nar y
semisolid	sem i **sol** id
sensational	sen **sa** tion al
sentimental	sen ti **men** tal
separation	sep a **ra** tion
Seraphina	Ser a **phi** na
serenity	se **ren** i ty
seventieth	**sev** en ti eth
significance	sig **nif** i cance
significant	sig **nif** i cant
simplicity	sim **plic** i ty
	*sim **pli** ci ty
sincerity	sin **cer** i ty
situation	sit u **a** tion
Slovenia	Slo **ve** ni a
society	so **ci** e ty
Somalia	So **ma** li a
	So **ma** li a
spectacular	spec **tac** u lar
speedometer	speed **om** e ter
spiritual	**spir** it u al
spontaneous	spon **ta** ne ous
stationary	**sta** tion ar y
stationery	**sta** tion er y
subordinate	sub **or** di nate
superficial	su per **fi** cial
superior	su **pe** ri or
superlative	su **per** la tive
supersonic	su per **son** ic
superstition	su per **sti** tion
superstitious	su per **sti** tious
supervisor	**su** per vi sor
sustainable	sus **tain** a ble
symbiosis	sym bi **o** sis
symmetrical	sym **met** ri cal
sympathetic	sym pa **thet** ic
syncopation	syn co **pa** tion
synonymous	syn **on** y mous
synthesizer	**syn** the siz er
systematic	sys tem **at** ic
Tajikistan	Ta **ji** ki stan
	Ta **ji** ki stan
Tallahassee	Tal la **has** see
Tanzania	Tan za **ni** a
tapioca	tap i **o** ca
tarantula	ta **ran** tu la
technology	tech **nol** o gy
temperature	**tem** per a ture
temporary	**tem** por ar y
terrarium	ter **rar** i um
terrestrial	ter **res** tri al
territory	**ter** ri tor y
testimony	**tes** ti mo ny
theology	the **ol** o gy
Theophilus	The **oph** i lus
thermometer	ther **mom** e ter
tolerable	**tol** er a ble
traditional	tra **di** tion al
transformation	trans for **ma** tion
transportation	trans por **ta** tion
triangular	tri **an** gu lar
tributary	**trib** u tar y
triumphant	tri **um** phant
Turkmenistan	Turk **me** ni stan
	*Turk **men** is stan

ultrasonic	ul tra **son** ic
unaccustomed	un ac **cus** tomed
unanimous	u **nan** i mous
unbearable	un **bear** a ble
unbecoming	un be **com** ing
unbreakable	un **break** a ble
uncertainty	un **cer** tain ty
undecided	un de **cid** ed
understanding	un der **stand** ing
undertaken	un der **tak** en
undertaker	un der **tak** er
undoubtedly	un **doubt** ed ly
unemployment	un em **ploy** ment
unexpected	un ex **pect** ed
unfamiliar	un fa **mil** iar
unfortunate	un **for** tu nate
unicycle	**u** ni cy cle
universal	u ni **ver** sal
unlimited	un **lim** it ed
unnatural	un **nat** u ral
unoccupied	un **oc** cu pied
unpopular	un **pop** u lar
unscrupulous	un **scru** pu lous
unthinkable	un **think** a ble
unusual	un **u** su al
upholstery	up **hol** ster y
uranium	u **ra** ni um
usually	**u** su al ly
utility	u **til** i ty
Uzbekistan	Uz **bek** i stan
vaccination	vac ci **na** tion
Valencia	Va **len** ci a
Vanuatu	Van **ua** tu (US)
	Va nu **a** tu (UK)
variable	**var** i a ble
variation	var i **a** tion
variety	va **ri** e ty
vegetation	veg e **ta** tion
	*ve ge **ta** tion
velocity	ve **loc** i ty
	*ve **lo** ci ty
Venezuela	Ven e **zue** la
ventilation	ven ti **la** tion
ventilator	**ven** ti la tor
ventriloquist	ven **tril** o quist
Veronica	Ver **on** i ca
vicinity	vi **cin** i ty
Victoria	Vic **to** ri a
	*Vic **tor** i a
victorious	vic **tor** i ous
Vietnamese	Vi et nam **ese**
violinist	vi o **lin** ist
virtually	**vir** tu al ly
virtuoso	vir tu **o** so
voluntary	**vol** un tar y
vulnerable	**vul** ner a ble
watermelon	**wa** ter mel on
Zechariah	Zech a **ri** ah
Zephaniah	Zeph a **ni** ah
zoologist	zo **ol** o gist
zoology	zo **ol** o gy

5 Syllables

- In this list, the stressed syllable is indicated by **bold** print, and the schwa syllable is indicated by underlined print. These may vary based on dialect.
- In multi-syllable words, you will often find that one or more syllables in the word have a vowel schwa sound. This can be confusing for students who have learned that open syllables make a long vowel sound and closed syllables make a short vowel sound. Teaching students about the schwa sound is a valuable tool in teaching them to decode multi-syllable words.
- Five-syllable words often have more than one schwa sound. As student read longer words, they need to learn more how to "flex" the vowels. This means to try out different vowel sounds to see which one sounds like it fits in the word. The most common flex would be to try out the schwa sound for the different vowels in a multi-syllable word. Here are some examples of open vowel syllables that make the schwa sound instead of the long vowel sound:

  a pol o **get** ic al pha **bet** i cal Al ex **an** dri a

- The accent/stress in a 5 syllable word will vary, and will be especially influenced by the suffixes in the word.
- Words that end in the **-ED** suffix, but do not add an extra syllable are marked with a line in ex per i **enc-ed**. Those **-ED** suffixes are the ones that are pronounced **/d/** or **/t/.**
- Five-syllable words may have more than one schwa sound, and students will need to practice flexing vowel sounds to see if a schwa sound is the correct sound.

abbreviation	ab bre vi **a** tion	agricultural	ag ri **cul** tur al
abolitionist	ab o **li** tion ist	Alexandria	Al ex **an** dri a
abominable	a **bom** i na ble	alliteration	al lit er **a** tion
acceleration	ac cel er **a** tion	alphabetical	al pha **bet** i cal
accelerator	ac **cel** er a tor	ambiguity	am bi **gu** i ty
accidentally	ac ci **den** tal ly	amphitheater	**am** phi the a ter
accompaniment	ac **com** pa ni ment	anniversary	an ni **ver** sa ry
accumulation	ac cu mu **la** tion	annunciation	an nun ci **a** tion
administration	ad min is **tra** tion	anorexia	an or **ex** i a
administrator	ad **min** is tra tor	anthropology	an thro **pol** o gy

antibiotic	an ti bi **ot** ic
anticipation	an tic i **pa** tion
antiperspirant	an ti **per** spi rant
apologetic	a pol o **get** ic
appendicitis	ap pen di **ci** tis
appreciation	ap pre ci **a** tion
approximately	ap **prox** i mate ly
approximation	ap prox i **ma** tion
archaeologist	ar chae **ol** o gist
archaeology	ar chae **ol** o gy
archipelago	ar chi pel **a** go
aristocracy	ar is **toc** ra cy
assassination	as sas si **na** tion
association	as so ci **a** tion
astronomical	as tro **nom** i cal
auditorium	au di **tor** i um
authoritative	au **thor** i ta tive
authorization	au thor i **za** tion
bibliography	bib li **og** ra phy
biographical	bi o **graph** i cal
biological	bi o **log** i cal
cafeteria	caf e **te** ri a
	*caf e **ter** i a
ceremonial	cer e **mo** ni al
characteristic	char ac ter **is** tic
Christianity	Chris ti **an** i ty
chronological	chron o **log** i cal
circumnavigate	cir cum **nav** i gate
civilization	civ i li **za** tion
classification	clas si fi **ca** tion
communicable	com **mu** ni ca ble
communication	com mu ni **ca** tion
complementary	com ple **men** ta ry
complimentary	com pli **men** ta ry
condominium	con do **min** i um

confederacy	con **fed** er a cy
confederation	con fed er **a** tion
congratulations	con grat u **la** tions
considerable	con **sid** er a ble
consideration	con sid er **a** tion
constitutional	con sti **tu** tion al
contradictory	con tra **dic** to ry
cooperation	co op er **a** tion
coordination	co or di **na** tion
curiosity	cu ri **os** i ty
	*cur i **os** i ty
deliberation	de lib er **a** tion
delicatessen	del i ca **tes** sen
denomination	de nom i **na** tion
denominator	de **nom** i na tor
desegregation	de seg re **ga** tion
deteriorate	de **te** ri o rate
determination	de ter mi **na** tion
Deuteronomy	Deu ter **on** o my
dilapidated	di **lap** i dat ed
disability	dis a **bil** i ty
disagreeable	dis a **gree** a ble
discrimination	dis crim i **na** tion
dishonorable	dis **hon** or a ble
disinterested	dis **in** ter est ed
disobedient	dis o **be** di ent
dissatisfaction	dis sat is **fac** tion
documentary	doc u **men** ta ry
Ecclesiastes	Ec cle si **as** tes
economical	ec o **nom** i cal
editorial	ed i **tor** i al
educational	ed u **ca** tion al
electricity	e lec **tric** i ty
electromagnet	e lec tro **mag** net
elementary	el e **men** ta ry

emancipation	e man ci **pa** tion
enthusiastic	en thu si **as** tic
equatorial	e qua **to** ri al
	*e qua **tor** i al
equilibrium	e qui **lib** ri um
Ethiopia	E thi **o** pi a
etymology	et y **mol** o gy
experimental	ex per i **men** tal
fortification	for ti fi **ca** tion
genealogy	ge ne **al** o gy
generosity	gen er **os** i ty
geographical	ge o **graph** i cal
hereditary	he **red** i tar y
hippopotamus	hip po **pot** a mus
hospitality	hos pi **tal** i ty
hydroelectric	hy dro e **lec** tric
imaginary	im **ag** i nar y
imagination	im ag i **na** tion
imaginative	im **ag** i na tive
	im **a** gi na tive
immeasurable	im **meas** ur a ble
immediately	im **me** di ate ly
imperceptible	im per **cep** ti ble
inability	in a **bil** i ty
inappropriate	in ap **pro** pri ate
inauguration	in au gu **ra** tion
incidentally	in ci **den** tal ly
incinerator	in **cin** er a tor
inconsiderate	in con **sid** er ate
inconspicuous	in con **spic** u ous
indigestible	in di **gest** i ble
individual	in di **vid** u al
indivisible	in di **vis** i ble
industrialized	in **dus** tri al iz-ed
inequality	in e **qual** i ty
inevitable	in **ev** i ta ble
inexcusable	in ex **cus** a ble
inexperienced	in ex **pe** ri enc-ed
infatuation	in fat u **a** tion
ingenuity	in ge **nu** i ty
initiation	in i ti **a** tion
initiative	in **i** tia tive
innumerable	in **nu** mer a ble
insignificant	in sig **nif** i cant
intellectual	in tel **lec** tu al
intermediate	in ter **me** di ate
international	in ter **na** tion al
interpretation	in ter pre **ta** tion
introductory	in tro **duc** to ry
	*in tro **duct** or y
invaluable	in **val** u a ble
investigation	in ves ti **ga** tion
investigator	in **ves** ti ga tor
involuntary	in **vol** un tar y
irresistible	ir re **sist** i ble
irresponsible	ir re **spon** si ble
itinerary	i **tin** er ar y
laboratory	**lab** or a to ry
	lab **or** a tor y
Laodicea	La o di **ce** a
	La o di **ce** a
liability	li a **bil** i ty
Lithuania	Lith u **a** ni a
Louisiana	Lou i si **an** a
manifestation	man i fes **ta** tion
materialize	ma **te** ri al ize
mathematical	math e **mat** i cal
mathematician	math e ma **ti** cian
Mauritania	Mau ri **ta** ni a
melodramatic	mel o dra **mat** ic

metamorphosis	met a **mor** pho sis
metropolitan	met ro **pol** i tan
Minneapolis	Min ne **ap** o lis
miscellaneous	mis cel **la** ne ous
misunderstanding	mis un der **stand** ing
modification	mod i fi **ca** tion
momentarily	**mo** men tar i ly
multicultural	mul ti **cul** tur al
multimedia	mul ti **me** di a
multiplication	mul ti pli **ca** tion
nationality	na tion **al** i ty
necessarily	nec es **sar** i ly
observatory	ob **serv** a to ry
	*ob **serv** a tor y
oceanography	o cea **nog** ra phy
	*o cean **og** ra phy
opportunity	op por **tu** ni ty
ordinarily	or di **nar** i ly
organization	or gan i **za** tion
orientation	or i en **ta** tion
originally	or **ig** i nal ly
	*or **i** gi nal ly
pandemonium	pan de **mo** ni um
paramecium	par a **me** ci um
participation	par tic i **pa** tion
	par ti ci **pa** tion
particularly	par **tic** u lar ly
pediatrician	pe di a **tri** cian
periodical	pe ri **od** i cal
perpendicular	per pen **dic** u lar
personality	per son **al** i ty
pharmaceutical	phar ma **ceu** ti cal
Philadelphia	Phil a **del** phi a
philosophical	phil o **soph** i cal
photosynthesis	pho to **syn** the sis

popularity	pop u **lar** i ty
possibility	pos si **bil** i ty
precipitation	pre cip i **ta** tion
preliminary	pre **lim** i nar y
premeditated	pre **med** i tat ed
preparatory	**pre** par a tor y
principality	prin ci **pal** i ty
probability	prob a **bil** i ty
productivity	pro duc **tiv** i ty
pronunciation	pro nun ci **a** tion
psychological	psy cho **log** i cal
quadrilateral	quad ri **lat** er al
qualification	qual i fi **ca** tion
realization	re al i **za** tion
recommendation	rec om men **da** tion
refrigerator	re **frig** er a tor
reincarnation	re in car **na** tion
representative	rep re **sent** a tive
satisfactory	sat is **fac** to ry
	*sat is **fact** or y
Scandinavian	Scan di **na** vi an
sedimentary	**sed** i men ta ry
similarity	sim i **lar** i ty
simultaneous	si mul **ta** ne ous
sophisticated	so **phis** ti cat ed
specifically	spe **cif** i cal ly
superintendent	su per in **tend** ent
temperamental	tem per a **men** tal
Thessalonians	Thes sa **lo** ni ans
transcontinental	trans con ti **nen** tal
tuberculosis	tu ber cu **lo** sis
unbelievable	un be **liev** a ble
uncomfortable	un **com** fort a ble
undeniable	un de **ni** a ble

unforgettable	un for **get** ta ble
university	u ni **ver** si ty
unmistakable	un mis **tak** a ble
unquestionable	un **ques** tion a ble
unreasonable	un **rea** son a ble
unreliable	un re **li** a ble
vegetarian	veg e **tar** i an
	ve ge **tar** i an
visibility	vis i **bil** i ty
vocabulary	vo **cab** u lar y
	vo **cab** u lar y

6 or 7 Syllables

- In this list, the stressed syllable is indicated by **bold** print, and the schwa syllable is indicated by underlined print. These may vary based on dialect.

- In multi-syllable words, you will often find that one or more syllables in the word have a vowel schwa sound. This can be confusing for students who have learned that open syllables make a long vowel sound and closed syllables make a short vowel sound. Teaching students about the schwa sound is a valuable tool in teaching them to decode multi-syllable words.

- Six-syllable words often have more than one schwa sound. As student read longer words, they need to learn more how to "flex" the vowels. This means to try out different vowel sounds to see which one sounds like it fits in the word. The most common flex would be to try out the schwa sound for the different vowels in a multi-syllable word. Here are some examples of open vowel syllables that make the schwa sound instead of the long vowel sound:

Mes o po **ta** mi a   me te or **ol** o gist   pa le on **tol** o gist

- The accent/stress in a 6 or 7 syllable word will vary, and will be especially influenced by the suffixes in the word.

- The words in this word list dictionary are the ones that are typically found in middle school or early high school texts. Once students get up to higher level high school and college level texts, they will find there are many more 6 or 7 syllable words.

autobiography	au to bi **og** ra phy	originality	or ig i **nal** i ty
biodegradable	bi o de **grad** a ble		or i gi **nal** i ty
biodiversity	bi o di **ver** si ty	paleontology	pa le on **tol** o gy
biotechnology	bi o tech **nol** o gy	peculiarity	pe cu li **ar** i ty
encyclopedia	en cy clo **pe** di a	reconciliation	rec on cil i **a** tion
environmentalist	en vi ron **men** tal ist	responsibility	re spon si **bil** i ty
identification	i den ti fi **ca** tion	revolutionary	rev o **lu** tion ar y
	i den ti fi **ca** tion	superiority	su pe ri **or** i ty
Indianapolis	In di an **ap** o lis	transubstantiation	tran sub stan ti **a** tion
individuality	in di vid u **al** i ty	unconstitutional	un con sti **tu** tion al
Mesopotamia	Mes o po **ta** mi a	unsatisfactory	un sat is **fac** to ry
meteorologist	me te or **ol** o gist		*un sat is **fact** or y
naturalization	nat u ral i **za** tion	veterinarian	vet er i **nar** i an

ION/TION

and

Related Endings

Different Approaches

-ION or -TION?

There are three different approaches to teaching words with **ION/TION** and similar letter teams **(TIAL, SION, CIOUS**, etc). Two of those approaches focus on phonics and the third focuses on morphology.

In the following descriptions I focus on the letter groups **TION** and **ATION,** but the concepts would apply to all similar letter groups.

The three approaches are:

1) **Traditional Syllable Division Approach** (whole letter team)

Traditionally, teachers have taught their students that **TION** is a letter team that is pronounced **/shun/.** Some teachers have called **-TION** a suffix, although the true suffix is **-ION**. Traditional syllable division divides **TION** as a syllable:

e lec **tion,** par ti **tion.**

The traditional syllable division approach is a phonics approach because each letter team is matched with a pronunciation. This Syllables book is focused on syllables, and therefore divides **TION** as a syllable. In my Morphology books, I divide words into prefix, root, and suffix, which includes suffix **-ION**. (Due for publication in 2022 is a Morphology series by the same author).

2) **Phoneme/Grapheme Approach** (divided letter team)

Some teachers break **TION** down into smaller sounds (phonemes), and their associated letters (graphemes).

TI	O	N
/sh/	/ə/	/n/

The letter **i** in these words is a connective vowel that connects the base of a word to the suffix of a word. It also has another job of signaling the letters **T**, **S** and **C** to change their sound. Those different sounds are based on Latin pronunciations because the words in this section were brought into English from Latin.

Below are some examples of words divided into phoneme boxes for sound/symbol mapping. The **TI** and **CI** each go in one box that symbolizes the sound **/sh/.**

nation

/n/ /ā/ /sh/ /ŭ/ /n/

n	a	ti	o	n

precious

/p/ /r/ /ĕ/ /sh/ /ŭ/ /s/

p	r	e	ci	ou	s

3) **Morphological Approach**
Teachers have started to take an interest lately in morphology. Morphs are the smallest units of meaning within a word. Usually those units are prefixes, roots, and suffixes. Teachers who focus on morphology teach their students that the true suffix is **-ION,** not **TION.** The **T** is a part of the base word, or the **T** comes from either the original Latin root, or a variation of the Latin root. This is a meaning/structure approach, not a phonics approach. The word **prescription** would be broken down in to **pre + script + ion. Collection** would be broken down into **col + lect + ion.**

Which approach is the best?

There is a lot of disagreement right now on which approach is the best. The people who focus on morphology have been especially critical of teaching **TION** as a syllable or a suffix. However, all three approaches have both positives and negatives, and therefore all three are valid teaching approaches for different reasons.

I provide you with card copying pages for all three approaches and I will describe the positives and negatives of each approach in more detail below so that you can make the best choice for your own teaching. I also hope this will encourage you that if you are required to use a certain program by your school or school district that does not use the approach that you think is best, you can still use that required program with confidence. You will know that whichever approach you are using, you are giving your students valuable information for reading and spelling.

Traditional Syllable Division (whole letter team)

The traditional phonics way to teach **TION** is to treat **TION** as a letter team that is pronounced **/shun/.** Students learn it as they would any other letter team. This is the approach that has traditionally been taught by Orton-Gillingham practitioners.

Positives to this approach:

-This approach supports orthographic mapping, because each letter group can be matched with its associated sound. Brain studies have shown that the way our brains learn to read is by matching letters with speech sounds. The letter team **TION** matches with the spoken sounds **/shun/.**

-It is uncomplicated and straight-forward. **TION** and **ATION** are used in so many words that recognizing them as a unit is efficient and it helps students to acquire a large number of words quickly.

Negatives to this approach:

-Connecting the **T** to **ION** can take the focus away from the base word and the meaning of a word. For example, in the word **connection**, the base word is **connect.** If you take off **TION** from the word **connection**, you only get **connec**, which is less obvious that the base word is **connect.**

-When you take the focus off the base word that ends in the letter **T**, you may have more difficulty determining spelling, when to use **TION** and when to use **SION**.

Phoneme/Grapheme Approach (split letter team)

A Phoneme/Grapheme approach teaches that **TI, SI,** and **CI** are all pronounced **/sh/,** and **O-N** is pronounced **/ ŭ / /n/.**

Positives to this approach:

-Making the connection that **TI** is pronounced **/sh/** helps with orthographic mapping because it helps to form the letter/sound connections in the brain. Making letter/sound connections in the brain is the number one most important thing you can do when you are teaching students to read, especially students with dyslexia. This Phoneme/Grapheme approach breaks down the **TION** into more specific phoneme/grapheme connections than it does when it is kept as a whole. Some teachers who teach with the more traditional whole **TION** will still point out to their students that the **TI** part of **TION** says **/sh/.**

- The phoneme/grapheme approach also connects **TI** to other word patterns. The **TI** as **/sh/** combination is found not only in **TION** and related words, but in other words, as well, such as **initiation** and **initiative**. It also connects to other sound groups. In words with **TI** or **TU**, the **T** often says **/sh/** and sometimes **/ch/**. For example, **TU** says **/choo/,** in words like **actual** and **situation.**

-Once students learn the different parts, they can mix and match the parts. For example, once you know **TI + OUS** is **TIOUS /shus/,** you can also read and spell **CI + OUS = CIOUS /shus/.** Once you know **TI + ENCE** is **TIENCE /shens/,** you can read and spell **CI + ENCE = CIENCE /shens/.**

Negatives to this approach:

-Dividing a word into small parts can take the focus away from the base word and the meaning of a word.

-When you take the focus off the base word, you may have more difficulty determining how to spell certain sounds. For example, when do you use **TION** and when do you use **SION**?

Morphological Approach

Morphology focuses on the meaning parts of the word and looks at words as a sum of prefix, root/base, and suffix. People who focus on morphology (especially those who do Structured Word Inquiry*) also focus on the history of the word.

People who use the morphological approach teach that the true suffix is **-ION** (not **TION**). They believe that students will understand vocabulary better and be better spellers if they understand that **-ION** is the suffix. If you take **-ION** off the word **connection**, you are left with the base word **connect**. This emphasizes the connection between the words **connection** and **connect**.

Positives to this approach:

- It focuses on the meaning of the word. When students know the meanings of prefixes, suffixes, and roots, they can make connections to the meaning of the word, which aids in comprehension.
-It helps students to understand the structure of words.
-It fosters connections across related words. For example. **act-ion, act-ing, act-ed, re-act.**
-When students understand the meaning of a word part, they can transfer that knowledge to other word parts. For example, when you learn that **bi** means **two,** you begin to understand words like **bicycle, biped, binomial.**
-In some cases, teaching **-ION** as the suffix helps the student to understand why words are spelled the way they are. For example, you know that the word confe**ss** has two **SS**'s at the end of the word and therefore will become confe**ss**ion. The word loca**t**e with a **T** will become loca**t**ion. (This does not work with all words, for example the word expan**d** becomes expan**s**ion).

Negatives to this approach:

1) The morphological approach causes some difficulty with the phoneme/grapheme connections. What phonics sounds go with -**ION**? Some teachers have chosen to say that **-ION** is pronounced **/shun/.** But identifying **-ION** as **/shun/** means that you are left with **T** as a silent letter. The word **connection** is pronounced /cune**c**-shun/, not /cunec**t**-shun/. This also becomes a problem with words do not pronounce -ion as /shun/, such as the word **onion**. You pronounce **-ION** as **/yun/.** It is not **/unshun/.** In fact, **ION** has many different pronunciations in different words. In addition, if you look at other Latin words, the **TI/SI/CI** is clearly pronounced **/sh/** and sometimes **/ch/ (initial, special).**

2) Although this approach is supposed to make spelling easier, it sometimes causes more confusion.

Some words can be easily broken down in to base and suffix, and therefore can help the student to choose the correct spelling. For example, do we spell /akshun/ as ac**t**ion or ac**s**ion? Looking at the base word **act** makes it easy. However, others are more complex. The word **action** can easily be divided into **act** and **ion**. But the word **invasion** is more complicated. **Invasion** comes from the word **invade**, but it is not broken down into **in + vade + ion**. There is no **S** in **invade**. The **S** comes from the Latin ***invasio***, and the ***vade*** is related to the Latin ***wade***, which means to go forward. Some teachers may enjoy pursuing these kinds of inquiries to deepen their students' understanding of spelling, but they do not always make spelling more easy or simple.

The morphological approach also teaches that **ATION** is "**A..T..E**, drop the **E**, add suffix **-ION**."

replic**ate** replic**ation**
medi**ate** medi**ation**

For students that are struggling, however, reading or spelling **ATION** /ayshun/ as a letter team pattern is much easier and simple than trying to understand the whole process of dropping the **E** and adding the suffix.

An addition, many other words do not break down into **ATE + TION**.

The word **classification** is related to **classify**, not **classificate**
The word **proclamation** is related to **proclaim**, not **proclaimate**

Most of morphology is very ordered and really does make reading more simple for students. But in the case of the **ion/ian** groups of words, that is not always the case.

Which approach should I choose?

As you can see from the positives and negative above, there is validity in all three of these approaches. Some teachers use a balanced approach in which they teach from one of the phonics-based approaches (**TION** or **TI+ON**) initially for reading. They do this to make the process simple and to emphasize the phoneme/grapheme connections that help with orthographic mapping. Then, as students become stronger readers and the focus switches to spelling, the teachers introduce the more advanced **-ION** morphology.

Whatever approach you take, it is wise to focus on letter patterns and teach spelling of words that have similar spellings first. Teach and practice the spelling of **TION** words one day, **ATION** words on another day, and **SION** words on another day. These are extremely complex words with a large variety of spellings.

I have provided a chart so that you can compare the three methods and also a chart with the spelling rules related to these endings. You can see that there really are too many rules to teach them all without students becoming overwhelmed. Teaching words together as patterns instead of rules helps students to understand and absorb those rules more naturally.

Comparison Chart of Three Approaches

Teaching ION/TION and Related Combinations

1 of 2

Traditional Syllable Division (whole letter team)	**Phoneme/Grapheme** (divided letter team)	**Morphological** (focus on meanings of roots, affixes) The descriptions below are very basic generalities, since morphology looks at each word individually.

/shun/

TION	TI + ON	base or Latin root that includes T + suffix ION
SION	SI + ON	base or Latin root that includes S + suffix ION
SSION or S + SION	S + SI + ION	base or Latin root that ends in SS + suffix ION
CIAN (I-CIAN)	CI + AN	base or Latin root that includes C + IAN (or connective I + suffix AN)
CION	CI + ON	base or Latin root includes C + suffix ION
XION	XI + ON	base or Latin root that includes X + suffix ION Sometimes an alternative for CT + ION

/shul/

TIAL	TI + AL	base or Latin root that includes T + IAL (or connective I + suffix AL)
CIAL	CI + AL	base or Latin root that includes C + IAL (or connective I + suffix AL)

/shus/

TIOUS	TI + OUS	base or Latin root that includes T + connective I + suffix OUS
CIOUS	CI + OUS	base word that includes C + connective I + suffix OUS

/shent/

TIENT	TI + ENT	base or Latin root that includes T + connective I + suffix ENT
CIENT	CI + ENT	base or Latin root that includes C + connective I + suffix ENT

/shens/

TIENCE	TI + ENCE	base or Latin root that includes T + connective I + suffix ENCE
CIENCE	CI + ENCE	base or Latin root that includes C + connective I + suffix ENCE

Comparison Chart of Three Approaches

Teaching ION/TION and Related Combinations

Traditional Syllable Division (whole letter team)	Phoneme/Grapheme (divided letter team)	Morphological (focus on meanings of roots, affixes)

Vowel plus letter team

ATION or A + TION	A + TI + ON	base or root ending in ATE (drop E) + suffix ION
ETON or E + TION	E + TI + ON	base or root ending in ETE (drop E) + suffix ION
ITION or I + TION	I + TI + ON	base or root ending that includes IT + suffix ION or base or root ending in ITE(drop E) + suffix ION
OTION or O + TION	O + TI + ON	base or root ending in OTE (drop E) + suffix ION base or root that includes OT + suffix ION
UTION or U + TION	U + TI + ON	base or root ending in UTE (drop E) + suffix ION or base or root ending in OVE (drop VE) + UTE (drop E) + suffix ION

ION /yun/

L + ION (syllable division L/ION)	L + ION	base or root that includes L + suffix ION
LL + ION or	LL + ION	base or root that includes LL + suffix ION
N + ION	N + ION	base or root that includes an N + suffix ION

/un/

GION	G+ ION	base or root includes G + suffix ION

- Note on Phoneme/Grapheme approach: **-ON** does not seem to be recognized in dictionaries as a genuine suffix for non-chemistry words, despite the fact that all the other combinations of **TI,SI,CI** are paired with recognized suffixes **(-AL, -OUS, -ENT, ENCE)**. The suffix **-ION** is recognized as a genuine suffix.

Spelling Guidelines

TION/SION/SSION/CIAN

Credit for some of the information below goes to the Farlex book: *Complete English Spelling and Pronunciation Rules.*

TION	SION	SSION	CIAN
TION is the most common spelling of the sound **/shun/.** Use **TION** for words that end in **PT**, **CT**, and **RT** (Exception – words that end in **VERT** are spelled with **SION**) ado**pt**/ado**pt**ion, extin**ct**/extin**ct**ion exe**rt**/exe**rt**ion Words that end in **N** or **R** can be spelled with either **TION,** or **SION.** **TION** is never pronounced **/zhun/**, but both **SION** and **TION** can be pronounced **/shun/.** Words that end in **CEIVE** change **VE** to **P** and add **TION** concei**ve**/conce**p**tion percei**ve**/perce**p**tion A word that ends in **TAIN**, **VENE** or **VENT** is spelled **TION.** Note the other spelling changes. re**tain**/re**tent**ion con**vene** – con**vent**ion in**vent** – in**vent**ion For words that end in **SUME**, drop the **E** and add **PTION.** assum**e**/assum**pt**ion presum**e**/presum**pt**ion When you add **TION** to a word that has a **B** near the end, the **B** changes to a **P** absor**b** – absor**p**tion descri**b**e/descri**p**tion	**Both SION** and **TION** can be pronounced **/shun/,** but only **SION** is pronounced **/zhun/.** Use **SION** when the ending is pronounced **/zhun/.** **vision** **occasion** Words that end in **N** or **R** can be spelled with either **TION** or **SION.** Use **SION** for words that end in **DE** or **SE** (**VCE** pattern) **ADE** – inva**de**/inva**s**ion **IDE** – colli**de**/colli**s**ion **ODE** – corro**de**/corro**s**ion **UDE** – exclu**de**/exclu**s**ion **USE** – confu**se**/confu**s**ion Words that end in **VERT**, (instead of just **RT**) are spelled with **SION** extro**vert/extroversion** sub**vert/subversion** Words that end in **PEL** are spelled with **SION** (note the **e** turns into **u**) ex**pel**/ex**pul**sion re**pel**/re**pul**sion Use **SION** for verbs ending in **MIT** ad**mit**/ad**miss**ion per**mit**/per**miss**ion	Use **SSION** with base words that end in double **SS** confe**ss** - confe**ss**ion Use **SSION** for verbs ending in **CEDE** (replace **DE** with **SS**) conce**de**/conce**ss**ion rece**de**/rece**ss**ion	Used only for a person who participates in an activity, usually an occupation. The base word ending is **IC.** mus**ic**/mus**ic**ian mag**ic**/mag**ic**ian

Traditional Syllable Division Cards

TION is a whole syllable and is learned as a unit.

tion	ation
sion	ssion

cian	ician
tian	itian

xion	cion
tial	cial

tious	cious
gion	

tient	cient
tience	cience

ation	etion
ition	otion

ution	ion

l	ll	n	g	

Phoneme/Grapheme Cards

TI, SI, or CI is pronounced /sh/ and is combined with a traditional suffix

-ON, -AN, -AL, -OUS, -ENT, -ENCE

ti	si
ci	xi

an	al
on	ous

ent	ence
ion	

a	e	i	o	u
l	ll	n	g	

Morphology Cards

T from **TION** stays with the base word (**react, reaction**)

In this model, some base word endings need to be changed (**conclude/conclusion**)

-ion	-ian
-ial	

i + ous	i + ent
i + ence	

atȇ+ ion	etȇ + ion
it + ion itȇ + ion	otȇ + ion

ut~~e~~ + ion	

tion

ti on

t + ion

- See notes at the beginning of this section, "Different Approaches **TION** or **ION**?"
- **-ION** changes verbs into nouns.
- Most suffixes become their own syllable when they are added to the end of a word. However, when **-ED** is added onto words and is pronounced **/d/** or **/t/**, it does not create a new syllable because there is no new vowel sound. For those words, I have separated **-ED** from the rest of the syllable by a dash (**cau tion-ed**).
- This list does not include **ATION** words, or other similar combinations. Those each have their own word list.

abduction	ab **duc** tion
absorption	ab **sorp** tion
abstention	ab **sten** tion
abstraction	ab **strac** tion
action	**ac** tion
actionable	**ac** tion a ble
adaption	a **dap** tion
addiction	ad **dic** tion
adoption	ad **op** tion
affection	af fec tion
affectionate	af **fec** tion ate
affectionately	af **fec** tion ate ly
affliction	af **flic** tion
apportion	ap **por** tion
apportioned	ap **por** tion ed
apportioning	ap **por** tion ing
apportionment	ap **por** tion ment
assertion	as **ser** tion
assumption	as **sump** tion
attention	at **ten** tion
attraction	at **trac** tion
auction	**auc** tion
auctioned	**auc** tion-ed
auctioneer	auc tion **eer**
auctioning	**auc** tion ing
bastion	**bas** tion
benediction	ben e **dic** tion
caption	**cap** tion
captioned	**cap** tion-ed
captioning	**cap** tion ing
caution	**cau** tion
cautionary	**cau** tion ar y
cautioned	**cau** tion-ed
cautioning	**cau** tion ing
circumspection	cir cum **spec** tion
circumvention	cir cum **ven** tion
collection	col **lec** tion
combustion	com **bus** tion
commotion	com **mo** tion

completion	com **ple** tion
compunction	com **punc** tion
conception	con **cep** tion
concoction	con **coc** tion
conduction	con **duc** tion
confection	con **fec** tion
confectionery	con **fec** tion er y
congestion	con **ges** tion
conjunction	con **junc** tion
connection	con **nec** tion
conscription	con **scrip** tion
constitution	con sti **tu** tion
constitutional	con sti **tu** tion al
constitutionalism	con sti **tu** tion al ism
constitutionally	con sti **tu** tion al ly
constriction	con **stric** tion
construction	con **struc** tion
consumption	con **sump** tion
contention	con **ten** tion
contortion	con **tor** tion
contortionist	con **tor** tion ist
contraction	con **trac** tion
contractions	con **trac** tions
contradiction	con tra **dic** tion
contraption	con **trap** tion
contravention	con tra **ven** tion
contribution	con tri **bu** tion
convention	con **ven** tion
conventional	con **ven** tion al
conventionality	con ven tion **al** i ty
conventionally	con **ven** tion al ly
conventioneer	con ven tion **eer**
conviction	con **vic** tion
convolution	con vo **lu** tion
correction	cor **rec** tion
correctional	cor **rec** tion al
corruption	cor **rup** tion
deception	de **cep** tion
decomposition	de com po **si** tion
deconstruction	de con **struc** tion
deconstructionism	de con struc tion ism
deconstructionist	de con struc tion ist
deduction	de **duc** tion
defection	de **fec** tion
deflationary	de **fla** tion ar y
deflection	de **flec** tion
dejection	de **jec** tion
denationalize	de **na** tion al ize
denationalized	de **na** tion al iz-ed
depiction	de **pic** tion
dereliction	der e **lic** tion
description	de **scrip** tion
deselection	de se **lec** tion
desertion	de **ser** tion
destruction	de **struc** tion
detection	de **tec** tion
detention	de **ten** tion
devotional	de **vo** tion al
diction	**dic** tion
dictionary	**dic** tion ar y
diffraction	dif **frac** tion
digestion	di **ges** tion
direction	di **rec** tion
directional	di **rec** tion al
directionless	di **rec** tion less
disaffection	dis af **fec** tion
disconnection	dis con **nec** tion
discretionary	dis **cre** tion ar y
disproportion	dis pro **por** tion
disproportionate	dis pro **por** tion ate
disproportionately	dis pro **por** tion ate ly
disruption	dis **rup** tion
dissatisfaction	dis sat is **fac** tion
dissection	dis **sec** tion
dissolution	dis so **lu** tion
distention	dis **ten** tion
distinction	dis **tinc** tion
distortion	dis **tor** tion

distraction	dis **trac** tion
dysfunction	dys **func** tion
dysfunctional	dys **func** tion al
ejection	e **jec** tion
election	e **lec** tion
electioneering	e lec tion **eer** ing
emotional	e **mo** tion al
emotionalism	e **mo** tion al ism
emotionally	e **mo** tion al ly
emotionless	e **mo** tion less
encryption	en **cryp** tion
eruption	e **rup** tion
eviction	e **vic** tion
exception	ex **cep** tion
exceptionable	ex **cep** tion a ble
exceptional	ex **cep** tion al
exceptionally	ex **cep** tion al ly
executioner	ex e **cu** tion er
exemption	ex **emp** tion
exertion	ex **er** tion
exhaustion	ex **haus** tion
expeditionary	ex pe **di** tion ar y
expeditions	ex pe **di** tions
extinction	ex **tinc** tion
extortion	ex **tor** tion
extortioner	ex **tor** tion er
extortionist	ex **tor** tion ist
extraction	ex **trac** tion
extradition	ex tra **di** tion
faction	**fac** tion
factional	**fac** tion al
factionalism	**fac** tion al ism
fiction	**fic** tion
fictional	**fic** tion al
fictionalize	**fic** tion al ize
fictionalized	**fic** tion al ized
fictionalizing	**fic** tion al iz ing
fraction	**frac** tion
fractional	**frac** tion al
fractionally	**frac** tion al ly
friction	**fric** tion
function	**func** tion
functional	**func** tion al
functionalism	**func** tion al ism
functionalist	**func** tion al ist
functionality	func tion **al** i ty
functionally	**func** tion al ly
functionary	**func** tion ar y
functioned	**func** tion-ed
functioning	**func** tion ing
genuflection	gen u **flec** tion
gumption	**gump** tion
imperfection	im per **fec** tion
inaction	in **ac** tion
inattention	in at **ten** tion
indigestion	in di **ges** tion
indiscretion	in dis **cre** tion
induction	in **duc** tion
infection	in **fec** tion
inflection	in **flec** tion
infliction	in **flic** tion
infraction	in **frac** tion
ingestion	in **ges** tion
injection	in **jec** tion
injunction	in **junc** tion
inscription	in **scrip** tion
insertion	in **ser** tion
inspection	in **spec** tion
institutional	in sti **tu** tion al
institutionalize	in sti **tu** tion al ize
institutionalized	in sti **tu** tion al iz-ed
institutionalizing	in sti **tu** tion al iz ing
instruction	in **struc** tion
instructional	in **struc** tion al
insurrection	in sur **rec** tion
intention	in **ten** tion
intentional	in **ten** tion al
intentionally	in **ten** tion al ly

interaction	in ter **ac** tion
interception	in ter **cep** tion
interconnection	in ter con **nec** tion
interdiction	in ter **dic** tion
interjection	in ter **jec** tion
international	in ter **na** tion al
internationalism	in ter **na** tion al ism
internationalist	in ter **na** tion al ist
internationalize	in ter **na** tion al ize
internationalized	in ter **na** tion al iz-ed
internationalizing	in ter **na** tion al iz ing
internationally	in ter **na** tion al ly
interruption	in ter **rup** tion
intersection	in ter **sec** tion
intervention	in ter **ven** tion
interventionism	in ter **ven** tion ism
interventionist	in ter **ven** tion ist
introduction	in tro **duc** tion
introspection	in tro **spec** tion
invention	in **ven** tion
irrational	ir **ra** tion al
irrationality	ir ra tion **al** i ty
irrationally	ir **ra** tion al ly
irresolution	ir res o **lu** tion
irruption	ir **rup** tion
junction	**junc** tion
jurisdiction	ju ris **dic** tion
juxtaposition	jux ta po **si** tion
locomotion	lo co **mo** tion
lotion	**lo** tion
malfunction	mal **func** tion
malfunctioned	mal **func** tion-ed
malfunctioning	mal **func** tion ing
mention	**men** tion
mentioned	**men** tion-ed
mentioning	**men** tion ing
midsection	**mid** sec tion
misconception	mis con **cep** tion
misconstruction	mis con **struc** tion
misdirection	mis di **rec** tion
motion	**mo** tion
motioned	**mo** tion-ed
motioning	**mo** tion ing
motionless	**mo** tion less
multinational	mul ti **na** tion al
nation	**na** tion
national	**na** tion al
nationalism	**na** tion al ism
nationalist	**na** tion al ist
nationalistic	na tion al **is** tic
nationality	na tion **al** i ty
nationalize	**na** tion al ize
nationalized	**na** tion al iz-ed
nationalizing	**na** tion al iz ing
nationally	**na** tion al ly
nationhood	**na** tion hood
nationwide	**na** tion wide
nonfiction	non **fic** tion
nonintervention	non in ter **ven** tion
notion	**no** tion
notionally	**no** tion al ly
nutritional	nu **tri** tion al
nutritionally	nu **tri** tion al ly
nutritionist	nu **tri** tion ist
objectionable	ob **jec** tion a ble
obstruction	ob **struc** tion
obstructionism	ob **struc** tion ism
obstructionist	ob **struc** tion ist
opposition	op po **si** tion
option	**op** tion
optional	**op** tion al
overproduction	o ver pro **duc** tion
overreaction	o ver re **ac** tion
perception	per **cep** tion
perfection	per **fec** tion
perfectionism	per **fec** tion ism
perfectionist	per **fec** tion ist
persecution	per se **cu** tion

petitioned — pe **ti** tion-ed
petitioner — pe **ti** tion er
portion — **por** tion
portioned — **por** tion-ed
portioning — **por** tion ing
positional — po **si** tion al
positioned — po **si** tion-ed
potion — **po** tion
practitioner — prac **ti** tion er
precaution — pre **cau** tion
precautionary — pre **cau** tion ar y
precognition — pre cog **ni** tion
preconception — pre con **cep** tion
precondition — pre con **di** tion
prediction — pre **dic** tion
predilection — pre di **lec** tion
predisposition — pre dis po **si** tion
prepositional — prep o **si** tion al
prescription — pre **scrip** tion
presupposition — pre sup po **si** tion
prevention — pre **ven** tion
production — pro **duc** tion
projection — pro **jec** tion
projectionist — pro **jec** tion ist
proportion — pro **por** tion
proportional — pro **por** tion al
proportionality — pro por tion **al** i ty
proportionally — pro **por** tion al ly
proportionate — pro **por** tion ate
proportionately — pro **por** tion ate ly
proportioned — pro por tion-ed
propositioning — pro po **si** tion ing
propositions — pro po **si** tions
proscription — pro **scrip** tion
protection — pro **tec** tion
protectionism — pro **tec** tion ism
protectionist — pro **tec** tion ist
question — **ques** tion
questionable — **ques** tion a ble
questioned — **ques** tion-ed
questioner — **ques** tion er
questioningly — **ques** tion ing ly
ration — **ra** tion
rational — **ra** tion al
rationalized — **ra** tion al ized
rationalizing — **ra** tion al iz ing
rationally — **ra** tion al ly
rationed — **ra** tion-ed
rationing — **ra** tion ing
reaction — re **ac** tion
reception — re **cep** tion
receptionist — re **cep** tion ist
recollection — re col **lec** tion
reconstruction — re con **struc** tion
redefinition — re def i **ni** tion
redemption — re **demp** tion
redistribution — re dis tri **bu** tion
reduction — re **duc** tion
reductionist — re **duc** tion ist
reflection — re **flec** tion
refraction — re **frac** tion
rejection — re **jec** tion
reproduction — re pro **duc** tion
resumption — re **sump** tion
resurrection — res ur **rec** tion
retention — re **ten** tion
retraction — re **trac** tion
retrospection — re tro **spec** tion
revolutionary — rev o **lu** tion ar y
revolutionize — rev o **lu** tion ize
revolutionized — rev o **lu** tion iz-ed
revolutionizing — rev o **lu** tion iz ing
sanction — **sanc** tion
sanctioned — **sanc** tion-ed
satisfaction — sat is **fac** tion
section — **sec** tion
sectional — **sec** tion al
sectioned — **sec** tion-ed

selection	se **lec** tion
subjection	sub **jec** tion
subscription	sub **scrip** tion
subsection	**sub** sec tion
substation	**sub** sta tion
suction	**suc** tion
suctioned	**suc** tion ed
suctioning	**suc** tion ing
suggestion	sug **ges** tion
traction	**trac** tion
transaction	trans **ac** tion
transcription	trans **scrip** tion
unconventional	un con **ven** tion al
unconventionally	un con **ven** tion al ly
undermentioned	un der **men** tion ed
unexceptionable	un ex **cep** tion a ble
unexceptional	un ex **cep** tion al
unintentional	un in **ten** tion al
unintentionally	un in **ten** tion al ly
unmentionable	un **men** tion a ble
unquestionable	un **ques** tion a ble
unquestionably	un **ques** tion a bly
unquestioned	un **ques** tion ed
unquestioning	un **ques** tion ing
unquestioningly	un **ques** tion ing ly

sion

/zhun/

si on

s + ion

- See notes at the beginning of this section, "Different Approaches **TION** or **ION**?"
- **-ION** changes verbs into nouns.
- **SION** can say **/shun/** or **/zhun/**. The words in this list say **/zhun/**.
- If the ending of a word is pronounced /zhun/, it is spelled **SION**, and never **TION**.
- **SION** is pronounced /zhun/ when following an open vowel or when following an **R**. It is pronounced /sion/ when following a consonant letter.

  invasion /in - v**a** – zhun/ (following open vowel)
  aversion /ah – ve**r** – zhun/ (following R)

  mission /mi**s** – shun/ (following consonant)

- When base words end in **DE**, the **DE** changes to **S**, then **-ION** is added.

  ADE – inva**de**/inva**sion**

  IDE – colli**de**/colli**sion**

  ODE – corro**de**/corro**sion**

  UDE – exclu**de**/exclu**sion**

- When base words end in **SE**, the **E** is dropped and **-ION** is added, resulting in **SION**.

  confu**se**/confu**sion**

  infu**se**/infu**sion**

- When a base word ends in **VERT,** the **T** changes to an **S** and **-ION** is added, resulting in **SION.**

  aver**t** – aver**s**ion
  diver**t** – diver**s**ion
  introver**t** – introver**s**ion

- Words that end in **SION** always have the accent/stress on the syllable proceeding the **SION** syllable.

abrasion	a **bra** sion
adhesion	ad **he** sion
allusion	al **lu** sion
aversion	a **ver** sion
cession	**ces** son
cohesion	co **he** sion
collision	col **li** sion
collusion	col **lu** sion
concision	con **ci** sion
conclusion	con **clu** sion
confusion	con **fu** sion
contusion	con **tu** sion
conversion	con **ver** sion
corrosion	cor **ro** sion
decision	de **ci** sion
delusion	de **lu** sion
derision	de **ri** sion
diffusion	dif **fu** sion
disillusion	dis il **lu** sion
disillusioned	dis il **lu** sion-ed
disillusioning	dis il **lu** sion ing
disillusionment	dis il **lu** sion ment
dispersion	dis **per** sion
diversion	di **ver** sion
diversionary	di **ver** sion ar y
division	di **vi** sion
divisional	di **vi** sion al
effusion	ef **fu** sion
envision	en **vi** sion
envisioned	en **vi** sion-ed
envisioning	en **vi** sion ing
erosion	e **ro** sion
evasion	e **va** sion
excision	ex **ci** sion
exclusion	ex **clu** sion
exclusionary	ex **clu** sion ar y
excursion	ex **cur** sion
explosion	ex **plo** sion
extrusion	ex tru sion
fusion	**fu** sion

illusion	il **lu** sion
illusionist	il **lu** sion ist
illusions	il **lu** sions
implosion	im **plo** sion
imprecision	im pre **ci** sion
incision	in **ci** sion
inclusion	in **clu** sion
incursion	in **cur** sion
indecision	in de **ci** sion
infusion	in **fu** sion
introversion	in tro ver sion
intrusion	in **tru** sion
invasion	in **va** sion
inversion	in **ver** sion
lesion	**le** sion
occasion	oc **ca** sion
occasional	oc **ca** sion al
occasionally	oc **ca** sion al ly
occasioned	oc **ca** sion-ed
occasioning	oc **ca** sion ing
precision	pre **ci** sion
preclusion	pre **clu** sion
profusion	pro **fu** sion
protrusion	pro **tru** sion
provision	pro **vi** sion
provisional	pro **vi** sion al
provisionally	pro **vi** sion al ly
provisioned	pro **vi** sion-ed
provisioning	pro **vi** sion ing
reversion	re **ver** sion
revision	re **vi** sion
revisionism	re **vi** sion ism
revisionist	re **vi** sion ist
seclusion	se **clu** sion
subdivision	sub di **vi** sion
subdivisions	sub di **vi** sions
submersion	sub **mer** sion
subversion	sub **ver** sion
supervision	su per **vi** sion
television	tel e **vi** sion
transfusion	trans **fu** sion
version	**ver** sion
vision	**vi** sion
visionary	**vi** sion ar y

sion

/shun/

si on

s + ion

- See notes at the beginning of this section, "Different Approaches **TION** or **ION**?"
- **-ION** changes verbs into nouns.
- **SION** can say **/shun/** or **/zhun/.** The words in this list are pronounced **/shun/.**
- The pronunciation **/zhun/** is the most common pronunciation for **SION** with one **S**. **SSION** with two **SS**'s is usually pronounced **/shun/.**
- **SION** is pronounced **/zhun/** when following an open vowel or when following an **R**. It is pronounced **/sion/** when following other consonant letters.

  invasion /in - v**a** – zhun/ (following open vowel)
  aversion /ah – ve**r** – zhun/ (following **R**)

  pension /pen – shun/ (following consonant)

- The majority of **SION** words that say **/shun/** fall in one of three categories:
  1) The base word ends in **SS** **(SSION)**
     discu**ss** – discu**ss**ion
  2) The base words ends in **-SE** (**E** is dropped)
     ten**se** - ten**s**ion
  3) The base word has a **D** that changes to **S**.
     apprehen**d** – apprehen**s**ion

- See **SSION** and **SION /zhun/** for more **SION** words.

- When base words end in **PEL**, the **E** changes to **U**, and **-ION** is added.

  ex**pel**/ex**pul**sion

  re**pel**/re**pul**sion

- Words that end in **SION** always have the accent/stress on the syllable proceeding the **SION** syllable.

apprehension	ap pre **hen** sion
ascension	a **scen** sion
comprehension	com pre **hen** sion
condescension	con de **scen** sion
convulsion	con **vul** sion
dimension	di **men** sion
distension	dis **ten** sion
emulsion	e **mul** sion
expansion	ex **pan** sion
expansionary	ex **pan** sion ar y
expansionism	ex **pan** sion ism
expansionist	ex **pan** sion ist
expulsion	ex **pul** sion
extension	ex **ten** sion
hypertension	hy per **ten** sion
immersion	im **mer** sion
imprecision	im pre **ci** sion
incomprehension	in com pre **hen** sion
mansion	**man** sion
misapprehension	mis ap pre **hen** sion
pension	**pen** sion
pensionable	**pen** sion a ble
pensioned	**pen** sion-ed
pensioner	**pen** sion er
pensioning	**pen** sion ing
pretension	pre **ten** sion
propulsion	pro **pul** sion
repulsion	re **pul** sion
revulsion	re **vul** sion
suspension	sus **pen** sion
tension	**ten** sion
torsion	**tor** sion

ssion

s si on

ss + ion

- See notes at the beginning of this section, "Different Approaches **TION** or **ION**?"
- **-ION** changes verbs into nouns.
- **SSION** words were primarily verbs that end in **SS**. When the **-ION** suffix was added, the words changed into nouns

  impress/impression

- Words that end in **SSION** always have the accent/stress on the syllable proceeding the **SION** syllable. The first **S** goes with the syllable that comes before the **SION**.

accession	ac **ces** sion	congressional	con **gres** sion al
admission	ad **mis** sion	decommission	de com **mis** sion
aggression	ag **gres** sion	decommissioned	de com **mis** sion ed
commission	com **mis** sion	decommissioning	de com **mis** sion ing
commissioned	com **mis** sion-ed	decompression	de com **pres** sion
commissioner	com **mis** sion er	depression	de **pres** sion
commissioning	com **mis** sion ing	digression	di **gres** sion
commissions	com **mis** sions	discussion	dis **cus** sion
compassion	com **pas** sion	dispassionate	dis **pas** sion ate
compassionate	com **pas** sion ate	dispassionately	dis **pas** sion ate ly
compassionately	com **pas** sion ate ly	dispossession	dis pos **ses** sion
compression	com **pres** sion	dissension	dis **sen** sion
concession	con **ces** sion	emission	e **mis** sion
concessionary	con **ces** sion ar y	expression	ex **pres** sion
concussion	con **cus** sion	expressionism	ex **pres** sion ism
confession	con **fes** sion	expressionist	ex **pres** sion ist
confessional	con **fes** sion al	expressionless	ex **pres** sion less

expressionlessly	ex **pres** sion less ly
fission	**fis** sion
impassioned	im **pas** sion-ed
impression	im **pres** sion
impressionable	im **pres** sion a ble
impressionism	im **pres** sion ism
impressionist	im **pres** sion ist
impressionistic	im **pres** sion is tic
intercession	in ter **ces** sion
intermission	in ter **mis** sion
mission	**mis** sion
missionary	**mis** sion ar y
obsession	ob **ses** sion
obsessional	ob **ses** sion al
obsessionally	ob **ses** sion al ly
omission	o **mis** sion
oppression	op **pres** sion
passion	**pas** sion
passionate	**pas** sion ate
passionately	**pas** sion ate ly
passionflower	**pas** sion flow er
passionless	**pas** sion less
percussion	per **cus** sion
percussionist	per **cus** sion ist
permission	per **mis** sion
possession	pos **ses** sion
procession	pro **ces** sion
processional	pro **ces** sion al
profession	pro **fes** sion
professional	pro **fes** sion al
professionalism	pro **fes** sion al ism
professionalization	pro **fes** sion al i za tion
professionalize	pro **fes** sion al ize
professionalized	pro **fes** sion al iz ed
professionalizing	pro **fes** sion al iz ing
professionally	pro **fes** sion al ly
progression	pro **gres** sion
recession	re **ces** sion
recessionary	re **ces** sion ar y
regression	re **gres** sion
remission	re **mis** sion
repercussion	re per **cus** sion
repossession	re pos **ses** sion
repression	re **pres** sion
retrogression	re tro **gres** sion
secession	se **ces** sion
secessionist	se **ces** sion ist
session	**ses** sion
submission	sub **mis** sion
succession	suc **ces** sion
suppression	sup **pres** sion
transgression	trans **gres** sion
transgressions	trans **gres** sions
transmission	trans **mis** sion
unprofessional	un pro **fes** sion al
unprofessionally	un pro **fes** sion al ly

cion, xion,

ci on, xi on

c + ion, x + ion

- See notes at the beginning of this section, "Different Approaches **TION** or **ION**?"
- **-ION** changes verbs into nouns.
- Words that end in **-ION** always have the accent/stress on the syllable proceeding the **-ION** syllable.

ION/CION/SCION

/zhun/, /shun/

coercion	co **er** cion
suspicion	sus **pi** cion
unconscionable	un **con** scion a ble
unconscionably	un **con** scion a bly

X-ION

/k-shun/

complexion	com **plex** ion
crucifixion	cru ci **fix** ion
inflexion	in **flex** ion

cian

(i-cian)

i ci an

ic + ian

- See notes at the beginning of this section, "Different Approaches **TION** or **ION**?"
- **-IAN** is a combination of connective **I** and the syllable **-AN.** It means "pertaining to."[7]
- **CIAN** is usually used for a person who is engaging in an occupation. The short I usually comes from the base word ending, **IC**.

  music - musician

  magic – magician

  clinic – clinician

- Words that end in **-IAN** always have the accent/stress on the syllable proceeding the-**IAN** syllable.

theoretician	*the or e **ti** cian	obstetrician	ob ste **tri** cian
academician	ac a de **mi** cian	optician	op **ti** cian
beautician	beau **ti** cian	patrician	pa **tri** cian
clinician	cli **ni** cian	pediatrician	pe di a **tri** cian
dietician	di e **ti** cian	physician	phy **si** cian
electrician	e lec **tri** cian	politician	pol i **ti** cian
geriatrician	ger i a **tri** cian	rhetorician	rhet o **ri** cian
magician	ma **gi** cian	statistician	stat is **ti** cian
mathematician	math e ma **ti** cian	tactician	tac **ti** cian
musician	mu **si** cian	technician	tech **ni** ican
musicianship	mu **si** cian ship	theoretician	the o re **ti** cian

[7] etymonline.com

tian

ti an

t + ian

- See notes at the beginning of this section, "Different Approaches **TION** or **ION**?"
- **-IAN** is a combination of a connective **I** and the syllable **-AN.** It means "pertaining to."[8]
- **TIAN** has at least three different pronunciations.

Titian	Ti tian
fustian	fus tian
gentian	gen tian
Christian	Chris tian
dalmatian	dal ma tian
dietitian	di e ti tian
Lilliputian	Lil li pu tian

[8] etymonline.com

ation

a ti on

at~~e~~ + ion

- See notes at the beginning of this section, "Different Approaches **TION** or **ION**?"
- The accent/stress in an **ATION** word are always on the syllable with the **A**. This is true, no matter how many suffixes are added.

con ser **va** tion	sen **sa** tion al
con ser **va** tion ist	sen **sa** tion al iz ing

- Many words that end in **ATION** are formed from the ending **ATE**, with the **E** dropped and **TION** added. This is not the only way to form **ATION** (see next note).

  educ**ate**/educ**ationa**l

  legistl**ate**/legisl**ation**

  negoti**ate**/negoti**ation**.

- Other words do not have English base words that end in **ATE**, but they still end in **-ATION**. There is some disagreement on whether or not this makes **-ATION** its own suffix. Many dictionaries, list **-ATION** as a legitimate suffix on its own. If you look back at the original Latin root of a word that is spelled **-ATION**, you can often find the "**at**" that is missing.
  - cancel (cancell**ate** is an uncommon usage) cancell**ation** (Latin *canell**at**io*)
  - prepare (prepar**ate** is an uncommon usage) prepar**ation** (Latin *prepar**at**io*)
  - accuse (no word accus**ate**) accus**ation** (Latin *accus**at**io*)
- When a word ending in **ATION** is divided into syllables with traditional syllable division, the **A** sometimes has its own syllable, and sometimes it joins the syllable before **TION.**

  ab bre ve **a** tion

  an no **ta** tion

- Some verb endings predictably add **-ATION.** They include

  Words that end in **IZE**

  author**ize** - authoriz**ation**

  immun**ize** - immuniz**ation**

  Words that end in **IFY**

  clarify - clarific**ation**

  falsify - falsific**ation**

  Words that end in **AIM**

  exclaim - exclam**ation**

  proclaim - proclam**ation**)

abbreviation	ab bre vi **a** tion
abdication	ab di **ca** tion
aberration	ab er **ra** tion
abnegation	ab ne **ga** tion
abomination	a bom i **na** tion
abrogation	ab ro **ga** tion
acceleration	ac cel er **a** tion
accentuation	ac cen tu **a** tion
acclimatization	ac cli ma ti **za** tion
accommodation	ac com mo **da** tion
accreditation	ac cred i **ta** tion
accumulation	ac cu mu **la** tion
accusation	ac cu **sa** tion
activation	ac ti **va** tion
adaptation	ad ap **ta** tion
adjudication	ad ju di **ca** tion
administration	ad min is **tra** tion
admiration	ad mi **ra** tion
adoration	ad or **a** tion
adulation	ad u **la** tion
affectation	af fec **ta** tion
affiliation	af fil i **a** tion
affirmation	af fir **ma** tion
afforestation	af for est **a** tion
agglomeration	ag glom er **a** tion
aggravation	ag gra **va** tion
aggregation	ag gre **ga** tion
agitation	ag i **ta** tion
alienation	a li en **a** tion
allegation	al le **ga** tion

alleviation	al le vi **a** tion
alliteration	al lit er **a** tion
allocation	al lo **ca** tion
alteration	al ter **a** tion
amortization	am or ti **za** tion
amplification	am pli fi **ca** tion
amputation	am pu **ta** tion
animation	an i **ma** tion
annexation	an nex **a** tion
annihilation	an ni hi **la** tion
annotation	an no **ta** tion
anticipation	an tic i **pa** tion
appellation	ap pel **la** tion
application	ap pli **ca** tion
appreciation	ap pre ci **a** tion
approbation	ap pro **ba** tion
approximation	ap prox i **ma** tion
arbitration	ar bi **tra** tion
argumentation	ar gu men **ta** tion
articulation	ar ti cu **la** tion
aspiration	as pi **ra** tion
assassination	as sas si **na** tion
assimilation	as sim i **la** tion
association	as so ci **a** tion
attenuation	at ten u **a** tion
attestation	at tes **ta** tion
augmentation	aug men **ta** tion
authentication	au then ti **ca** tion
authorization	au thor i **za** tion
automation	au to **ma** tion

aviation	a vi **a** tion
calculation	cal cu **la** tion
calibration	cal i **bra** tion
cancellation	can cel **la** tion
canonization	can on i **za** tion
capitalization	cap i tal i **za** tion
capitulation	cap it u **la** tion
castigation	cas ti **ga** tion
categorization	cat e gor i **za** tion
causation	cau **sa** tion
celebration	cel e **bra** tion
centralization	cen tral i **za** tion
certification	cer ti fi **ca** tion
cessation	ces **sa** tion
characterization	char ac ter i **za** tion
circulation	cir cu **la** tion
circumnavigation	cir cum nav i **ga** tion
citation	ci **ta** tion
civilization	civ i li **za** tion
clarification	clar i fi **ca** tion
classification	clas si fi **ca** tion
coagulation	co ag u **la** tion
codification	cod i fi **ca** tion
cogitation	cog i **ta** tion
collaboration	col lab o **ra** tion
collation	col **la** tion
collectivization	col lect ti vi **za** tion
coloration	col or **a** tion
colorization	col or i **za** tion
combination	com bi **na** tion
commemoration	com mem o **ra** tion
commendation	com men **da** tion
commercialization	com mer cial i **za** tion
commiseration	com mis er **a** tion
communication	com mu ni **ca** tion
commutation	com mu **ta** tion
compensation	com pen **sa** tion
compilation	com pi **la** tion
complication	com pli **ca** tion
computation	com pu **ta** tion
computational	com pu **ta** tion al
computerization	com put er i **za** tion
concentration	con cen **tra** tion
conceptualization	con cep tu al i **za** tion
conciliation	con cil i **a** tion
condemnation	con dem **na** tion
condensation	con den **sa** tion
confederation	con fed er **a** tion
configuration	con fig u **ra** tion
confirmation	con fir **ma** tion
confiscation	con fis **ca** tion
conflagration	con fla **gra** tion
conformation	con for **ma** tion
confrontation	con fron **ta** tion
confrontational	con fron **ta** tion al
conglomeration	con glom er **a** tion
congratulations	con grat u **la** tions
congregation	con gre **ga** tion
congregational	con gre **ga** tion al
conjugation	con ju **ga** tion
connotation	con no **ta** tion
consecration	con se **cra** tion
conservation	con ser **va** tion
conservationist	con ser **va** tion ist
consideration	con sid er **a** tion
consolation	con so **la** tion
consolidation	con sol i **da** tion
constellation	con stel **la** tion
consternation	con ster **na** tion
constipation	con sti **pa** tion
consultation	con sul **ta** tion
contamination	con tam i **na** tion
contemplation	con tem **pla** tion
contextualization	con tex tu al i **za** tion
continuation	con tin u **a** tion
contraindication	con tra in di **ca** tion
conversation	con ver **sa** tion
conversational	con ver **sa** tion al
conversationalist	con ver **sa** tion al ist
conversationally	con ver **sa** tion al ly
convocation	con vo **ca** tion
cooperation	co op er **a** tion
coordination	co or di **na** tion
coronation	cor o **na** tion
corporation	cor po **ra** tion
correlation	cor re **la** tion
corroboration	cor rob o **ra** tion
creation	cre **a** tion

creationism	cre **a** tion ism
creationist	cre **a** tion ist
crystallization	crys tal li **za** tion
culmination	cul mi **na** tion
cultivation	cul ti **va** tion
deceleration	de cel er **a** tion
decentralization	de cen tral i **za** tion
decimalization	dec i mal i **za** tion
decimation	dec i **ma** tion
declamation	dec la **ma** tion
declaration	dec la **ra** tion
declassification	de clas si fi **ca** tion
decolonization	de col o ni **za** tion
decoration	de co **ra** tion
decriminalization	de crim i nal i **za** tion
dedication	ded i **ca** tion
deflation	de **fla** tion
defoliation	de fo li **a** tion
deforestation	de for est **a** tion
deformation	de for **ma** tion
degeneration	de gen er **a** tion
dehumanization	de hu man i **za** tion
dehydration	de hy **dra** tion
deification	de i fi **ca** tion
delegation	del e **ga** tion
deliberation	de lib er **a** tion
delineation	de lin e **a** tion
demarcation	de mar **ca** tion
demilitarization	de mil i ta ri **za** tion
demobilization	de mo bi li **za** tion
democratization	de moc ra ti **za** tion
demonstration	dem on **stra** tion
demoralization	de mor al i **za** tion
demystification	de mys ti fi **ca** tion
denationalization	de na tion al iz **a** tion
denigration	den i **gra** tion
denomination	de nom i **na** tion
denominational	de nom i **na** tion al
denunciation	de nun ci **a** tion
depopulation	de pop u **la** tion
deportation	de por **ta** tion
depreciation	de pre ci **a** tion
depressurization	de pres sur i **za** tion
deprivation	dep ri **va** tion
deputation	dep u **ta** tion
deregulation	de reg u **la** tion
derivation	der i **va** tion
desalination	de sal i **na** tion
desecration	des e **cra** tion
desegregation	de seg re **ga** tion
desensitization	de sen si ti **za** tion
designation	des ig **na** tion
desolation	des o **la** tion
desperation	des per **a** tion
destabilization	de sta bi li **za** tion
destination	des ti **na** tion
deterioration	de te ri or **a** tion
determination	de ter mi **na** tion
detestation	des ti **na** tion
detonation	det o **na** tion
detoxification	de tox i fi **ca** tion
devaluation	de val u **a** tion
devastation	dev as **ta** tion
deviation	de vi **a** tion
dictation	dic **ta** tion
differentiation	dif fer en ti **a** tion
dilapidation	di lap i **da** tion
dilation	di **la** tion
disapprobation	dis ap pro **ba** tion
discoloration	dis col or **a** tion
discrimination	dis crim i **na** tion
disinclination	dis in cli **na** tion
disinformation	dis in for **ma** tion
disintegration	dis in te **gra** tion
dislocation	dis lo **ca** tion
disorganization	dis or gan i **za** tion
disorientation	dis o ri en **ta** tion
dispensation	dis pen **sa** tion
disputation	dis pu **ta** tion
disqualification	dis qual i fi **ca** tion
dissemination	dis sem i **na** tion
dissertation	dis ser **ta** tion
dissipation	dis si **pa** tion
dissociation	dis so ci **a** tion
distillation	dis til **la** tion
diversification	di ver si fi **ca** tion
documentation	doc u men **ta** tion
domestication	do mes ti **ca** tion

domination	dom i **na** tion
donation	do **na** tion
dramatization	dram a ti **za** tion
duplication	du pli **ca** tion
duration	du **ra** tion
evaporation	e vap or **a** tion
edification	ed i fi **ca** tion
education	ed u **ca** tion
educational	ed u **ca** tion al
educationalist	ed u **ca** tion al ist
educationally	ed u **ca** tion al ly
elaboration	e lab or **a** tion
elation	e **la** tion
electrification	e lec tri fi **ca** tion
elevation	el e **va** tion
elimination	e lim i **na** tion
elongation	e lon **ga** tion
elucidation	e lu ci **da** tion
emaciation	e ma ci **a** tion
emanation	em a **na** tion
emancipation	e man ci **pa** tion
emigration	em i **gra** tion
emulation	em u **la** tion
encapsulation	en cap su **la** tion
encrustation	en crus **ta** tion
enunciation	e nun ci **a** tion
equalization	e qual i **za** tion
equation	e **qua** tion
equivocation	e qui vo **ca** tion
eradication	e rad i **ca** tion
escalation	es ca **la** tion
estimation	es ti **ma** tion
evacuation	e vac u **a** tion
evaluation	e val u **a** tion
evaporation	e vap o **ra** tion
exacerbation	ex ac er **ba** tion
exaggeration	ex ag ger **a** tion
exaltation	ex al **ta** tion
examination	ex am i **na** tion
exasperation	ex as per **a** tion
excavation	ex ca **va** tion
exclamation	ex cla **ma** tion
excommunication	ex com mu ni **ca** tion
exemplification	ex em pli fi **ca** tion
exfoliation	ex fol i **a** tion
exhalation	ex ha **la** tion
exhilaration	ex hil a **ra** tion
exhortation	ex hor **ta** tion
exoneration	ex on er **a** tion
expectation	ex pec **ta** tion
experimentation	ex per i men **ta** tion
expiration	ex pir **a** tion
explanation	ex pla **na** tion
explication	ex pli **ca** tion
exploitation	ex ploi **ta** tion
exploration	ex plo **ra** tion
exportation	ex por **ta** tion
expostulation	ex pos tu **la** tion
expropriation	ex pro pri **a** tion
extemporization	ex tem po ri **za** tion
extenuation	ex ten u **a** tion
extermination	ex ter mi **na** tion
externalization	ex ter nal i **za** tion
extrapolation	ex trap o **la** tion
extrication	ex tri **ca** tion
exultation	ex ul **ta** tion
fabrication	fab ri **ca** tion
facilitation	fa cil i **ta** tion
falsification	fal si fi **ca** tion
familiarization	fa mil iar i **za** tion
fascination	fas ci **na** tion
federation	fed er **a** tion
fermentation	fer men **ta** tion
fertilization	fer ti li **za** tion
fictionalization	fic tion al i **za** tion
filtration	fil **tra** tion
finalization	fi na li **za** tion
fixation	fix **a** tion
flirtation	flir **ta** tion
fluctuation	fluc tu **a** tion
fluoridation	fluor i **da** tion
formalization	for mal i **za** tion
formation	for **ma** tion
formulation	for mu **la** tion
fortification	for ti fi **ca** tion
fossilization	fos sil i **za** tion
foundation	foun **da** tion
fragmentation	frag men **ta** tion

frustration	frus **tra** tion
fulmination	ful mi **na** tion
fumigation	fu mi **ga** tion
generalization	gen er al i **za** tion
generation	gen er **a** tion
generational	gen er **a** tion al
gentrification	gen tri fi **ca** tion
germination	ger mi **na** tion
gestation	ges **ta** tion
gesticulation	ges tic u **la** tion
glaciation	gla ci **a** tion
globalization	glob al i **za** tion
glorification	glo ri fi **ca** tion
gradation	gra **da** tion
graduation	grad u **a** tion
gratification	grat i fi **ca** tion
gravitation	grav i **ta** tion
gravitational	grav i **ta** tion al
habitation	hab i **ta** tion
hallucination	hal lu ci **na** tion
harmonization	har mo ni **za** tion
hesitation	hes i **ta** tion
hibernation	hi ber **na** tion
hospitalization	hos pi tal i **za** tion
humiliation	hu mil i **a** tion
hydration	hy **dra** tion
hyperinflation	hy per in **fla** tion
hyperventilation	hy per ven ti **la** tion
hyphenation	hy phen **a** tion
idealization	i de al i **za** tion
identification	i den ti fi **ca** tion
illumination	il lu mi **na** tion
illustration	il lus **tra** tion
imagination	im ag i **na** tion
imitation	im i **ta** tion
immigration	im mi **gra** tion
immobilization	im mo bi li **za** tion
impersonation	im per son **a** tion
implantation	im plan **ta** tion
implementation	im ple men **ta** tion
implication	im pli **ca** tion
importation	im por **ta** tion
improvisation	im prov i **sa** tion
imputation	im pu **ta** tion
inauguration	in au gu **ra** tion
incantation	in can **ta** tion
incarceration	in car cer **a** tion
incarnation	in car **na** tion
incineration	in cin er **a** tion
inclination	in cli **na** tion
incorporation	in cor por **a** tion
incrimination	in crim i **na** tion
incrustation	in crus **ta** tion
incubation	in cu **ba** tion
indemnification	in dem ni fi **ca** tion
indentation	in den **ta** tion
indexation	in dex **a** tion
indication	in di **ca** tion
indignation	in dig **na** tion
indoctrination	in doc tri **na** tion
industrialization	in dus tri al i **za** tion
infatuation	in fat u **a** tion
infestation	in fes **ta** tion
infiltration	in fil **tra** tion
inflammation	in flam **ma** tion
inflation	in **fla** tion
inflationary	in **fla** tion ar y
information	in for **ma** tion
informational	in for **ma** tion al
inhalation	in ha **la** tion
initiation	in i ti **a** tion
innovation	in no **va** tion
inoculation	in oc u **la** tion
insinuation	in sin u **a** tion
inspiration	in spi **ra** tion
inspirational	in spi **ra** tion al
installation	in stal **la** tion
instigation	in sti **ga** tion
institutionalization	in sti tu tion al i **za** tion
instrumentation	in stru men **ta** tion
insubordination	in sub or di **na** tion
insulation	in su **la** tion
integration	in te **gra** tion
intensification	in ten si fi **ca** tion
intercommunication	in ter com mu ni **ca** tion
interdenominational	in ter de nom i **na** tion al
internalization	in ter nal i **za** tion
interpretation	in ter pre **ta** tion

interrelation	in ter re **la** tion
interrelationship	in ter re **la** tion ship
interrogation	in ter ro **ga** tion
intimation	in ti **ma** tion
intimidation	in tim i **da** tion
intonation	in to **na** tion
intoxication	in tox i **ca** tion
inundation	in un **da** tion
invalidation	in val i **da** tion
investigation	in ves ti **ga** tion
invitation	in vi **ta** tion
invitational	in vi **ta** tion al
invocation	in vo **ca** tion
ionization	i on i **za** tion
irradiation	ir ra di **a** tion
irrigation	ir ri **ga** tion
irritation	ir ri **ta** tion
isolation	i so **la** tion
isolationism	i so **la** tion ism
isolationist	i so **la** tion ist
jubilation	ju bi **la** tion
justification	jus ti if **ca** tion
laceration	lac er **a** tion
lactation	lac **ta** tion
lamentation	lam en **ta** tion
legalization	le gal i **za** tion
legation	le **ga** tion
legislation	leg is **la** tion
liberation	lib er **a** tion
limitation	lim i **ta** tion
liquidation	liq ui **da** tion
litigation	lit i **ga** tion
location	lo **ca** tion
lubrication	lu bri **ca** tion
magnification	mag ni fi **ca** tion
maladministration	mal ad min is **tra** tion
malformation	mal for **ma** tion
manifestation	man i fes **ta** tion
manipulation	ma nip u **la** tion
marginalization	mar gin al i **za** tion
materialization	ma te ri al i **za** tion
matriculation	ma tric u **la** tion
maturation	mat u **ra** tion
maximization	max i mi **za** tion
mechanization	mech a ni **za** tion
mediation	me di **a** tion
medication	med i **ca** tion
meditation	med i **ta** tion
migration	mi **gra** tion
miniaturization	min i a tur i **za** tion
misapplication	mis ap pli **ca** tion
misappropriation	mis ap pro pri **a** tion
miscalculation	mis cal cu **la** tion
misinformation	mis in for **ma** tion
misinterpretation	mis in ter pre **ta** tion
mispronunciation	mis pro nun ci **a** tion
misquotation	mis quo **ta** tion
misrepresentation	mis rep re sen **ta** tion
mitigation	mit i **ga** tion
mobilization	mo bi li **za** tion
moderation	mod er **a** tion
modernization	mod ern i **za** tion
modification	mod i fi **ca** tion
modulation	mod u **la** tion
monopolization	mo nop i **za** tion
mortification	mor ti fi **ca** tion
motivation	mo ti **va** tion
multiplication	mul ti pli **ca** tion
mutation	mu **ta** tion
mutilation	mu ti **la** tion
mystification	mys ti fi **ca** tion
narration	nar **ra** tion
naturalization	nat ur al i **za** tion
nationhood	**na** tion hood
nationwide	**na** tion wide
naturalization	nat u ral i **za** tion
navigation	nav i **ga** tion
navigational	nav i **ga** tion al
negation	ne **ga** tion
negotiation	ne go ti **a** tion
neutralization	neu tral i **za** tion
nomination	nom i **na** tion
normalization	nor mal i **za** tion
notation	no **ta** tion
notification	no ti fi **ca** tion
obligation	ob li **ga** tion
obliteration	ob lit er **a** tion
observation	ob ser **va** tion

occupation	oc cu **pa** tion
occupational	oc cu **pa** tion al
occupationally	oc cu **pa** tion al ly
operation	op er **a** tion
operational	op er **a** tion al
operationally	op er **a** tion al ly
oration	or **a** tion
orchestration	or ches **tra** tion
ordination	or di **na** tion
organization	or gan i **za** tion
organizational	or gan i **za** tion al
orientation	or i en **ta** tion
ornamentation	or na men **ta** tion
oscillation	os cil **la** tion
ossification	os si fi **ca** tion
ostentation	os ten **ta** tion
ovation	o **va** tion
overestimation	o ver es ti **ma** tion
overpopulation	o ver pop u **la** tion
oversimplification	o ver sim pli fi **ca** tion
overvaluation	o ver val u **a** tion
ovulation	ov u **la** tion
oxidation	ox i **da** tion
oxygenation	ox y gen **a** tion
pacification	pac i fi **ca** tion
pagination	pag i **na** tion
palpation	pal **pa** tion
palpitation	pal pi **ta** tion
participation	par tic i **pa** tion
pasteurization	pas teur i **za** tion
pedestrianization	ped es tri an i **za** tion
perambulation	per am bu **la** tion
perforation	per for **a** tion
permeation	per me **a** tion
permutation	per mu **ta** tion
perpetration	per pe **tra** tion
personification	per son i fi **ca** tion
perspiration	per spi **ra** tion
perturbation	per tur **ba** tion
pigmentation	pig men **ta** tion
plantation	plan **ta** tion
polarization	po lar i **za** tion
politicization	po lit i ci **za** tion
pollination	pol li **na** tion
popularization	pop u lar i **za** tion
population	pop u **la** tion
precipitation	pre cip i **ta** tion
predestination	pre des ti **na** tion
predetermination	pre de ter mi **na** tion
prefabrication	pre fab ri **ca** tion
premeditation	pre med i **ta** tion
preoccupation	pre oc cu **pa** tion
preparation	pre par **a** tion
preregistration	pre reg is **tra** tion
presentation	pres en **ta** tion
preservation	pres er **va** tion
preservationist	pres er **va** tion ist
pressurization	pres sur i **za** tion
prevarication	pre var i **ca** tion
prioritization	pri or i ti **za** tion
privation	pri **va** tion
privatization	pri va ti **za** tion
probation	pro **ba** tion
probationary	pro **ba** tion ar y
probationer	pro **ba** tion er
proclamation	pro cla **ma** tion
procrastination	pro cras ti **na** tion
procreation	pro cre **a** tion
professionalization	pro fes sion al i **za** tion
prognostication	prog nos ti **ca** tion
proliferation	pro lif er **a** tion
prolongation	pro lon **ga** tion
promulgation	prom ul **ga** tion
pronunciation	pro nun ci **a** tion
propagation	prop a **ga** tion
propitiation	pro pi ti **a** tion
prostration	pros **tra** tion
protestation	prot es **ta** tion
provocation	prov o **ca** tion
publication	pub li **ca** tion
pulsation	pul **sa** tion
pulverization	pul ver i **za** tion
punctuation	punc tu **a** tion
purification	pu ri fi **ca** tion
qualification	qual i fi **ca** tion
quantification	quan ti fi **ca** tion
quotation	quo **ta** tion
radiation	ra di **a** tion

ramification	ram i fi **ca** tion
ratification	rat i fi **ca** tion
reaffirmation	re af fir **ma** tion
reaffirmations	re af fir **ma** tions
reafforestation	re af for es **ta** tion
realization	re al i **za** tion
recantation	re can **ta** tion
recapitalization	re cap i tal i **za** tion
recapitulation	re ca pit u **la** tion
recitation	rec i **ta** tion
reclamation	rec la **ma** tion
recommendation	rec om men **da** tion
reconciliation	re con cil li **a** tion
reconsideration	re con sid er **a** tion
recreation	rec re **a** tion
recreational	rec re **a** tion al
recrimination	re crim i **na** tion
rectification	rec ti fi **ca** tion
recuperation	re cu per **a** tion
redecoration	re dec o **ra** tion
reflationary	re **fla** tion ar y
reforestation	re for est **a** tion
reformation	ref or **ma** tion
refrigeration	re frig er **a** tion
refutation	ref u **ta** tion
regeneration	re gen er **a** tion
regimentation	reg i men **ta** tion
registration	reg is **tra** tion
regularization	reg u lar i **za** tion
regulation	reg u **la** tion
regurgitation	re gur gi **ta** tion
rehabilitation	re ha bil i **ta** tion
reinterpretation	re in ter pre **ta** tion
reiteration	re it er **a** tion
rejuvenation	re ju ve **na** tion
relation	re **la** tion
relational	re **la** tion al
relationship	re **la** tion ship
relaxation	re lax **a** tion
relegation	rel e **ga** tion
relocation	re lo **ca** tion
remuneration	re mu ner **a** tion
renovation	ren o **va** tion
renunciation	re nun ci **a** tion
reorganization	re or gan i **za** tion
reparation	rep a **ra** tion
repatriation	re pa tri **a** tion
replication	rep li **ca** tion
representation	rep re sen **ta** tion
representational	rep re sen **ta** tion al
repudiation	re pu di **a** tion
reputation	re pu **ta** tion
reservation	re ser **va** tion
resignation	res ig **na** tion
respiration	res pi **ra** tion
restoration	res to **ra--** tion
resuscitation	re sus ci **ta** tion
retaliation	re tal i **a** tion
reticulation	re tic u **la** tion
reunification	re u ni fi **ca** tion
revaluation	re val u **a** tion
revelation	rev e **la** tion
reverberation	re ver ber **a** tion
revocation	rev o **ca** tion
rotation	ro **ta** tion
ruination	ru in **a** tion
rumination	ru mi **na** tion
salivation	sal i **va** tion
salutation	sal u **ta** tion
salvation	sal **va** tion
sanctification	sanc ti fi **ca** tion
sanitation	san i **ta** tion
saturation	sat u **ra** tion
secularization	sec u lar i **za** tion
sedation	se **da** tion
sedimentation	sed i men **ta** tion
segmentation	seg men **ta** tion
segregation	seg re **ga** tion
segregationist	seg re **ga** tion ist
sensation	sen **sa** tion
sensational	sen **sa** tion al
sensationalism	sen **sa** tion al ism
sensationalist	sen **sa** tion al ist
sensationalize	sen **sa** tion al ize
sensationalized	sen **sa** tion al iz-ed
sensationalizing	sen **sa** tion al iz ing
sensationally	sen **sa** tion al ly
sensitization	sen si it **za** tion

separation	se par **a** tion
sequestration	se ques **tra** tion
serialization	se ri al i **za** tion
signification	sig ni fi **ca** tion
simplification	sim pli fi **ca** tion
simulation	sim u **la** tion
situation	sit u **a** tion
socialization	so cial i **za** tion
solemnization	sol em ni **za** tion
solidification	so lid i fi **ca** tion
sophistication	so phis ti **ca** tion
specialization	spe cial i **za** tion
specification	spec i fi **ca** tion
speculation	spec u **la** tion
stabilization	st bi li **za** tion
stagnation	stag **na** tion
standardization	stan dard i **za** tion
starvation	star **va** tion
station	**sta** tion
stationary	**sta** tion ar y
stationed	**sta** tion-ed
stationery	**sta** tion er y
stationing	**sta** tion ing
stationmaster	**sta** tion mas ter
sterilization	ster i li **za** tion
stigmatization	stig ma ti **za** tion
stimulation	stim u **la** tion
stipulation	stip u **la** tion
strangulation	stran gu **la** tion
stratification	strat i fi **ca** tion
striation	stri **a** tion
subjugation	sub ju **ga** tion
sublimation	sub li **ma** tion
subordination	sub or di **na** tion
subsidization	sub si di **za** tion
substantiation	sub stan ti **a** tion
substation	sub **sta** tion
suffocation	suf fo **ca** tion
summation	sum **ma** tion
superannuation	su per an nu **a** tion
supplementation	sup ple men **ta** tion
supplication	sup pli **ca** tion
synchronization	syn chro ni **za** tion
syncopation	syn co **pa** tion
syndication	syn di **ca** tion
systematization	sys tem a ti **za** tion
tabulation	tab u **la** tion
taxation	tax **a** tion
telecommunication	te le com mu ni **ca** tion
temptation	temp **ta** tion
termination	ter mi **na** tion
tessellation	tes sel **la** tion
toleration	tol er **a** tion
transfiguration	trans fig u **ra** tion
transformation	trans for **ma** tion
translation	trans **la** tion
transliteration	trans lit er **a** tion
transmigration	trans mit i **ga** tion
transmutation	trans mu **ta** tion
transpiration	tran spi **ra** tion
transportation	trans por **ta** tion
transubstantiation	trans sub stan ti **a** tion
trepidation	trep i **da** tion
triangulation	tri an gu **la** tion
tribulation	trib u **la** tion
truncation	trun **ca** tion
ulceration	ul cer **a** tion
underestimation	un der es ti **ma** tion
undulation	un du **la** tion
unification	u ni fi **ca** tion
unionization	un ion i **za** tion
urbanization	ur ban i **za** tion
usurpation	u sur **pa** tion
utilization	u ti li **za** tion
vacation	va **ca** tion
vacationed	va **ca** tion-ed
vacationer	va **ca** tion er
vacationing	va **ca** tion ing
vaccination	vac ci **na** tion
vacillation	vac i **la** tion
validation	val i **da** tion
valuation	val u **a** tion
vaporization	va por i **za** tion
variation	var i **a** tion
vegetation	veg e **ta** tion
veneration	ven er **a** tion
ventilation	ven ti **la** tion
verification	ver i fi **ca** tion

vexation	vex **a** tion	visualization	vis u al i **za** tion
vibration	vi **bra** tion	vocalization	vo cal i **za** tion
victimization	vic tim i **za** tion	vocation	vo **ca** tion
vilification	vil i fi **ca** tion	vocational	vo **ca** tion al
vindication	vin di **ca** tion	vocationally	vo **ca** tion al ly
violation	vi o **la** tion	westernization	west ern i **za** tion
visitation	vis it **a** tion	workstation	work **sta** tion

etion

e ti on

et~~e~~ + ion

- See notes at the beginning of this section, "Different Approaches **TION** or **ION**?"
- Words that end in **-ETE** drop the ending **E** and add **-ION**, resuting in **ETION**.

  compl**ete**/compl**etion**

  depl**ete**/depl**etion**

- Words that end in **ETION** always have the accent/stress on the syllable with the letter **E.**

accretion	ac **cre** tion
completion	com **ple** tion
deletion	de **le** tion
depletion	de **ple** tion
discretion	dis **cre** tion
discretionary	dis **cre** tion ar y
excretion	ex **cre** tion
indiscretion	in dis **cre** tion
secretion	se **cre** tion

ition

i ti on

it-ion/ it~~e~~ + ion

- See notes at the beginning of this section, "Different Approaches **TION** or **ION**?

- For words that end in **ITION:**

  -If the base word ends in the letters **IT** (not **MIT**), the ending will be spelled with a **T** (**TION**).

  fru**it** - fruit**ition**

  trans**it** - trans**ition**

  -If the base word ends in **MIT** instead of just **IT** the ending will be spelled with an **S** (**SION**).

  trans**mit**/transm**ission**

  ad**mit**/adm**ission**

  If the base word ends in **ITE,** the ending will be spelled with a **T (TION)**

  ign**ite** - ign**ition**

  exped**ite** – exped**ition**

- Words that end in **ITION** always have the accent/stress on the syllable with the letter **I.**

abolition	ab o **li** tion	ambition	am **bi** tion
abolitionist	ab o **li** tion ist	ammunition	am mu **ni** tion
acquisition	ac qui **si** tion	apparition	ap pa **ri** tion
addition	ad **di** tion	apposition	ap po **si** tion
additional	ad **di** tion al	attrition	at **tri** tion
additionally	ad **di** tion al ly	audition	au **di** tion
additions	ad **di** tions	auditioned	au **di** tion-ed
admonition	ad mo **ni** tion	auditioning	au **di** tion ing

coalition	co a **li** tion
cognition	cog **ni** tion
competition	com pe **ti** tion
composition	com po **si** tion
condition	con **di** tion
conditional	con **di** tion al
conditionally	con **di** tion al ly
conditioned	con **di** tion-ed
conditioner	con **di** tion er
conditioning	con **di** tion ing
contrition	con **tri** tion
decomposition	de com po **si** tion
definition	def i **ni** tion
demolition	dem o **li** tion
deposition	dep o **si** tion
disposition	dis po **si** tion
edition	e **di** tion
erudition	er u **di** tion
exhibition	ex hi **bi** tion
expedition	ex pe **di** tion
expeditionary	ex pe **di** tion ar y
exposition	ex po **si** tion
extradition	ex tra **di** tion
ignition	ig **ni** tion
imposition	im po **si** tion
indisposition	in dis po **si** tion
inhibition	in hi **bi** tion
inquisition	in qui **si** tion
intuition	in tu **i** tion
juxtaposition	jux ta po **si** tion
malnutrition	mal nu **tri** tion
munition	mu **ni** tion
munitions	mu **ni** tions
nutrition	nu **tri** tion
nutritional	nu **tri** tion al
nutritionally	nu **tri** tion al ly
nutritionist	nu **tri** tion ist
opposition	opp o **si** tion
partition	par **ti** tion
partitioned	par **ti** tion-ed
partitioning	par **ti** tion ing
perdition	per **di** tion
petition	pe **ti** tion
petitioned	pe **ti** tion-ed
petitioner	pe **ti** tion er
petitioning	pe **ti** tion ing
position	po **si** tion
positional	po **si** tion al
positioned	po **si** tion-ed
positioning	po **si** tion ing
practitioner	prac **ti** tion er
precognition	pre cog **ni** tion
precondition	pre con **di** tion
predisposition	pre dis po **si** tion
premonition	pre mo **ni** tion
preposition	pre po **si** tion
prepositional	pre po **si** tion al
presupposition	pre sup po **si** tion
prohibition	pro hi **bi** tion
proposition	pro po **si** tion
propositioned	pro po **si** tion-ed
propositioning	pro po **si** tion ing
recognition	re cog **ni** tion
recondition	re con **di** tion
reconditioned	re con **di** tion-ed
reconditioning	re con **di** tion ing
redefinition	re def i **ni** tion
rendition	ren **di** tion
repetition	rep e **ti** tion
requisition	req ui **si** tion

requisitioned	req ui **si** tion-ed
requisitioning	req ui **si** tion ing
sedition	se **di** tion
superstition	su per **sti** tion
supposition	sup po **si** tion
tradition	tra **di** tion
traditional	tra **di** tion al
traditionalism	tra **di** tion al ism
traditionalist	tra **di** tion al ist
traditionally	tra **di** tion al ly
transition	tran **si** tion
transitional	tran **si** tion al
transposition	trans po **si** tion
tuition	tu **i** tion
unconditional	un con **di** tion al
unconditionally	un con **di** iton al ly
volition	vo **li** tion

otion

o ti on

otẹ̸ + ion

- See notes at the beginning of this section, "Different Approaches **TION** or **ION**?"
- Base words ending in **-OTE**, will drop the **E** when they add **-ION,** resulting in **-OTION**

  dev**ote** – dev**otion**
  prom**ote** – prom**otion**
  em**ote** – em**otion**

- Words that end in **OTION** always have the accent/stress on the syllable with the letter **O.**

demotion	de **mo** tion
devotion	de **vo** tion
devotional	de **vo** tion al
devotional	de **vo** tion al
emotion	e **mo** tion
emotional	e **mo** tion al
emotionalism	e **mo** tion al ism
emotionally	e **mo** tion al ly
emotionally	e **mo** tion al ly
emotionless	e **mo** tion less
locomotion	lo co **mo** tion
promotion	pro **mo** tion
promotional	pro **mo** tion al
unemotional	un e **mo** tion al
unemotionally	un e **mo** tion al ly

ution

u ti on

ut~~e~~ + ion

- Base words ending in **UTE** will drop the **E** when adding the suffix **-ION**.

  attrib**ute** – attrib**ution**

  substit**ute** – substit**ution**

  constit**ute** - constit**ution**

- Base words that end in **OLVE** will drop the **VE** before adding **-UTE** and **-ION,** resulting in **UTION**

  ev**olve** – evol**ution**

  res**olve** – resol**ution**

  rev**olve** - revol**ution**

- Words that end in **UTION** always have the accent/stress on the syllable with the letter **U.**

absolution	ab so **lu** tion
attribution	at tri **bu** tion
circumlocution	cir cum lo **cu** tion
constitution	con sti **tu** tion
constitutional	con sti **tu** tion al
constitutionalism	con sti **tu** tion al ism
constitutionality	con sti **tu** tion al it y
constitutionally	con sti **tu** tion al ly
contribution	con tri **bu** tion
convolution	con vo **lu** tion
counterrevolution	coun ter rev o **lu** tion
destitution	des ti **tu** tion
devolution	dev o **lu** tion
dilution	di **lu** tion
dissolution	dis so **lu** tion
distribution	dis tri **bu** tion
distributional	dis tri **bu** tion al
electrocution	e lec tro **cu** tion
elocution	el o **cu** tion
evolution	ev o **lu** tion
evolutionary	ev o **lu** tion ar y
execution	ex e **cu** tion
executioner	ex e **cu** tion er
institution	in sti **tu** tion
institutional	in sti **tu** tion al
institutionalization	in sti **tu** tion al i za tion
institutionalize	in sti **tu** tion al ize
institutionalized	in sti **tu** tion al iz-ed
institutionalizes	in sti **tu** tion al iz es
institutionalizing	in sti **tu** tion al iz ing

irresolution	ir res o **lu** tion	revolution	rev o **lu** tion
locution	lo **cu** tion	revolutionaries	rev o **lu** tion ar ies
persecution	per se **c**u tion	revolutionary	rev o **lu** tion ar y
pollution	pol **lu** tion	revolutionize	rev o **lu** tion ize
prosecution	pros e **cu** tion	revolutionized	rev o **lu** tion iz-ed
prostitution	pros ti **tu** tion	revolutionizes	rev o **lu** tion iz es
reconstitution	re con sti **tu** tion	revolutionizing	rev o **lu** tion iz ing
redistribution	re dis tri **bu** tion	solution	so **lu** tion
resolution	res o **lu** tion	substitution	sub sti **tu** tion
restitution	res ti **tu** tion	unconstitutional	un con sti **tu** tion al
retribution	ret ri **bu** tion	unconstitutionally	un con sti **tu** tion al ly

lion/llion

li on, lli on

l + ion, ll + ion

- See notes at the beginning of this section, "Different Approaches **TION** or **ION?**"
- Words that end in **-ION** always have the accent/stress on the syllable proceeding the **-ION** syllable. That includes the first **L** if the word ends in **LION** or **LLION**.

LION

battalion	bat **tal** ion
pavilion	pa **vil** ion
Vermilion	Ver **mil** ion

LLION

billion	**bil** lion
billionaire	**bil** lion **aire**
billionths	**bil** lionths
bullion	**bul** lion
medallion	me **dal** lion
million	**mil** lion
millionaire	**mil** lion aire
millionairess	mil lion **air** ess
millionth	**mil** lionth
millionths	**mil** lionths
multimillionaire	mul ti **mil** lion aire
rebellion	re **bel** lion
scallion	**scal** lion
stallion	**stal** lion
trillion	**tril** lion
zillion	**zil** lion

nion

n ion

n + ion

- See notes at the beginning of this section, "Different Approaches **TION** or **ION**?"
- Words that end in **-ION** always have the accent/stress on the syllable proceeding the **-ION** syllable. That syllable includes the **N** in **NION**.

bunion	**bun** ion	pinioned	**pin** ion ed
communion	com **mun** ion	pinioning	**pin** ion ing
companion	com **pan** ion	reunion	re **un** ion
companionable	com **pan** ion a ble	union	**un** ion
companionably	com **pan** ion a bly	unionism	**un** ion ism
companionship	com **pan** ion ship	unionist	**un** ion ist
dominion	do **min** ion	unionization	**un** ion i **za** tion
onion	**on** ion	unionize	**un** ion ize
opinion	o **pin** ion	unionized	**un** ion iz-ed
opinionated	o **pin** ion ate ed	unionizes	**un** ion iz-es
pinion	**pin** ion	unionizing	**un** ion iz-ing

gion

g ion

g + ion

- See notes at the beginning of this section, "Different Approaches **TION** or **ION**?"
- This combination is rare.

contagion	con **ta** gion	region	**re** gion
legion	**le** gion	regional	**re** gion al
legionaries	le gion **air** ies	regionalism	**re** gion al ism
legionary	**le** gion ar y	regionally	**re** gion al ly
legionnaire	le gion **naire**	religion	re **li** gion

tial

ti al

t + ial

- See notes at the beginning of this section, "Different Approaches **TION** or **ION**?"
- **TIAL** is pronounced two different ways: **/shul/** or **/chul/.**
- Most of the **TIAL** words are formed because of one of the following:
  1) They have the letter **T** at the end of the base word, with **-IAL** added.
     residen**t** - residen**tial**
  2) They have **T-IAL** in the Latin root
     Latin root *mar**tial**is* – mar**tial**
     Latin root *nup**tial**is* - nup**tial**s
  3) They have the letters **-CE** at the end of the base word. (**CIAL** can also be formed in this way)
     consequen**ce** – consequen**tial**
     circumstan**ce** – circumstan**tial**
- Words that end in **IAL/TIAL** always have the accent/stress on the syllable proceeding the **IAL/TIAL** syllable.

celestial	ce **les** tial	differential	dif fer **en** tial
circumstantial	cir cum **stan** tial	differentials	dif fer **en** tials
confidential	con fi **den** tial	essential	es **sen** tial
consequential	con se **quen** tial	essentially	es **sen** tial ly
consequentially	con se **quen** tial ly	existential	ex is **ten** tial
credential	cre **den** tial	existentialism	ex is **ten** tial ism
credentialed	cre **den** tial-ed	existentialist	ex is **ten** tial ist
credentialing	cre **den** tial ing	existentialists	ex is **ten** tial ists
deferential	de fer **en** tial	experiential	ex pe ri **en** tial
deferentially	de fer **en** tial ly	exponential	ex po **nen** tial

exponentially	ex po **nen** tial ly
impartial	im **par** tial
impartially	im **par** tial ly
inconsequential	in con se **quen** tial
inconsequentially	in con se **quen** tial ly
inertial	in **er** tial
inessential	in es **sen** tial
influential	in flu **en** tial
initial	in **i** tial
initialed	in **i** tial-ed
initialing	in **i** tial ing
initially	in **i** tial ly
insubstantial	in sub **stan** tial
martial	**mar** tial
nonessential	non es **sen** tial
nuptials	**nup** tials
palatial	pa **la** tial
partial	**par** tial
penitential	pen i **ten** tial
pestilential	pes ti **len** tial

potential	po **ten** tial
potentially	po **ten** tial ly
preferential	pre fer **en** tial
preferentially	pre fer **en** tial ly
presidential	pres i **den** tial
providential	prov i **den** tial
providentially	prov i **den** tial ly
quintessential	quin tes **sen** tial
quintessentially	quin tes **sen** tial ly
residential	res i **den** tial
reverential	rev er **en** tial
reverentially	rev er **en** tial ly
sequential	se **quen** tial
sequentially	se **quen** tial ly
spatial	**spa** tial
spatially	**spa** tial ly
substantial	sub **stan** tial
substantially	sub **stan** tial ly
tangential	tan **gen** tial
torrential	tor **ren** tial

cial

ci al

c + ial

- See notes at the beginning of this section, "Different Approaches **TION** or **ION**?"
- Most of the **CIAL** words are formed because of one of the following:
  1) They have the letters **-CE** at the end of the base word. (**TIAL** can also be formed from **-CE** words).

     finan**ce** – finan**cial**

     ra**ce** - ra**cial**
  2) They have **CIAL** in the Latin root.

     Latin root *artifi**ciali**s* - ar ti fi **cial**

     Latin root *gla**ciali**s* - gla **cial**

- Words that end in **IAL/CIAL** always have the accent/stress on the syllable proceeding the **IAL/CIAL** syllable.

antisocial	an ti **so** cial	especially	es **pe** cial ly
artificial	ar ti **fi** cial	extrajudicial	ex tra ju **di** cial
artificially	ar ti **fi** cial ly	facial	**fa** cial
beneficial	ben e **fi** cial	facially	**fa** cial ly
commercial	com **mer** cial	financial	fi **nan** cial
commercialism	com **mer** cial ism	financially	fi **nan** cial ly
commercialization	com **mer** cial i za tion	glacial	**gla** cial
commercialize	com **mer** cial ize	infomercial	**in** fo mer cial
commercialized	com **mer** cial iz-ed	interracial	in ter **ra** cial
commercializing	com **mer** cial iz ing	judicial	ju **di** cial
commercially	com **mer** cial ly	judicially	ju **di** cial ly
crucial	**cru** cial	multiracial	mul ti **ra** cial
crucially	**cru** cial ly	official	of **fi** cial
especial	es **pe** cial	officialese	of **fi** cial ese

officially	of **fi** cial ly
prejudicial	pre ju **di** cial
provincial	pro **vin** cial
provincialism	pro **vin** cial ism
provincially	pro **vin** cial ly
racial	**ra** cial
racialism	**ra** cial ism
racialist	**ra** cial ist
racially	**ra** cial ly
sacrificial	sac ri **fi** cial
sacrificially	sac ri **fi** cial ly
social	**so** cial
socialism	**so** cial ism
socialist	**so** cial ist
socialistic	so cial **is** tic
socialite	**so** cial ite
socialization	so cial i **za** tion
socialize	**so** cial ize
socialized	**so** cial iz-ed
socializes	**so** cial iz es
socializing	**so** cial iz ing
socially	**so** cial ly
special	**spe** cial
specialist	**spe** cial ist
specialization	spe cial i **za** tion
specializations	spe cial i **za** tions
specialize	**spe** cial ize
specialized	**spe** cial i z-ed
specializes	**spe** cial iz es
specializing	**spe** cial iz ing
specially	**spe** cial ly
specialties	**spe** cial ties
specialty	**spe** cial ty
superficial	su per **fi** cial
superficially	su per **fi** cial ly
unofficial	un of **fi** cial
unofficially	un of **fi** cial ly
unsocial	un **so** cial

tious

ti ous

t + ious

- See notes at the beginning of this section, "Different Approaches **TION** or **ION**?"
- Most **TIOUS** words are formed because of one of the following:
  1) The base word ends in the letter **T** or **D**

     conten**d** – conten**tious**

     infec**t** - infec**tious**
  2) The base word ends in the letters **CE**

     preten**ce** – pretentious

     conscien**ce** - conscien**tious**
  3) They have **T** or **C** in the bound Latin root.

     Latin root *cautio* - cau**tious**

     Latin root *nutricius* – nutri**tious**
- Words that end in **IOUS/TIOUS** always have the accent/stress on the syllable proceeding the **IOUS/TIOUS** syllable.

adventitious	ad ven **ti** tious	contentious	con **ten** tious
adventitiously	ad ven **ti** tious ly	contentiously	con **ten** tious ly
ambitious	am **bi** tious	contentiousness	con **ten** tious ness
ambitiously	am **bi** tious ly	expeditious	ex pe **di** tious
captious	**cap** tious	expeditiously	ex pe **di** tious ly
cautious	**cau** tious	facetious	fa **ce** tious
cautiously	**cau** tious ly	facetiously	fa **ce** tious ly
cautiousness	**cau** tious ness	facetiousness	fa **ce** tious ness
conscientious	con sci **en** tious	factitious	fac **ti** tious
conscientiously	con sci **en** tious ly	fictitious	fic **ti** tious
conscientiousness	con sci **en** tious ness	flirtatious	flir **ta** tious

flirtatiously	flir **ta** tious ly
flirtatiousness	flir **ta** tious ness
fractious	**frac** tious
fractiousness	**frac** tious ness
incautious	in **cau** tious
incautiously	in **cau** tious ly
infectious	in **fec** tious
infectiously	in **fec** tious ly
nutritious	nu **tri** tious
ostentatious	os ten **ta** tious
ostentatiously	os ten **ta** tious ly
pretentious	pre **ten** tious
pretentiously	pre **ten** tious ly
pretentiousness	pre **ten** tious nes
repetitious	re pe **ti** tious
seditious	se **di** tious
superstitious	su per **sti** tious
superstitiously	su per **sti** tious ly
surreptitious	sur rep **ti** tious
surreptitiously	sur rep **ti** tious ly
surreptitiousness	sur rep **ti** tious ness
unambitious	un am **bi** tious
unpretentious	un pre **ten** tious
vexatious	vex a tious
vexatiously	vex a tious ly

cious

ci ous

c + ious

- See notes at the beginning of this section, "Different Approaches **TION** or **ION**?"
- Most **CIOUS** words are formed because of one of the following:
  1) The base word ends in the letters **CE**

     gra**ce** – gra**ci**ous

     spa**ce** - spa**ci**ous

  2) The Latin root includes **CE** or **CI**.

     Latin root *auda**ce*** – auda**ci**ous

     Latin root *deli**ci**a* - deli**ci**ous
- Words that end in **IOUS/CIOUS/SCIOUS** always have the accent/stress on the syllable proceeding the **IOUS/CIOUS/SCIOUS** syllable.
- Some **CIOUS** syllables have an extra **S – SCIOUS**. All the **SCIOUS** words are related to the word **conscious** which is from the Latin ***conscius***.

atrocious	a **tro** cious
atrociously	a **tro** cious ly
audacious	au **da** cious
audaciously	au **da** cious ly
auspicious	au **spi** cious
avaricious	av a **ri** cious
avariciously	av a **ri** cious ly
capacious	ca **pa** cious
capricious	ca **pri** cious
capriciously	ca **pri** cious ly
capriciousness	ca **pri** cious ness
conscious	**con** scious
consciously	**con** scious ly
consciousness	**con** scious ness
consciousness	**con** scious ness
delicious	de **li** cious
deliciously	de **li** cious ly
efficacious	ef fi **ca** cious
fallacious	fal **la** cious
fallaciously	fal **la** cious ly
ferocious	fer **o** cious
ferociously	fer **o** cious ly
ferociousness	fer **o** cious ness
gracious	**gra** cious
graciously	**gra** cious ly
graciousness	**gra** cious ness
inauspicious	in aus **pi** cious
inauspiciously	in aus **pi** cious ly

injudicious	in ju **di** cious
injudiciously	in ju **di** cious ly
judicious	ju **di** cious
judiciously	ju **di** cious ly
loquacious	lo **qua** cious
loquaciously	lo **qua** cious ly
malicious	ma **li** cious
maliciously	ma **li** cious ly
mendacious	men **da** cious
officious	of **fi** cious
officiously	of **fi** cious ly
officiousness	of **fi** cious ness
pernicious	per **ni** cious
perspicacious	pers pi **ca** cious
pertinacious	per ti **na** cious
precious	**pre** cious
preciously	**pre** cious ly
preciousness	**pre** cious ness
precocious	pre **co** cious
precociously	pre **co** cious ly
precociousness	pre **co** cious ness
pugnacious	pug **na** cious
pugnaciously	pug **na** cious ly
rapacious	ra **pa** cious
rapaciously	ra **pa** cious ly
rapaciousness	ra **pa** cious ness
sagacious	sa **ga** cious
sagaciously	sa **ga** cious ly
salacious	sa **la** cious
salaciously	sa **la** cious ly

salaciousness	sa **la** cious ness
semiprecious	sem i **pre** cious
spacious	**spa** cious
spaciously	**spa** cious ly
spaciousness	**spa** cious ness
subconscious	sub **con** scious
subconscious	sub **con** scious
subconsciously	sub **con** scious ly
subconsciously	sub **con** scious ly
suspicious	sus **pi** cious
suspiciously	sus **pi** cious ly
tenacious	ten **a** cious
tenaciously	ten **a** cious ly
unconscious	un **con** scious
unconscious	un **con** scious
unconsciously	un **con** scious ly
unconsciously	un **con** scious ly
unconsciousness	un **con** scious ness
unconsciousness	un **con** scious ness
ungracious	un **gra** cious
ungraciously	un **gra** cious ly
vicious	**vi** cious
viciously	**vi** cious ly
viciousness	**vi** cious ness
vivacious	vi **va** cious
vivaciously	vi **va** cious ly
voracious	vor **a** cious
voraciously	vor **a** cious ly
voraciousness	vor **a** cious ness

tient/tience

ti ent / ti ence

t + ient / t + ience

- See notes at the beginning of this section, "Different Approaches **TION** or **ION**?"
- Most **TIENT** words are related to the word **patient**, which comes from the Latin ***patientem***. Quotient comes from the Latin ***quotiens***. Sentient comes from the Latin ***sentiens***.

TIENT

/shent/

impatient	im **pa** tient
impatiently	im **pa** tient ly
outpatient	out **pa** tient
patient	**pa** tient
patiently	**pa** tient ly
quotient	**quo** tient
sentient	**sen** tient

(pronounced /tee-ent/

TIENCE

/shens/

impatience	im **pa** tience
patience	**pa** tience

cient/cience

ci ent / ci ence

c + ient / c + ience

- See notes at the beginning of this section, "Different Approaches **TION** or **ION**?"
- **CIENT** is pronounced two different ways: **/shent/** or **/chent/.** The **E** may make a schwa sound.
- Most **CIENT** words have a Latin root that includes **CIEN**

  effi**cien**t – Latin *effi**cien**s*

  suffi**cien**t – Latin *suffi**cien**s*

- The combination **CIENCE** is rare and pronounced different ways.
- The word **science** does not end in the **CI + ENCE** combination. **Science** comes from the Old French ***science***, which derives from the Latin ***scientia***.[9]

CIENT		**CIENCE/SCIENCE**	
ancient	**an** cient	conscience	**con** science
coefficient	co ef **fi** cient	prescience	**pre** sci ence
deficient	de **fi** cient	(pronounced /pre-se-uns/ or /pre-she-uns/	
efficient	ef **fi** cient	omniscience	om **nis** cience
efficiently	ef **fi** cient ly		
inefficient	in ef **fi** cient		
inefficiently	in ef **fi** cient ly		
insufficient	in suf **fi** cient		
insufficiently	in suf **fi** cient ly		
omniscient	om **nis** cient		
proficient	pro **fi** cient		
sufficient	suf **fi** cient		
sufficiently	suf **fi** cient ly		

[9] etmonline.com

Resources

Contractions
not - set 1

Building contractions - these pages can be printed on card stock, cut out, and used as a manipulative to build contractions. The apostrophe can be used to cover up the letters that are removed to make the contraction. The apostrophe box may need to be trimmed on the right to fit over the vowel.

did	not	’	didn’t
are	not	’	aren’t
can	not	’	can’t
did	not	’	didn’t
do	not	’	don’t

Matching contractions

did not	didn’t
are not	aren’t
can not	can’t
did not	didn’t
do not	don’t

Contractions

not - set 2

Building contractions

does	not	’	doesn’t
has	not	’	hasn’t
have	not	’	haven’t
is	not	’	isn’t
was	not	’	wasn’t
were	not	’	weren’t

Changing **will not** to **won’t** involves replacing the **ill** with **on**. This contraction change can be confusing for some students. There were many changes with the vowel on this particular word through history. The Old English word **willan** referred to **willing** or **wishing** in the present and **wold** referred to **willing** in the past. At one time **willn’t** was the contraction. Another time **woll not** was used instead of **wold not**. The best way to approach this is to remind students that they say “won’t” naturally when they speak. They do not say “willn’t.”[10] See next page for matching contractions

will	not	’	on	won’t

[10] Okrent, Arika. Why Does “Will Not” Become Won’t”? www.mentalfloss.com.

Contractions
not - set 2

Matching contractions

does not	doesn’t
has not	hasn’t
have not	haven’t
is not	isn’t
was not were not will not	wasn’t weren’t won’t

Contractions

will - set 1

I	will	’	I’ll
you	will	’	you’ll
he	will	’	he’ll
we	will	’	we’ll

Matching contracitons

I will	I’ll
you will	you’ll
he will	he’ll
we will	we’ll

Contractions
will - set 2

Building contractions

they	will	’	they’ll
she	will	’	she’ll
we	will	’	we’ll
it	will	’	it’ll

Matching contracitons

they will	they’ll
she will	she’ll
we will	we’ll
it will	it’ll

Contractions
am/is - set 1

am/is – set 1

Building contractions

I	am	’	I’m
who	is	’	who’s
she	is	’	she’s
he	is	’	he’s
when	is	’	when’s

Matching contracitons

I am	I’m
who is	who’s
she is	she’s
he is	he’s
when is	when’s

Contractions
am/is - set 2

Building contractions

how	is	’	how’s
what	is	’	what’s
that	is	’	that’s
where	is	’	where’s

Matching contracitons

how is	how’s
what is	what’s
that is	that’s
where is	where’s

Contractions
have/has

Building contractions

I	have	’	I’ve
you	have	’	you’ve
we	have	’	we’ve
they	have	’	they’ve
he	has	’	he’s
it	has	’	it’s
she	has	’	she’s

See next page for matching contractions.

Contractions
have/has

Matching contracitons

I have	I’ve
you have	you’ve
we have	we’ve
they have	they’ve
he has	he’s
it has	it’s
she has	she’s

Contractions
had

Building contractions

I	had	’	I’d
you	had	’	you’d
he	had	’	he’d
she	had	’	she’d
it	had	’	it’d
we	had	’	we’d
they	had	’	they’d

See next page for matching contractions.

Contractions
had

Matching contracitons

I had	I'd
you had	you'd
he had	he'd
she had	she'd
it had	it'd
we had	we'd
they had	they'd

Contractions
are

Building contractions

they	are	’	they’re
we	are	’	we’re
you	are	’	you’re
we	are	’	we’re
let	us	’	let’s

Matching contracitons

they are	they’re
we are	we’re
you are	you’re
we are	we’re
let us	let’s

Contractions
mixed - set 1

Building contractions

did	not	’	didn’t
has	not	’	hasn’t
you	will	’	you’ll
she	will	’	she’ll
I	am	’	I’m
she	is	’	she’s
what	is	’	what’s
I	have	’	I’ve
she	is	’	she’s
I	had	’	I’d

Contractions
mixed - set 1

Matching contracitons

did not	didn’t
has not	hasn’t
you will	you’ll
she will	she’ll
I am	I’m
she is	she’s
what is	what’s
I have	I’ve
she is	she’s
I had	I’d

Contractions
mixed - set 2

Building contractions

do	not	’	don’t
I	will	’	I’ll
they	will	’	they’ll
he	is	’	he’s
that	is	’	that’s
we	have	’	we’ve
it	is	’	it’s
we	had	’	we’d
they	are	’	they’re
you	are	’	you’re

Contractions
mixed - set 2

Matching contracitons

do not	don’t
was not	wasn’t
I will	I’ll
they will	they’ll
he is	he’s
that is	that’s
we have	we’ve
it is	it’s
we had	we’d
they are	they’re
you are	you’re

Simple possessives

cat	s	'	
dog	s	'	
Dan	s	'	
Jen	s	'	
	s	'	
	s	'	

2-1-1- Rule

When students are working with single syllable words, they learn the **1-1-1** rule. When adding a vowel suffix to the end of a word, they double the ending consonant if the word has 1 syllable, 1 vowel, and 1 ending consonant.

bat batting
pop popped

The **2-1-1** rule applies to multi-syllable rules, but it is similar.

When a word has:

2 or more syllables
and the last syllable is stressed (accented) and has
1 vowel
1 ending consonant
then they double the ending consonant.

un **wash** un wash ed
fur nish fur nish ing

(There is no doubling in the above words because there are 2 consonants at the end. Also, furnish has the accent on the first syllable)

re **can** recan**n**ing
com **pel** compel**l**ing

(The last consonant is doubled in the above words, because the last syllable is stressed and the last syllable has 1 vowel and 1 ending consonant).

Vowel Suffix Spelling Rules

1-1-1 Rule (for single syllable words)

When you add a vowel suffix, and the root word has:

1 – syllable

1 - vowel letter

1 – consonant (after the vowel)

then the last consonant is doubled before adding the vowel suffix.

Note: X, W and Y do not double. The U in QU does not count as a vowel.

The **2-1-1** rule is very similar to the **1-1-1** rule, but it applies to words of 2 or more syllables, where the accent is on the last syllable.

2-1-1 Rule (for multi-syllable words)

When you add a vowel suffix to a word, and the word has:

2 or more syllables <u>and the **accent/stress** is on the last syllable,</u>

1 - vowel letter

1 - consonant (after the the vowel)

then the last consonant is doubled before adding the vowel suffix.

Note: X, W and Y do not double. The U in QU does not count as a vowel.

2-1-1 Checklist - Example

Root word	Suffix	Adding Vowel suffix? Y/N	2 or more syllables? Y/N	Look at last syllable in the word			Final Word (2 Yes & 3 checks = double the end consonant)
				Stressed ✓	1 Vowel letter ✓	1 Ending Consonant (not X, W, Y) ✓	
open	-ed	Y	Y		✓	✓	opened
forget	-ing	Y	Y	✓	✓	✓	forgetting
permit	-ed	Y	Y	✓	✓	✓	permitted
dislike	-s	N					dislikes
profit	-able	Y	Y		✓	✓	profitable
benefit	-ing	Y	Y		✓	✓	benefitting
shiver	-s	N					shivers
result	-ed	Y	Y	✓	✓		resulted
reboot	-ing	Y	Y	✓		✓	rebooting
index	-ing	Y	Y		✓	X	indexing
tax	-able	Y	N				taxable

Explanations:

Only the words **forget** and **permit** met all the requirements for doubling.

For the words **dislike** and **shiver**, the suffix was not a vowel suffix, so the student just crossed out the rest of the requirements. For the word **tax**, the word had only one syllable, so the student just crossed out the rest of the requirements.

For the words **open, profit,** and **benefit**, and **index**, the accent/stress was on the first syllable, so the last consonant did not double. The word **index** also ended in the letter **X**, so the last consonant did not double.

For the word **reboot**, there was more than one vowel letter, so the last consonant did not double.

For the word **result**, there was more than one ending consonant after the vowel, so the last consonant did not double.

2-1-2 Checklist

Root word	Suffix	Adding Vowel suffix?	2 or more syllables?	**Look at last syllable in the word**			Final Word
		Y/N	Y/N	Stressed ✓	1 Vowel letter ✓	1 Ending Consonant (not X, W, Y) ✓	2 Yes & 3 checks = double the end consonant

CLOVER

Syllable Boxes

Syllable Boxes can be used in multiple ways. There are a variety of different configurations of boxes on the next several pages. Below are some ideas on how to use the syllable boxes.

1) The teacher writes words in the boxes (divided into syllables) for the students to practice reading.
2) The teacher writes words in the boxes (divided into syllables) on one worksheet template, and makes as many copies as she needs for the group. The teacher also provides each student with a blank syllable boxes worksheet. The teacher or the student then cuts out the syllables and mixes them up. The teacher says the words out loud one at a time, and the students find the syllables (cut out slips of paper) that are needed to make that word. The student places the slips of paper in the boxes on the blank template to make the word.
3) The teacher prepares the materials in the same way as #2, but instead of providing the words, the teachers have the students try to figure out what the words are. I have found that students really enjoy this activity, and it helps them to read the individual syllables several times as they try to create words.
4) The teacher provides the students with a blank worksheet page. The teacher says the name of a word out loud. The students pound out the syllables of the word on the table. The students then write the letters in the syllable boxes.
5) Some of the syllable boxes show circles above the boxes. To use these sheets, the teacher provides a blank worksheet page to each student and gives students circles (or some other manipulative). The teacher has the students put one circle in each syllable box. The teacher then says a word out loud, and the students push up the circles from the box into the circle shape above, while saying the syllable out loud. (See Multi-Sensory Syllable Spelling). Teachers may also have the students write the syllables in the boxes, similar to #4. The circles may also be used to color in above the syllables, or to mark with an X for each syllable.

Syllable Boxes Example

ho	tel

but	ter	fly

in	tel	li	gent

Syllable Boxes

Syllable Boxes

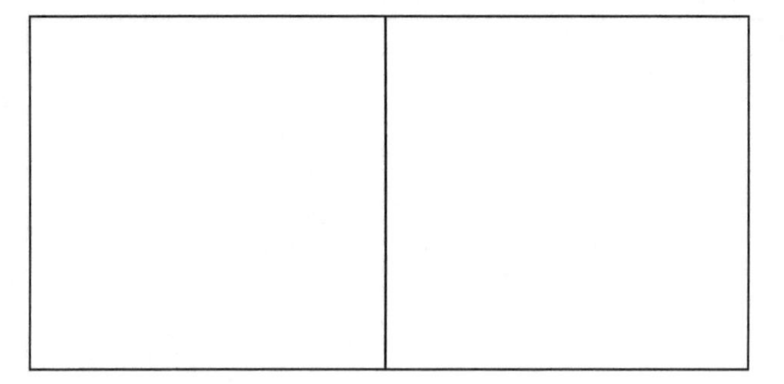

Syllable Boxes

Syllable Boxes

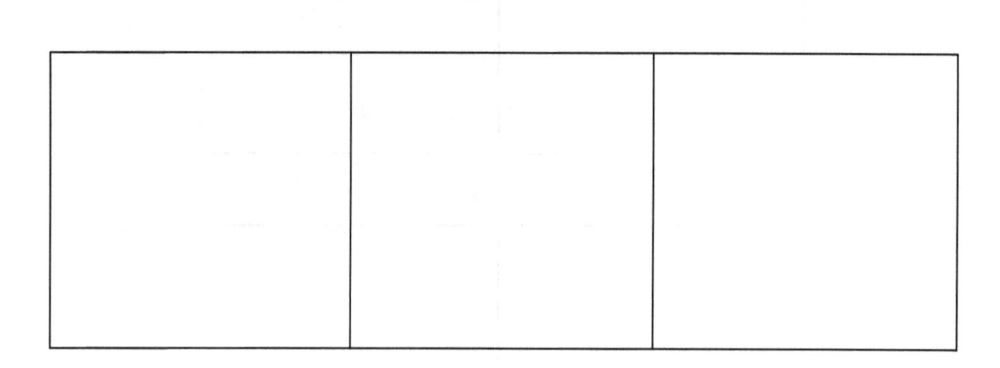

Syllable Boxes

Syllable Boxes

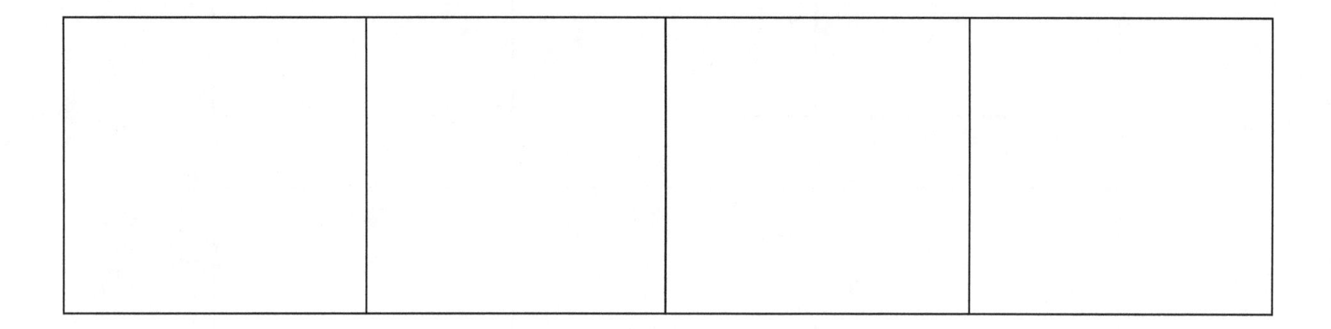

Syllable Boxes

Syllable Boxes

Syllable Boxes

Syllable Boxes with Chips Example

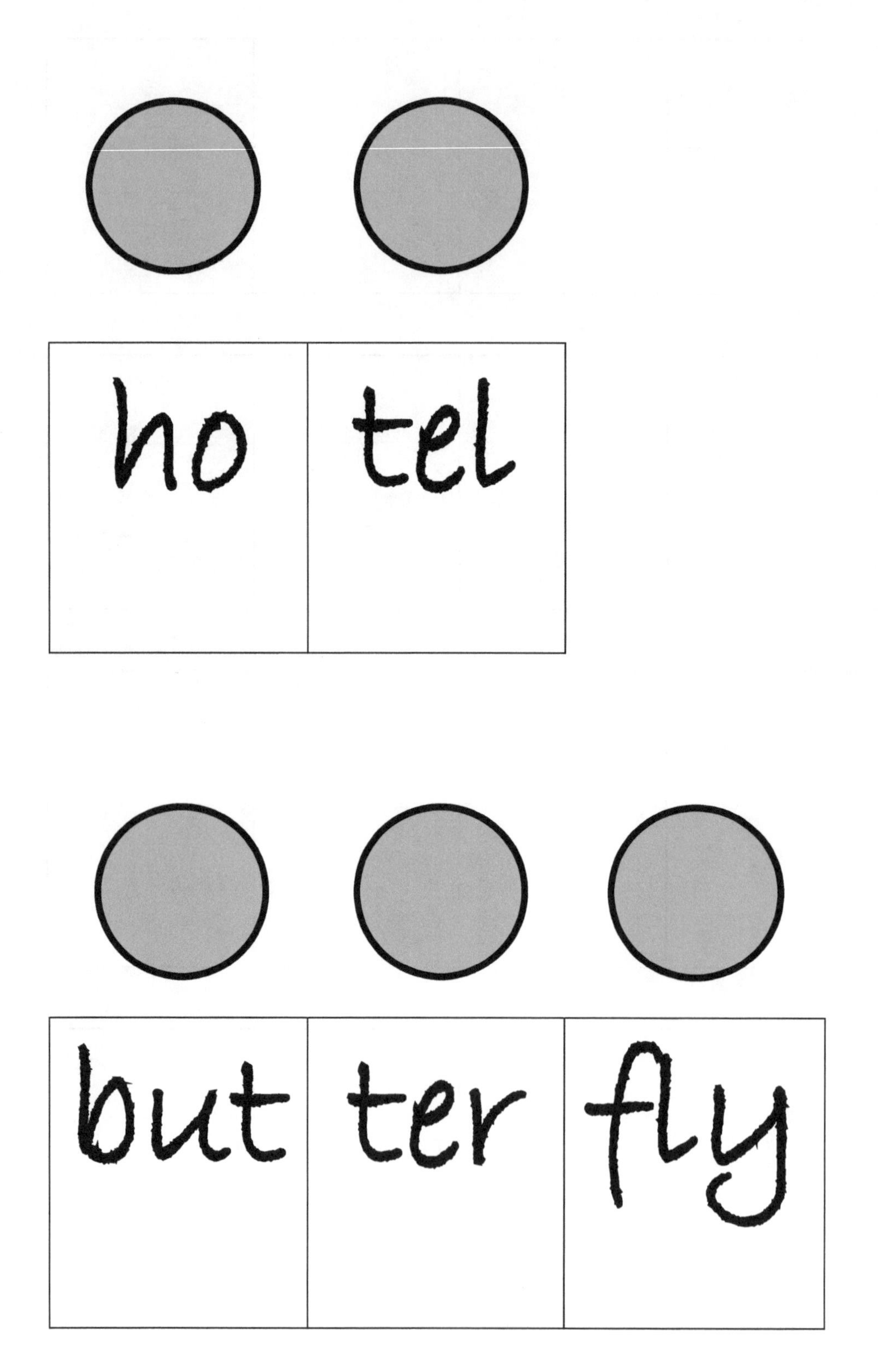

Syllable Boxes with Chips Example

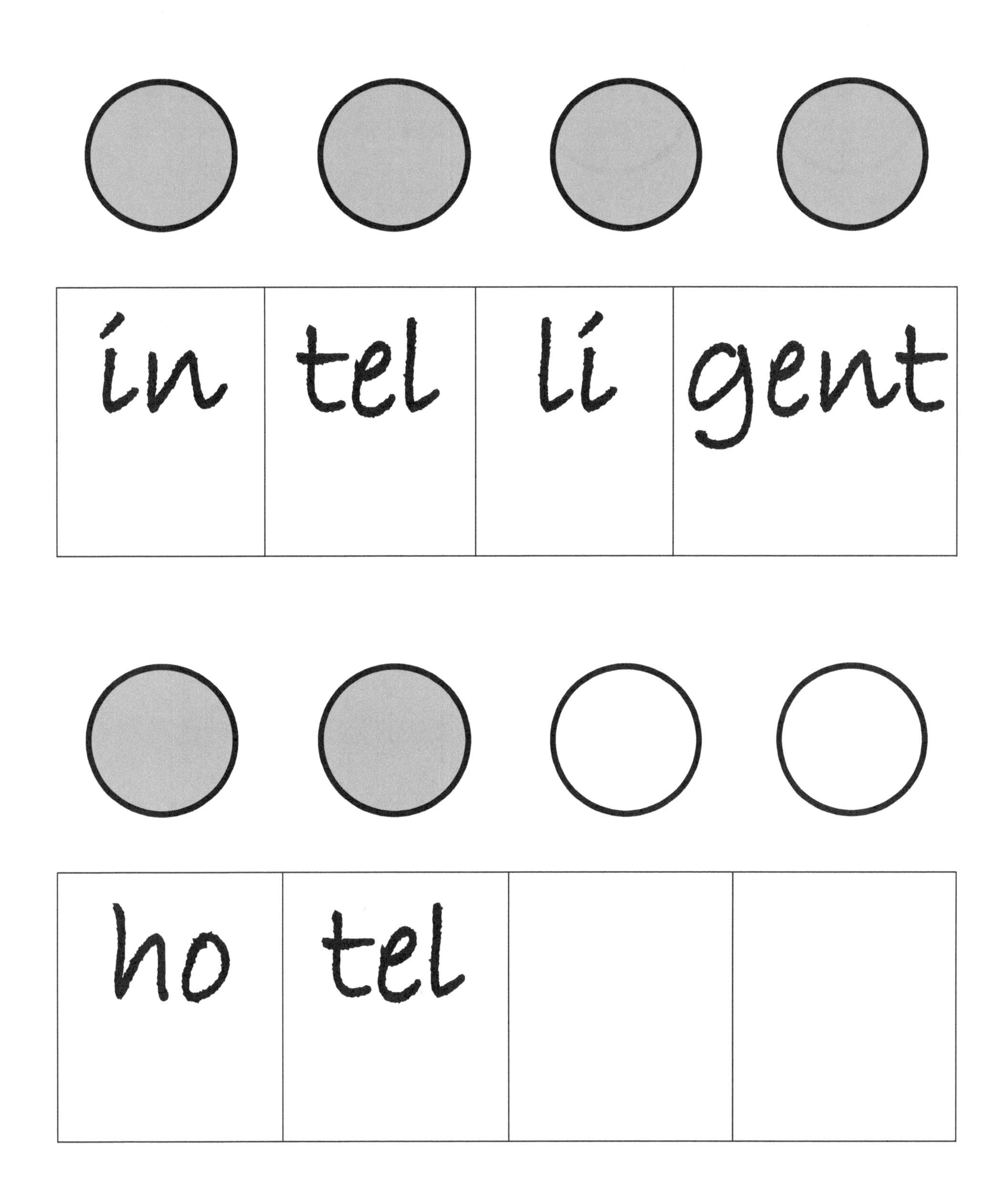

Syllable Boxes with Chips

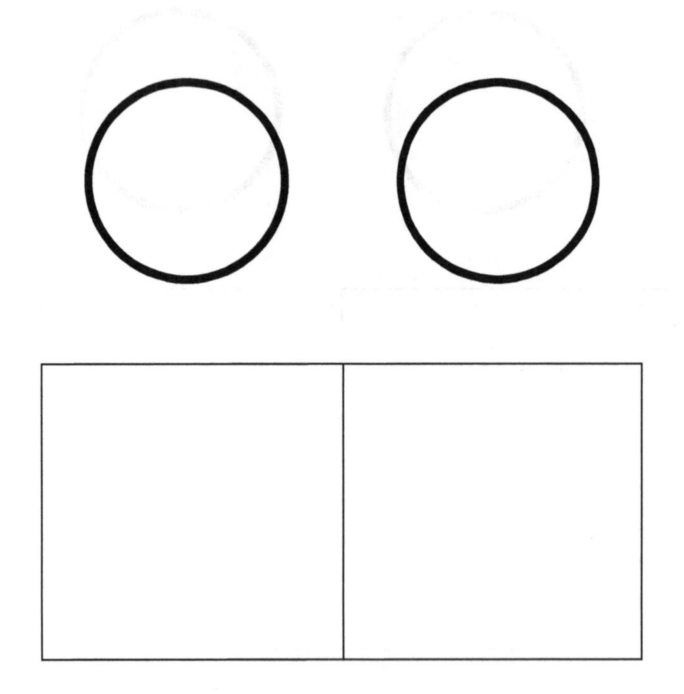

Syllable Boxes with Chips

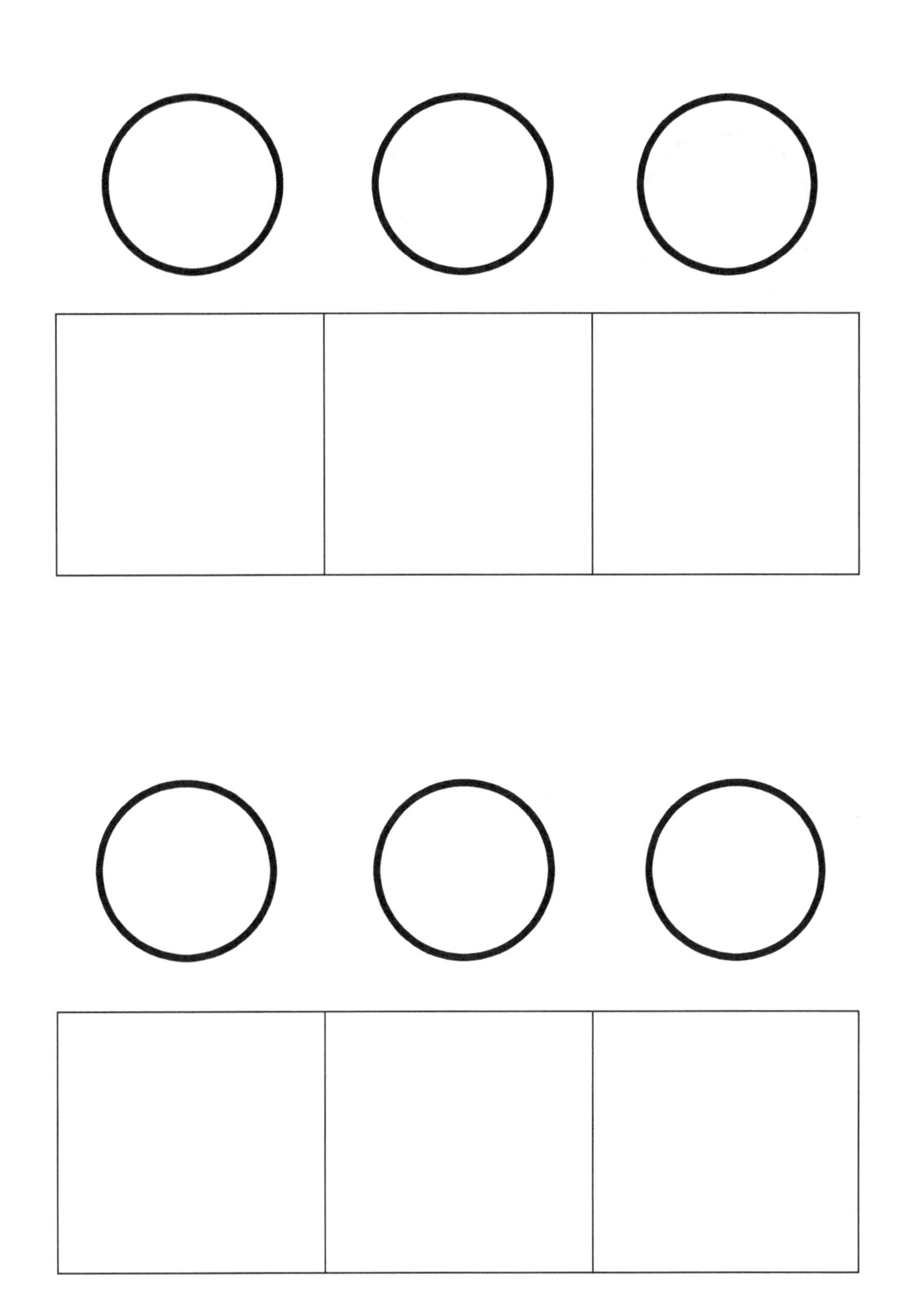

Syllable Boxes with Chips

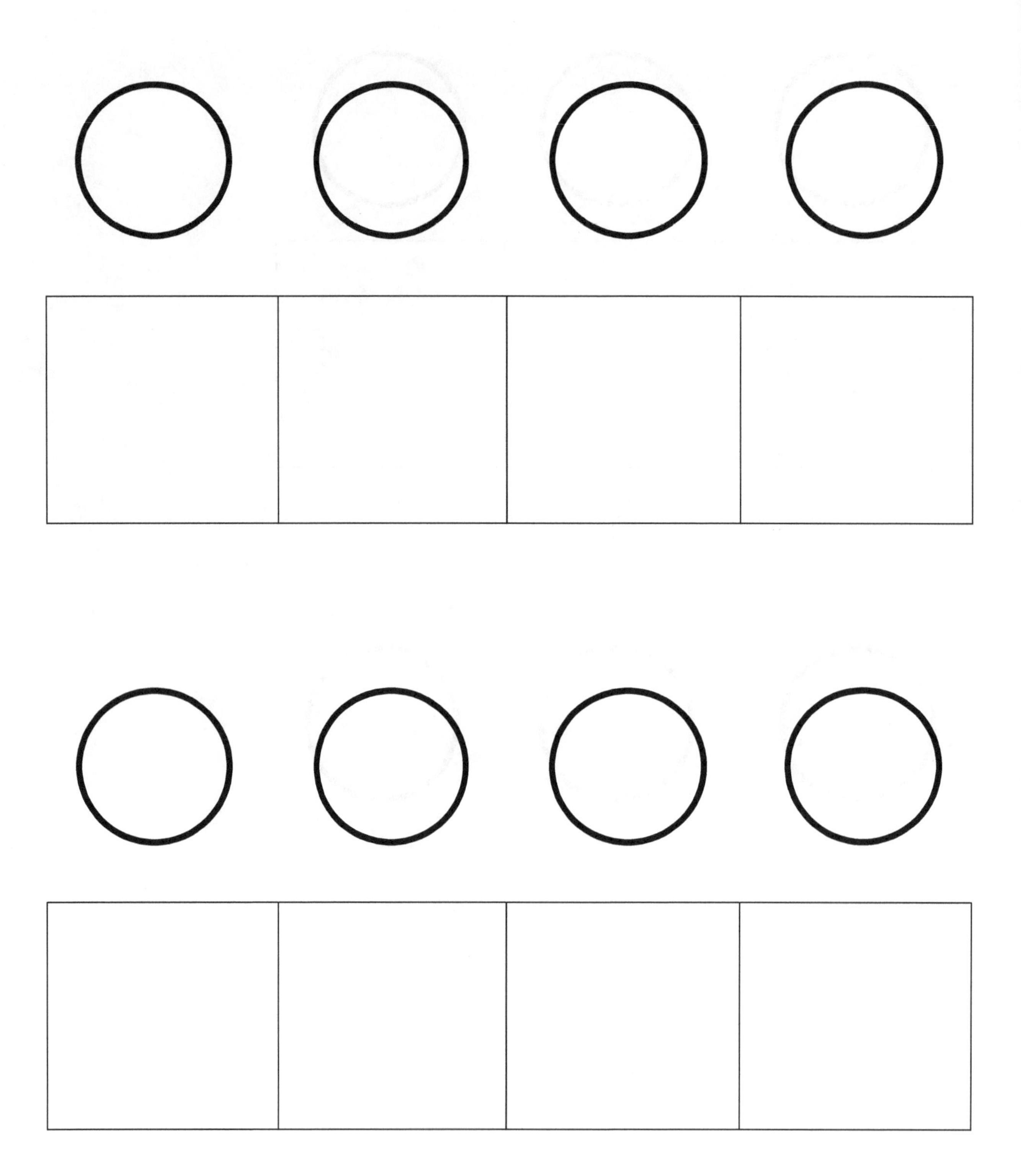

Cut-Out Manipulatives – Circles

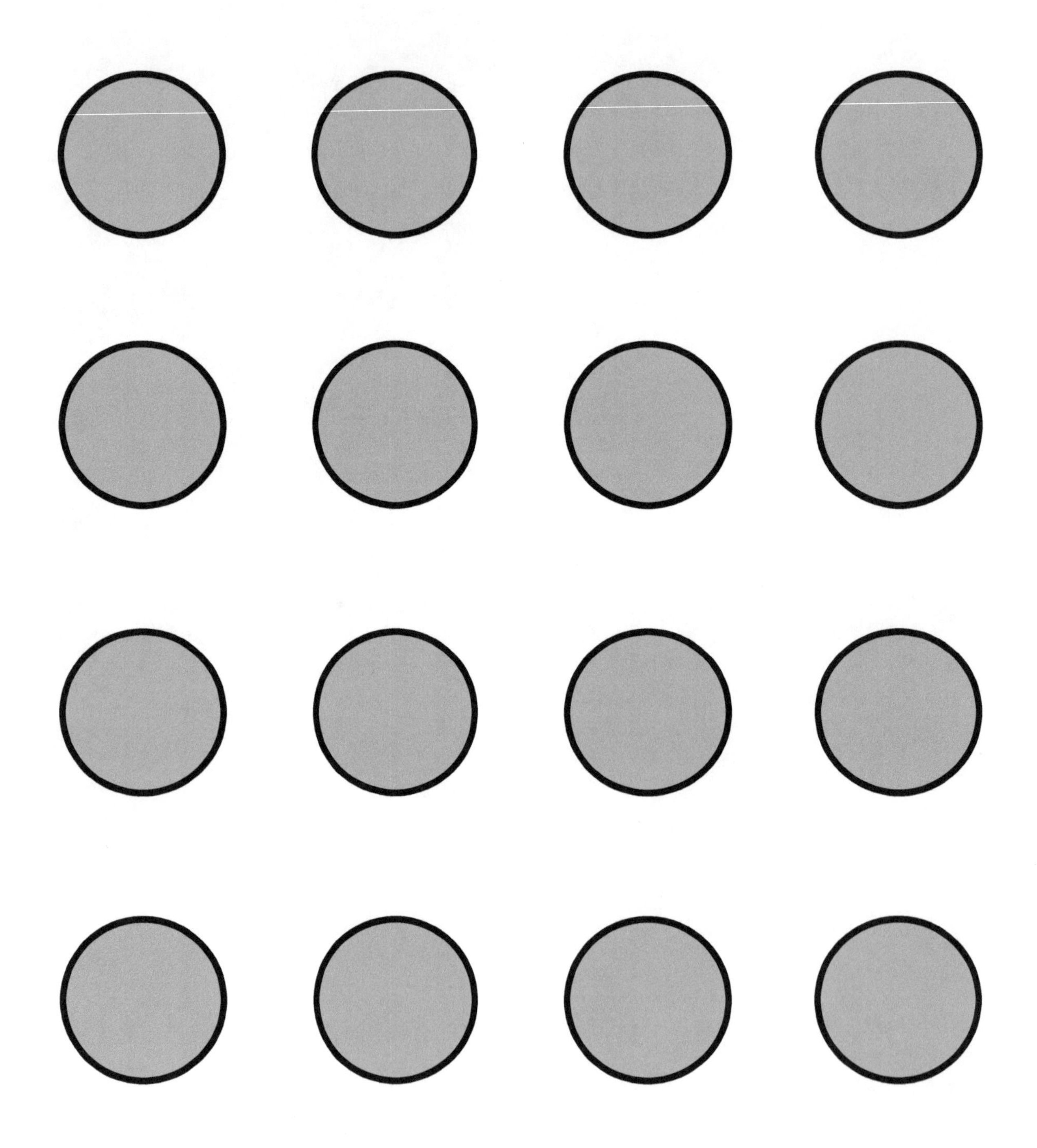

Cut-Out Manipulatives – Circles

Photocopy onto colored tagboard

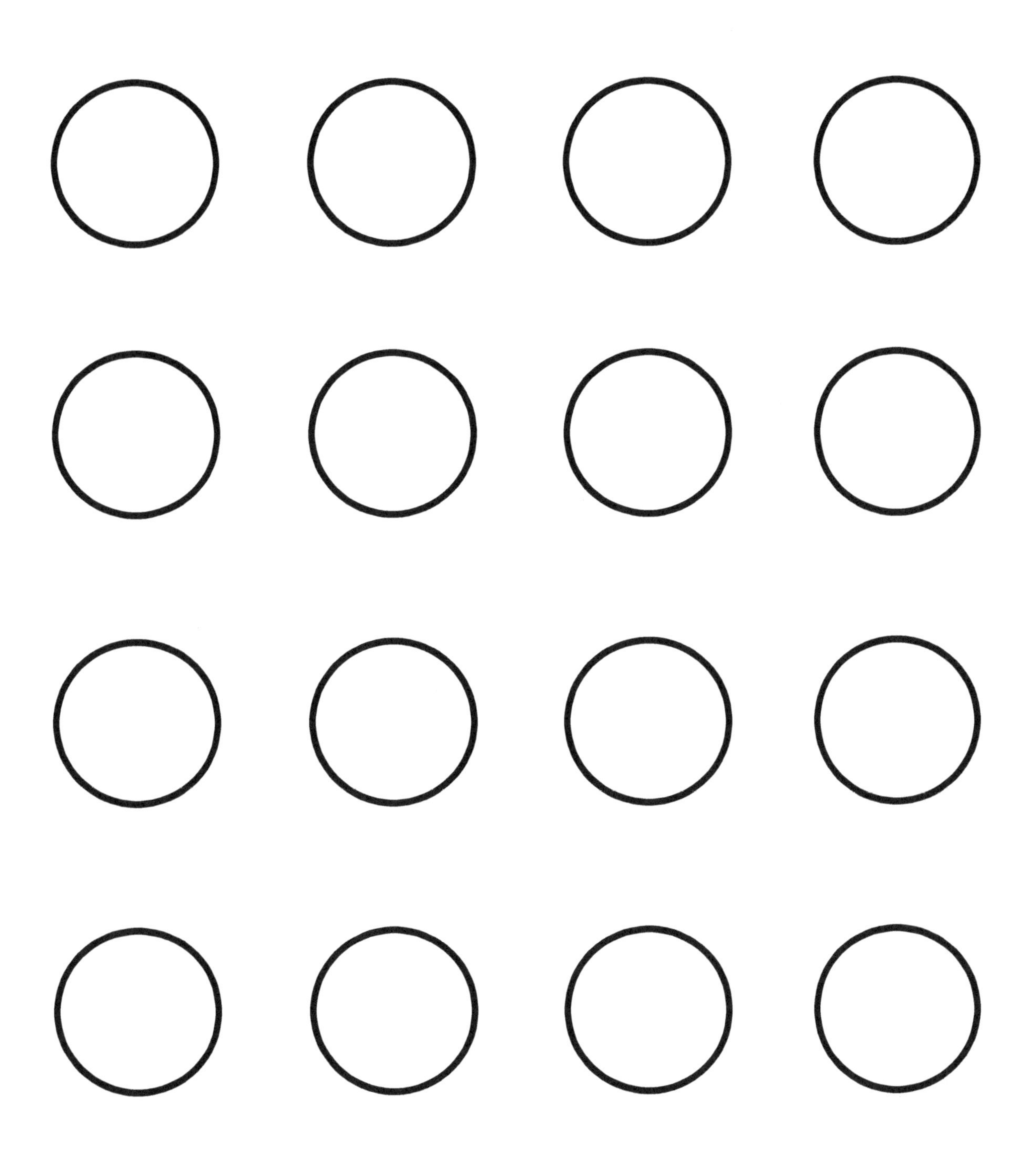

Cut-out Manipulatives – Syllable Rectangles

Photocopy onto colored tagboard.

Cut-out Manipulatives – Syllable Rectangles

Syllable Matching - Beginner

For the Syllable Matching Worksheet, the teacher divides words into two syllables, and writes the first syllable of the word in the first box, and the second syllable of the word in the second box. The student matches the first and second syllables by drawing and line, and then writes the words that they make on the lines below. This is an especially good practice, because the student naturally has to read each syllable in order to complete the task. This worksheet template is good for beginners, and the Syllable Matching template that follows is good for more advanced students. In this example, the teacher is having the student practice words with closed syllables, however this template can be used for a variety of concepts.

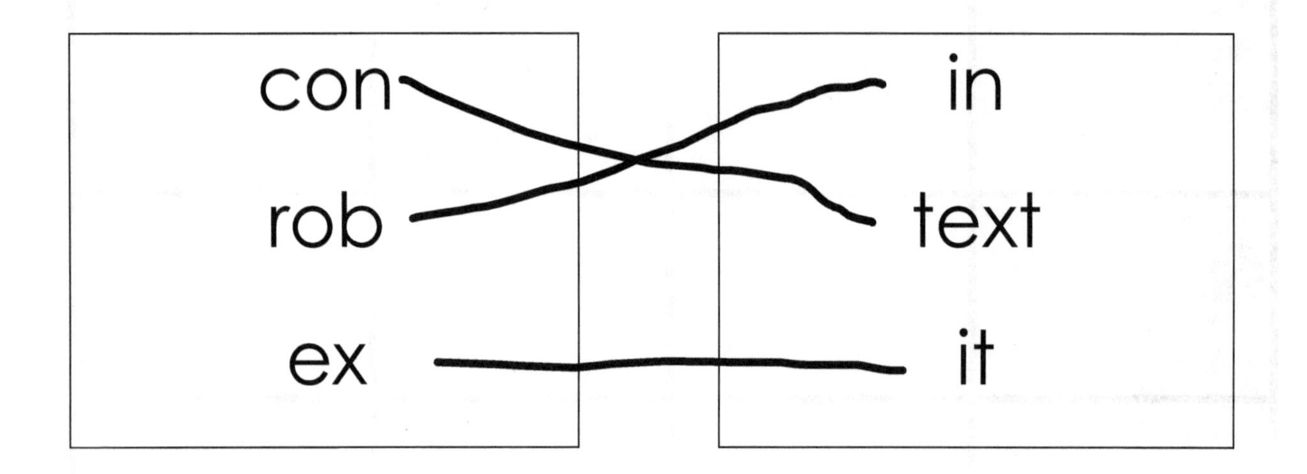

context

robin

exit

Syllable Matching

Syllable Matching Advanced

For the Syllable Matching Worksheet, the teacher divides words into two syllables, and writes the syllables in the box. The student matches the first and second syllables by drawing and line, and then writes the words that they made on the lines below. This is an especially good practice, because the student has to read each syllable in isolation in order to complete the task. The examples show four words in each box, but you can use any number of words that fit in the box. In this example, the student is practicing words with the **CLE** syllable, but you can use this worksheet template for any number of concepts.

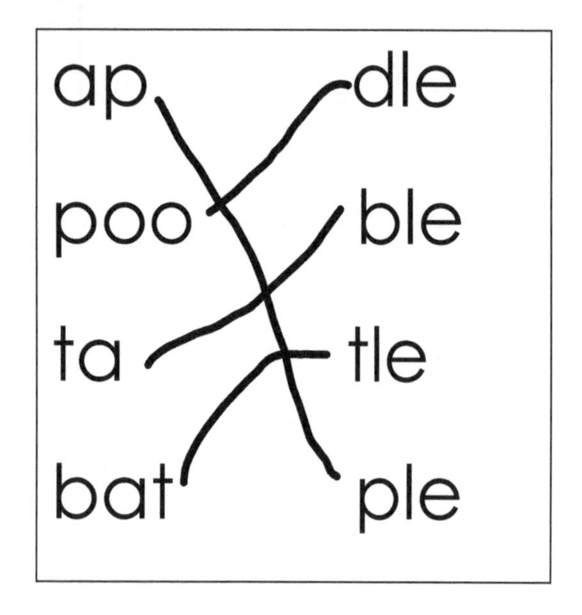

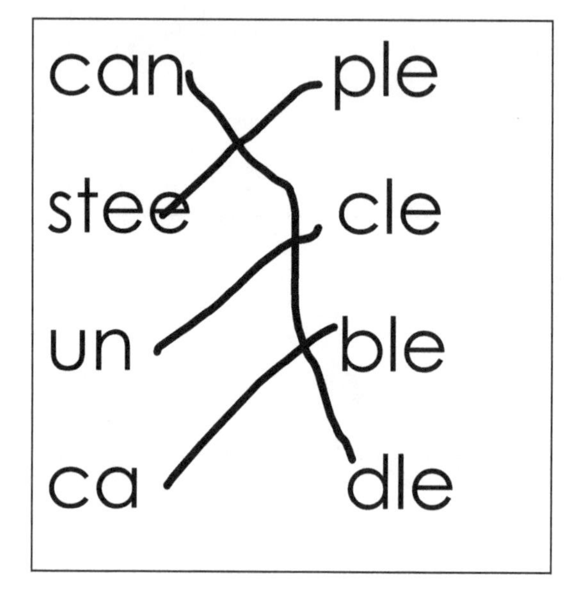

apple

candle

poodle

steeple

table

uncle

battle

cable

Syllable Matching

______________________________________ - ______________________________________ -

______________________________________ - ______________________________________ -

______________________________________ - ______________________________________ -

______________________________________ - ______________________________________ -

Syllable Division (Two Syllables)

For this Syllable Division worksheet, the teacher writes a whole word on the first line. The student divides the word into syllables and writes each individual syllable on the following two lines. In this sample worksheet, the teacher is having the student practice dividing after an open syllable. It is helpful, especially for beginners, to have the students underline or highlight the vowels in the word before they divide them into syllables.

proton	pro	ton
prefer	pre	fer
motel	mo	tel
music	mu	sic
local		
Lucy		

Syllable Division (Two Syllables)

Syllable Division (Three syllables)

For this Syllable Division worksheet, the teacher writes a whole word on the first line. The student divides the word into syllables and writes each individual syllable on the following three lines. In this sample worksheet, the teacher has chosen words that have one consonant between vowels, and the students must choose whether the division line is before or after the vowel. This template, however, can be used to practice a variety of different concepts.

meteor	me	te	or
migration	mi	gra	tion
mineral	min	er	al
momentum			

Syllable Division (Three syllables)

Two Syllable Blending

In Two Syllable Blending, the teacher writes the syllables on the first two lines of the worksheet template and the teacher also writes the whole word on the final line. The student reads the syllables as parts while pointing to each part, then the student points to the whole word on the third line and reads the word as a whole. Some programs have similar worksheets where they only provide the first two syllables and then they expect the student to write the word as a whole on the last line. However, using the worksheet template in that manner does nothing to further learning, because all the student is doing is copying the letters.

pic	nic	picnic
pen	cil	pencil
kid	nap	kidnap
hec	tic	hectic
hel	met	helmet
cos	mic	cosmic
fun	gus	fungus
Jus	tin	Justin

Two Syllable Blending

Three Syllable Blending

In Three Syllable Blending, the teacher writes the syllables on the first three lines of the worksheet template and the teacher also writes the whole word on the final line. The student reads the syllables as parts while pointing to each part, then the student points to the whole word on the fourth line and reads the word as a whole. Some programs have similar worksheets where they only provide the first three syllables and then they expect the student to write the word as a whole on the last line. However, using the worksheet template in that manner does nothing to further learning, because all the student is doing is copying the letters.

in	fan	try	infantry
in	field	er	infielder
in	fi	nite	infinite
in	fla	tion	inflation
in	flu	ence	influence

Three Syllable Blending

Cut-apart Table Example

Syllable types lesson – VC/CV (twin) example

Teacher List	Word Cards	Syllables	
happen	happen	hap	pen
muffin	muffin	muf	fin
button	button	but	ton
lesson	lesson	les	son
bottom	bottom	bot	tom
hidden	hidden	hid	den
kitten	kitten	kit	ten

Cut-apart Table – two syllables

Teacher List	Word Cards	Syllables	

Teacher List	Word Cards	Syllables	

Content Passage Lesson example

Teacher List	Word Cards	Syllables				
ribosome	ribosome	ri	bo	some		
cellular	cellular	cel	lu	lar		
particle	particle	par	ti	cle		
genetic	genetic	ge	net	ic		
amino	amino	a	mi	no		
messenger	messenger	mes	sen	ger		
synthesis	synthesis	syn	the	sis		

Cut-apart Table – up to 5 syllables

Teacher List	Word Cards	Syllables				

Teacher List	Word Cards	Syllables				

Spinner Game – 4 in a row

Place a clear spinner over top of the circle, or use a pencil and paperclip to make a spinner. Spin a prefix or other word part, and X off a box with a word that contains that word part. 4 in a row in any direction wins the game.

prefer	regroup	unusual	immense	unfounded
relax	prewash	immobile	reload	preheat
unbound	impossible	predate	unbutton	remake
imperfect	uncertain	relive	prefix	import

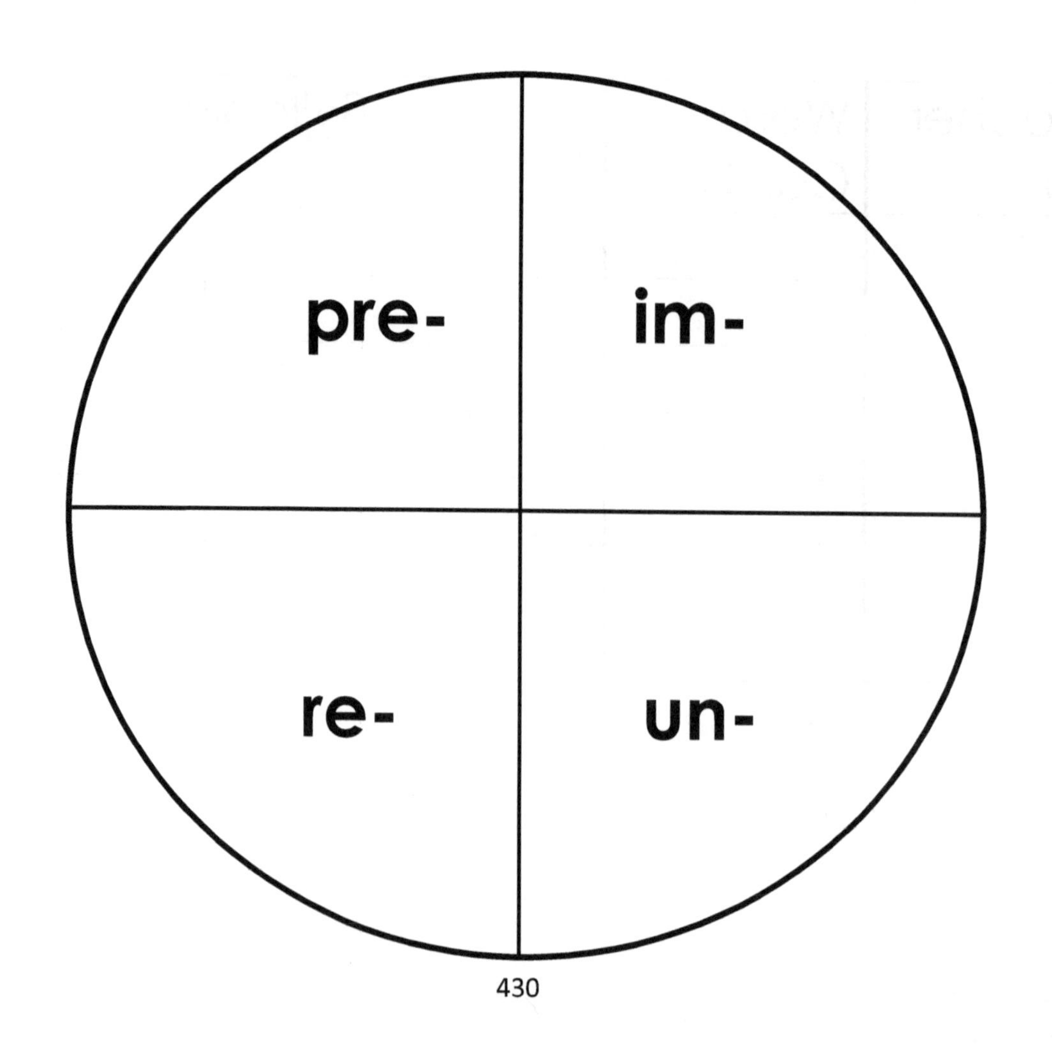

Spinner Game – 4 in a row

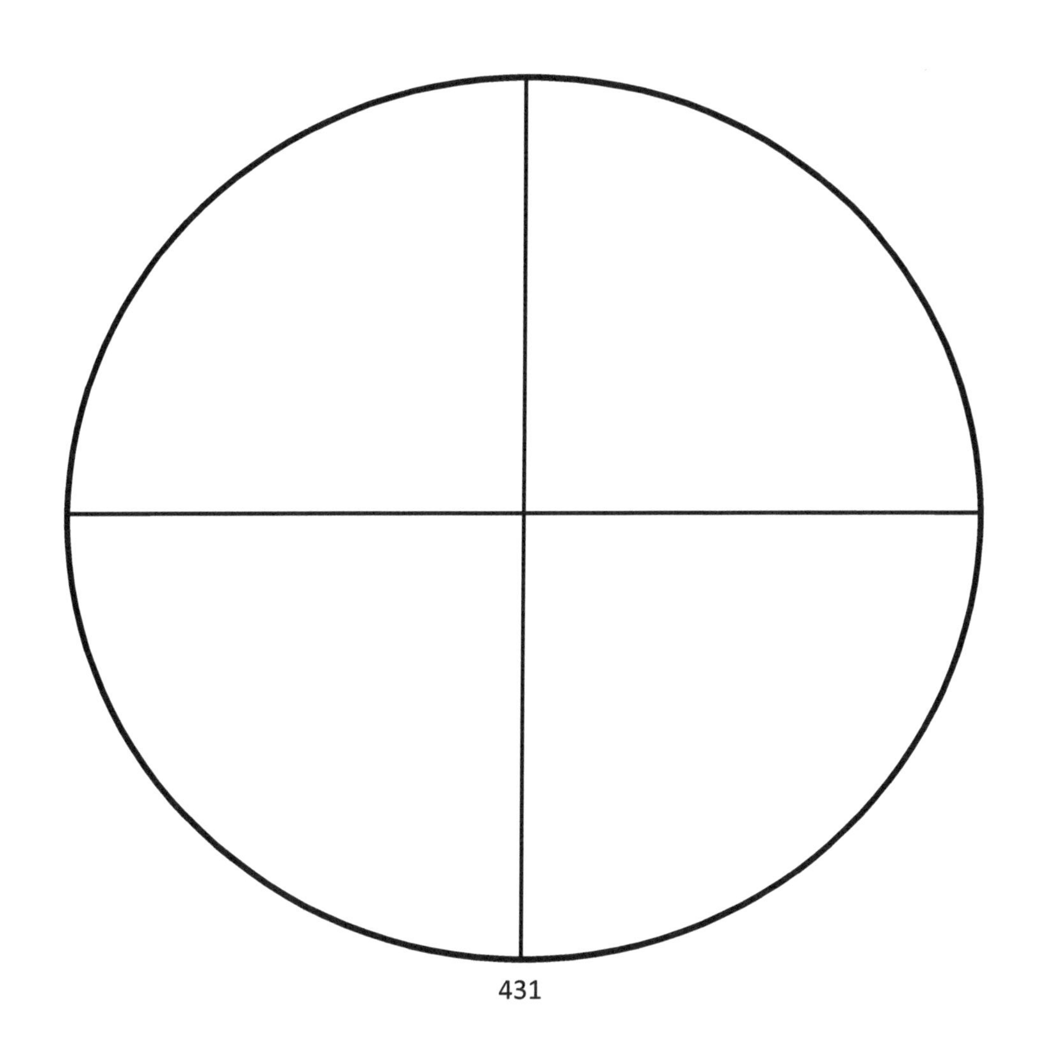

Bibliography & Resources

for Dyslexia, Phonics, and Word Study

American Heritage Students's Dictionary (2019). Houghton Mifflin Harcourt Publishing Company.

Arredondo, Valerie. (2019). *Orton-Gillingham Word List Dictionary Volume 1, 2 and 3.* Campbell Curriculum.

Ayers, Donald M. (1986). *English Words from Latin and Greek Elements.* University of Arizona Press.

Ayto, John. (2011). *Dictionary of Word Origins.* Arcade Publishing.

Barton Reading & Spelling System. www.bartonreading.com

Bauer, Laurie, et al. (2015). *The Oxford Reference Guide to English Morphology.* Oxford University Press.

Berninger, Virginia. (2016). *Teaching Students with Dyslexia, Dysgraphia, OWL, LD and Dyscalculia.* Paul H. Brookes Publishing Co.

Birsh, Judith. (2011). *Multisensory Teaching of Basic Language Skills.* Paul H. Brookes Publishing Company.

Bishop, Margaret. (1986). *The ABC's and All Their Tricks: The Complete Reference Book of Phonics and Spelling.* Mott Media.

Blevins, Wiley. (2017). *Teaching Phonics & Word Study.* Scholastic.

Borrer, Donald J. (1988). *Dictionary of Word Roots and Combining Forms.* Mayfield Publsihing Company.

Bower, Peter. (2013). *Teaching How the Written Word Works.*

Carver, Lin & Pantoja, Lauren. (2009). *Teaching Syllable Patterns.* Capstone Publishing, Inc

Dehaene, Stanislas. (2009). *Reading in the Brain: The New Science of How We Read and The New Science of How We Read.* (2010). Penguin Books

Dictionary by Merriam-Webster. www.merriam-webster.com

Dictionary.com

Dyslexia Training Institute. www.dyslexiatraininginstitute.org

Eide, Brock & Eide, Fernette. (2011). *The Dyslexic Advantage.* Plume.

Eide, Denise. (2012). *Uncovering the Logic of English*. Pedia Learning, Inc.

Etymonline (Word Etymology/History & Origins dictionary) www.etymonline.com

Farrell, Linda and Hunter, Michael. *Readsters* (reading program) www.readsters.com

Fox, Barbara. (2014). *Phonics and Word Study for the Teacher of Reading*. Pearson.

Freeman, David & Freeman, Yvonne. *Essential Linguistics*. Heinemann.

Fulford, John. (2012). *The Complete Guide to English Spelling Rules*. Astoria Press.

Galaburda, Albert, et al. (2018). *Dyslexia and Neuroscience*. Paul H. Brookes Publishing Co.

Geffner, Donna. (2019). *Auditory Processing Disorders: Assessment, Management, and Treatment*. Plural Publishing.

Gillingham, Anna & Stillman, Bessie. *The Gillingham Manual*. Educators Publishing Service.

Haspelmath, Martin and Sims, Andrea. (2002). *Understanding Morphology* (Understanding Language Series). Routledge.

Henry, Marcia. (2010). *Unlocking Literacy: Effective Decoding & Spelling Instruction.* Paul H. Brookes Publishing Co.

Henry, Marcia. (2010). Words: *Integrated Decoding and Spelling Instruction Based on Word Origin and Word Structure.* Pro-Ed.

How Many Syllables. howmanysyllables.com

Institute for Multi-Sensory Education. www.orton-gillingham.com

International Dyslexia Association. www.dyslexiaida.org

Johnson, Kristin and Bayrd, Polly. (2010). *Megawords* (series). *Educators Publishing Service.*

Honig, Bill & Diamond, Linda. (2019). *Teaching Reading Sourcebook* (Core Literacy Library). Academic Therapy Publications; Third edition.

Kilpatrick, David, et al. (2019). *Reading Development and Difficulties: Bridging the Gap Between Research and Practice.*

Kilpatrick, David. (2016). *Equipped for Reading Success*. Casey & Kirsch Publishers.

Kilpatrick, David. (2015). *Essentials of Assessing, Preventing, and Overcoming Reading Difficulties.* John Wiley & Sons, Inc.

Leu, Donald & Kinzer, Charles. (2017). *Phonics, Phonemic Awareness, and Word Analysis.* Pearson Education, Inc.

Lewis, Norman. (2014). Word Power Made Easy. Anchor Press.

Mather, Nancy and Wendling, Barbara. (2012). *Essentials of Dyslexia Assessment and Intervention*. John Wiley & Sons, Inc.

Mather, Nancy. (2009). Writing Assessment and Instruction for Students with Learning Disabilities. Jossey-Bass (Wiley).

Minkova, Donka (2004). "Philology, linguistics, and the history of /hw/~/w/". In Anne Curzan; Kimberly Emmons (eds.). Studies in the History of the English language II: Unfolding Conversations.

Moats, Louisa Cook. (2010). *Speech to Print: Language Essentials for Teachers*. Paul H. Brookes Publishing Co.

Moats, Louisa & Toman, Carol. *LETRS* training program for teachers.

O'Connor, Rollanda E. (2020). *Teaching Word Recognition*. The Guildord Press.

Orton Gillingham Online Academy. www.ortongillinghamonlinetutor.com

Pennington, Mark. Pennington Publishing Blog. blog.penningtonpublishing.com

Ramsden, Neil. Word Microscope. www.neilramsden.co.uk

Ramsden, Neil. Word Searcher. www.neilramsden.co.uk

Reid, Gavin & Guise, Jennie. (2017). *The Dyslexia Assessment*. Bloomsbury.

Rippel, Marie. *All About Learning* curriculum. www.allaboutlearningpress.com

Rome, Paula & Osman, Jean. (2000). *Advanced Language Tool Kit*. Educators Publishing Services.

Rome, Paula & Osman, Jean. (2004). *Language Tool Kit*. Educators Publishing Services.

Ruding, Joanne. (2017). *Spelling Rules Workbook*. How to Spell Publishing.

Seidenberg, Mark. (2018). *Language at the Speed of Sight*. Basic Books.

Shaywitz, Sally. (2003). *Overcoming Dyslexia*. Vintage Books.

Stockwell, Robert, and Minkova, Donka. (2001). *English Words: History and Structure*. Cambridge University Press.

Syllable Count. www.syllablecount.com

The Yale Center for Dyslexia & Creativity. www.dyslexia.yale.edu

Venezky, Richard. (1999). *The American Way of Spelling: The Structure and Origins of American English Orthography*. Guilford Press.

Wilson Reading System. www.wilsonlanguage.com

Made in United States
Troutdale, OR
01/11/2024